Investigating Famines in North Bengal (1866-1909)

A Study on Ecology, Economic Transformations and the Colonial State

Investigating Famines in North Bengal (1866-1909)

A Study in Ecology, Economic Transformations and the Colonial State

Investigating Famines in North Bengal (1866-1909)

A Study on Ecology, Economic Transformations and the Colonial State

Tirthankar Ghosh

ABHIJEET PUBLICATIONS
NEW DELHI 110002

ABHIJEET PUBLICATIONS
4658-A, First Floor, Ambika Bhawan,
21 Ansari Road, New Delhi 110002
Phone: 011-23259444
E-mail: abhijeetpublication@gmail.com
www.abhijeetpublications.com

INVESTIGATING FAMINES IN NORTH BENGAL (1866-1909): A STUDY ON ECOLOGY, ECONOMIC TRANSFORMATIONS AND THE COLONIAL STATE

First Published 2021

ISBN 978-81-950909-7-6

PRINTED IN INDIA

Published by J.K. Singh for Abhijeet Publications, New Delhi-110002, Lasertypeset by Abhijeet Typesetters, New Delhi and Printed at Milan Enterprises, New Delhi.

Dedicated to the

memory of my late father

Sri Dipak Kumar Ghosh

Acknowledgements

The idea for writing this book developed during the days of my doctoral research which I have completed at the University of North Bengal. The present book derives from my doctoral dissertation which includes a chapter on famines in colonial North Bengal. I am grateful to Dr. Dahlia Bhattacharya for supervising my doctoral work. This book would not have been possible without the active support of my teacher, Professor Ichhimuddin Sarkar, who always remains helpful during the writing of this book. I express my sincere gratitude to him for his critical and thought-provoking comments that contribute a lot for the development of this work. I would like to thank my teachers namely Professor Chhanda Chakrabarti, Professor Ratna Roy Sanyal, Professor Ananda Gopal Ghosh, Professor Anita Bagchi, Professor Bijoy Kumar Sarkar, Dr. Sudas Lama, and Dr. Varun Kumar Roy, at the Department of History, University of North Bengal. I thank to the Department of History, University of North Bengal once again where I have begun my Ph. D research as a Junior Research Fellow.

I am grateful to Richard Alford, Secretary of Charles Wallace India Trust (CWIT), who was kind enough to offer me a grant to visit and work in the libraries and institutions of the United Kingdom. The CWIT grant enables me to go through a vast literature of archival and secondary sources stored in the Asian and African Studies section of the British Library, London. I express my sincere gratitude to the staffs of the British Library for their extensive support, help and warmth during my work there. I am thankful to Professor

Ranjan Chakrabarti, Vice-Chancellor of Vidyasagar University for his constant support and encouragement. Professor Tirthankar Roy of London School of Economics has enriched my ideas and understandings through his expert comments and suggestions which are of great importance for this research. I acknowledge my sincere gratitude to Professor Anindya Sekhar Purakayastha, Dr. Manas Datta, Professor Raj Sekhar Basu, and Professor Arun Bandopadhyay for their generous help and support. I am also thankful to Anjashi Sarkar and Ayesha Sarkar for their kind involvement in this work.

I also thank to the librarians, archivists and staffs of the Central Library, Centre for Himalayan Studies, and Akshay Kumar Maitreya Museum of the University of North Bengal; the National Library (Kolkata) and the West Bengal State Archives, Kolkata. I am also grateful to my colleagues namely Amitava Chatterjee, Sk. Maidul Rahman, Priyanka Guha Roy, and Pradip Kumar Das for their continuous support. I have been immensely benefitted by the discussions with my students and research scholars namely Biswadip Nag, Debasree Dhar, Aparna Halder, Bapan Mal, Aditi Banerjee, Soumen Bhadra, Kalyan Pandit, Kamalesh Majumdar, whose critical comments provide fresh insights to my work.

Portions of Chapter 3 have been published previously in the journals namely - *Quarterly Review of Historical Studies* (Vol. LIV, No. 1&2, April -September, 2014, pp. 4-19) and *Crossroads: The Journal of Transdisciplinary Studies* (Vol. I, No. I, May 2015, pp. 47-63). I acknowledge my sincere gratitude to the editors of these journals for giving me the kind permission to include a revised and enlarged version of these articles. An earlier version of chapter 4 of this book has been accepted for publication in the journal *Contemporary Voice of Dalit* (Sage publications). This chapter is, however, a revised and modified version of the article. Many of the sources, information and interpretations of this chapter can be found in the accepted article. Therefore, I am grateful to the editor and publisher of the journal for giving me the permission to include a revised and modified version of the article as a chapter in this book.

This work would not have been possible without the blessings and love of my late father, my mother and sister. I am thankful to my in-laws who have helped me in many ways during the writing of this book. I would acknowledge my deepest gratitude to my wife and my daughter who always spare me in all circumstances despite of my long absence from the family duties and responsibilities.

This book does not promise a comprehensive history of famines in North Bengal. I wish I could give more time and effort to this work for making it more critical. There may be some errors in this book. Nonetheless, for the error and mistakes in this work the responsibility are mine.

Lastly, I would like to thank Mr. J. K. Singh of Abhijeet Publications, New Delhi for carrying out this volume till the publication.

Tirthankar Ghosh

Contents

List of Tables

List of Figures

Glossary

adivasi	indigenous people, tribal people
aman	winter rice
anna	fraction of rupee
aus	autumn rice
bania	trader
barind	upland tract of Malda and Rajshahi district
bheels	deep water
bil	water-body, marsh
boro	summer rice
char	alluvial land
chhit	piece of land
chaukidar	village police
cutcha	mud-house
dhan	paddy
diara	fluvial deposited land found in Malda district
gola	granary
hat	village market
jalkar	water tax
jote	Cultivable land

jotedar	landholder or holder of cultivable land
kachari/kutcheri	Office of landlord or sometime government officers
khal	water channel drawn from river to land, canal
khas mahal	government estate
khiyar/khiar	Sapless or hard tract of land found in Bogra district
mahajan	creditor/noble man
mofussil	countryside
mauza	village revenue unit
naib	officer of landlord
pali	silt-covered
patni	a type land tenure or contract
patnidar	holder of *patni*
ryot/raiyat	peasants
tal/taal	Low / swampy tract of land found in Malda district
taluk	rent collecting unit of district
thana	police station
zamindar	Landlord/landed magnet

Abbreviations

BL	British Library
CEHI	The Cambridge Economic History of India
EBR	Eastern Bengal Railway
EPW	Economic and Political Weekly
IESHR	Indian Economic and Social History Review
FRC	Famine Relief Committee
HMSO	Her Majesty's Stationary Office
IOR	Indian Office Records
LG	Lieutenant Governor
MSS EUR	Private Papers
MAS	Modern Asian Studies
Offg.	Officiating
Progs.	Proceedings
Secy.	Secretary
WBSA	West Bengal State Archives

Introduction

Famine signifies a situation which was caused by acute shortage in subsistence and even starvation that ultimately led to mortality or crisis in human existence. The ecological dislocations, produced by the nature or human factors, which are intensified by famine and subsistence crisis, have been very crucial for identifying and analyzing the severity of famine.[1] Ecology is the systematic relationship between human and natural situations. When this methodical (or regular) connection breaks it creates crisis and aberrations in the socio-economic pattern. As the world ecology has been profoundly changed by the western capitalism, first through trade and later by colonialism, in view of this alteration the ecological transformations in India during the colonial period deserve special interest in regard to the intimate connection that recent research has made between British imperialism and environmental degradation.[2] However, this could not be attributed exclusively to the natural causes while artificial or human elements had played a decisive role in the outcome of famine or making ecological crises so intense. Rajat Datta has aptly categorised dearth and famine in the following words:

> "Famine was typically a situation when a subsistence and mortality crisis became combined in a critical conjuncture lasting for a length of time, which stretched beyond the critical threshold of a food shock...Dearth, on the other hand, constituted a more

> continuous saga of smaller scarcities. Although periods of dearth had lesser impact than famines, they were nevertheless important since their periodicity created major problems of subsistence among the...the artisans, labourers and the town poor.., women and children in the household, as well as among a section of the peasantry."[3]

Famine was a periodic event in British Indian history and since 1860s it grew in frequency and dimension. Famine-literature on colonial India is fairly rich by having diverse interpretations, varied from colonial officials to the nationalists and modern scholars; however, a few have dealt with the vital questions of regional peculiarities and problems. Among the official versions of the colonial Government, the work of G. W. Forrest (1897) highlights the Government policy and relief measures during the famines of 1866, 1873-74, and 1896-97 in Bengal. Though Forrest has supported government's policy of non-interference in private grain trade during famines but at the same time he criticized government's attitude of such general principles irrespective of local circumstances, as it was evident during the Orissa famine of 1866.[4] Another representation from the British official circle shows a clear outlook of political bias. While justifying his own work, McMinn asserted that, this work (his book) is 'not a monogram on famines' but an effort to 'expose' the so-called famine falsehoods which had been 'employed by several Bengali writers and Congress orators to blacken the character of English officials and administration.'[5] On the other hand nationalist economic thinkers like, Romesh Chandra Dutt and Dadabhai Naoroji underscored the over assessment or revenue pressure on Indian peasants and drain of wealth from India to England as the chief causes of famines. Nationalist arguments of increased food shortages due to growing food export and peasants' inclination towards non-food crop for its high export-value has been vehemently countered by the colonial administration. The British government had justified their policy of export of food crops by arguing that food exports increased in times of low prices and fell in times of high prices which eventually stabilized food prices and helped the peasants to get the actual returns.[6] However, ecological crisis did not receive any official consideration from the part of the colonial administration.

Datta argues that 'there has been a connection between ecological dislocations...and subsistence crisis' for the analysis of 'famine-causation.'[7] Among the modern scholars, Michelle Burge McAlpin (1979), while explaining the famines in western India between 1870 and 1920, emphasizes the role of climatological factor in causing crop failures. This work, based on rainfall statistics and climate influence, underlines the natural or ecological issues, rather than the institutional or policy background of famines.[8] However, by eschewing the theory of 'climatic determinism', David Arnold (1988) has assigned the climatic conditions as an 'instrumental' and not 'a causative role' in stimulating crises of production or subsistence.[9] It is also important to note that the agricultural dependence on natural supply of water sometimes had aggravated the risk of crop failure and the system of single cropping heightened the failure tendency of the monsoon crops. Moreover, El Nino – type disturbances of the tropical oceanic atmospheric occurrence could make rainfall more erratic.[10] Davis argues that though famine can be caused by floods (Bengal, 1883) or war (Bengal, 1943), 'drought is the proximate cause of most Indian subsistence crises, and twenty-one out of twenty-six droughts since 1877 have been attributed to El Ninos.'[11]

The Malthusian theory of disparity between production (and resources) and population (or demand) in a region illustrates the interrelation between the total output, current supply and per capita consumption (or availability) of food grains as the central point of famine. Ambirajan, on the other hand, showing the disparity between the Malthusian population theory and the Indian population, argues that 'India's population was anywhere near the Malthusian limit.'[12] But an essential rather more valuable argument has been put forward by Amartya Sen in his entitlement thesis where entitlement relations in a private ownership market economy involve *'trade-based entitlement'*, *'productions based entitlement'*, *own labour entitlement'*, and *'inheritance transfer entitlement'*.[13] Sen in his theory of the Failure of Exchange Entitlements (FEE) questions the above approach of Food Availability Decline (FAD). He is of the opinion that "[I]n a market economy, a person...can do [the] exchange either through trading, or through production, or through a combination of the two. The set of all the alternative bundles of commodities that he can acquire in exchange for what he owns may be called the 'exchange entitlement' of what he owns."[14] Sen, thus, argues that most famines are caused largely by an unexpected blow in the prevailing pattern of exchange relations rather than by a decline in food supply. Ghose, on the other hand, argues that 'famines are caused not generally by absolute food shortages but by sudden increases in inequality of food distribution.'[15] This changes in equality of food distribution according to Ghose, 'are most often brought about by a decline in food production and sometimes by a rise in the relative price of food.'[16] Bose argues that 'it was the role of the state and the economically powerful in effecting declines in entitlements to food of vulnerable social groups that turned the 'dearth into a famine.'[17] In another work on famines in western India, David Hall-Mathews while designating famines 'as process' and 'not as events', argues that the famines had produced 'the economic, social and political marginalisation of parts of populations to the extent that entitlements to food and other subsistence necessities are lost.'[18]

The reason for the recurrence of food-shortages during the late-eighteenth century have been attributed to the 'unknown ecological' factors which 'were more intense and…had more pervasive social consequences.'[19] While commenting on the Famine of 1770, Vinita Damodaran has remarked that 'the 1768–1770 droughts and famines were a profound blow not only to the system of revenue but also to the whole rationale of empire', as 'they provided an impetus for the evolution of a famine policy.'[20] Famine in colonial India had unleashed a continuous disagreement between the dominator and the dominated, when the later had to frequently adapt with their subsistence level and further survival. Bhatia argues that between 1858 and 1914 India 'went through a commercial revolution' and this revolution was brought out by the rapid spread of railways and the opening of Suez Canal.[21] In this process of commercialization, the competition of market forces had started to shape 'the relations between producers and consumers, lenders and borrowers, landlords and tenants, property owners and landless workers.'[22] Sugata Bose has argued that 'the structures and trends of demography, commercialization, production and appropriation were fashioned by the contest between the forces of domination and resistance.'[23] The ever-increasing lust of revenues in form of several taxes imposed upon the peasantry heightened tensions among the peasant society of Bengal as well as in India. R. C. Dutt was of the opinion that: 'The uncertainty of the State demand hangs like the sword of Damocles over the heads of Indian agriculturists, deadens their energy, and withdraws all motives for improvement.'[24] Exchange of money, credit relations and cash-based economy appeared to be most powerful elements in the realm of market economy under the colonial rule. Famine had, time to time, provided a major blow to the continuation of these elements which were collapsed or shattered either by the human exploitation or ecological disruptions, or sometimes by the combination of both of these.

Governmental concern for famine relief was, however, motivated by a single agenda – to normalize the source of revenue as fast as possible from the ruins of the economic disaster caused by the natural abnormalities. But governmental response in terms of famine relief was not identical throughout the colonial rule, in fact, it varied so widely that any single explanation could hardly reveal the mechanism and dynamics of colonial justification of 'charitable' or 'gratuitous' relief. Along with Governmental relief operations, there were also numerous instances of active private charities which contributed to the lessening of the intensity and duration of famines in colonial India. Georgina Brewis argues that the unwillingness of the administration to acknowledge full accountability for saving lives, and the apprehensions regarding the increase of impoverishment, provided the background for the appearance of a parallel system of charitable relief which included indigenous traditions of relief with British models of organizing philanthropy.[25] The chief aspects of voluntary famine relief in the 1890s 'was careful selection of recipients, the principle that labour should be exacted in exchange for relief, and strict discipline and routine in poor-houses or kitchens.'[26] Mike Davis emphasizes the importance of the state's role to regulate the prices of food grains that had always a negative impact upon the livelihood of the famine victims.[27] Over the last few decades, famine studies have been appeared as a distinctive genre of study which deserve to be treated as a separate 'discipline' with an interdisciplinary approach. Among these there are many recent studies that delve into the regional famine conditions in several parts of colonial Bengal which became vulnerable to the ecological and environmental changes that acted as the catalyst of the famines.[28] But there is hardly any attempt to explore the critical aspects of famine in northern Bengal where one may come across the existence of diverse complexities and elements which were not only distinctive for the region, but also provide the scopes for the development of new arguments and interpretations for the famine-studies.

The existing literature on Bengal-Orissa famine of 1866 overwhelmingly deals with the region of Orissa[29], and does not focus on the conditions of climate, crops and population of Bengal proper during the famine years. Jill Bender has made an interesting study of the 1873-74 Bengal famine which he relates with the Irish potato famine and other famines in Ireland. Bender has also situated the 1873-74 famine in the context of Irish parliamentary nationalism that was in opposition with the British imperialism.[30] It must be noted here that since the closing decades of the nineteenth century the colonial government had started to gather detailed information about the trends of crop-production, impact of rainfall upon the crop production and per acre production of crops in different parts of India. George Blyn argues that 'government interest in famine control and commercial needs for information led to central publication of coordinated agricultural series for British India and provinces.'[31] Vinita Damodaran in her essay titled *Famine in a Forest Tract* has shown the larger implications of colonial forest policy among the tribes of Chotanagpur region where colonial denial of forest use for the tribals triggered famines as a result of the absence of even minimum access to the forest products during the times of scarcities. Constant reduce of forest areas and openings of new coal mines in the cultivable land made the tribal population more vulnerable to any slightest fall in their entitlement. Though the famines of 1866-67 and 1873-74 were mitigated by the use of forest product but the 1896-97 famine, which had 'developed in the context of a failure of the monsoon' and was intensified by the destruction of forests had 'led to a decrease of jungle products and ... deprived the people of one of their chief means of resistance to famine.'[32] However, most ironically, 'specific regulations with regard to forests and fodder were proposed during the famine of 1896-97.'[33] The famine in Chotanagpur was accompanied by cholera epidemic which took a heavy toll due to the 'hesitancy in instituting relief' by the colonial state that 'reluctantly set in motion a system of famine relief.'[34] The consecutive famines in this area since 1866 had contributed to a large scale migration of tribal population as coolies for the tea garden areas of northern Bengal and Assam which eventually resulted in the increase of population in the later areas.[35] The most authoritative study on 1896-97 famine has come from Malavika Chakrabarty who in her book *Famine of 1896-97 in Bengal: The Availability or Entitlement Crisis* has vividly depicted all the aspects of 1896-97 famine in Bengal. The book has provided new insights in studying the famine of 1896-97 and adds new dimension in the realm of famine-studies. Though there is hardly any space left by the book in discussing the famine of 1896-97, but the distinctive and critical conditions which prevailed in the districts of northern Bengal deserve to be mentioned and analyzed separately.

An agricultural economy, like Bengal, which relied almost exclusively on the natural supply of waters or the monsoons for irrigating its fields, was naturally sensitive to the periodic cycles of droughts or floods. These ecological or environmental phenomena had an inevitable impact on the production and prices of the food grains. There are four chief harvests in the Bengali agricultural year – a). the *Aus* rice, sown in April-May (in the Bengali month of *Baisakh*), reaped in August or September (*Bhadro*); b). the *Aman* rice or the winter rice (the great harvest of the year), sown in lowlands in April, May, and June or on highlands in June or July (*Assar*); reaped in November and December (*Aghrahan*); c). the *Boro* rice, an intermediate crop producing the coarsest quality of rice, sown in March-April (*Chaitra*), and harvested in either *Assar* (i.e. June-July) or *Srawan* (i.e. July-August); and d). the *Rabi*, or spring crops, consisting of peas, pulses, oilseeds, and miscellaneous green crops, sown in October, reaped in February.

Ecological factors played an important role towards the causation of the famine and also towards the intensification of the famine. Shortage of rainfall, drought and subsequent decline in availability or entitlement had exposed the complexities of the social relations of production more overtly. However, this natural or ecological dislocations and their subsequent impact on the economy or production system during the colonial period were not confined only to the concerned regions but demonstrated an eclectic tendency that was caused by their ultimate link with the broader world economic structure which was dominated by the British colonialism. Thus it is evident that though a drought or shortage of rainfall persists for a shorter time or it affects the human life of a specific area, this cannot be confined within a precise 'scale' of time or space, because, according to Hughes, 'no case study, however small, may be considered in isolation."[36] During the second half of the nineteenth century north Bengal had been severely affected by two major famines – the Bihar-Bengal famine (1873-74) and the Bengal Famine of 1896-97. These two famines had considerably ravaged a greater part of colonial north Bengal. Apart from the famines, during the second half of the nineteenth century and first decade of the twentieth century, north Bengal had to witness several small-scale dearth or scarcities (1854, 1866, 1884, 1892, and 1908-09) that significantly affected the agriculture and population of this region.

Outline of the Book

In the above historical backdrop, the present book intends to critically explore the issues of droughts, subsistence and scarcities in colonial north Bengal during the second half of the nineteenth century. This book also seeks to examine the vulnerabilities and sufferings of the north Bengal districts in the major famines of 1866, 1873-74 and 1896-97. At the very outset it is important to say few words about the objectives of this present work. Famine-studies, over the years, have been emerging as a separate discipline in the realm of economic history of colonial India. This book, however, attempts to shed lights on the local or micro-level history of famines that occurred in a less known geographical or political area. Scarcities, till date, do not receive any serious historical intervention due to their so-called incapacity to provide materials for writing big histories. Thus, the present work intends to bring about the ecological and economic trajectories of a peripheral region like North Bengal where political economy of natural calamities (droughts and famines) can be studied on the basis of local variations of rainfall, market and subsistence crisis.

The objective of this book is fourfold – firstly, there is a remarkable absence of any famine-studies exclusively on North Bengal, and therefore, the present study, in a way, is a district-wise study of famines, scarcities and subsistence crises. Secondly, the existing literature focuses on the big aspects of famine that took away millions of lives or had ushered great rupture in the society and economy of colonial Bengal as well as in India. However, the famines and scarcities which had not been always attended with great casualty in some regions, like the districts of North Bengal, are also crucial for understanding the local or micro-level histories of capital, market, and populations. The inter-relations between these factors can be studied with more depth and criticality through the perspectives of local or regional ecological dislocations that further aggravated the vulnerability of a peripheral colonialized society. Thirdly, emphasis has been given so far on the big famines, but the stories of smaller scarcities or subsistence crisis that prevailed in the comparatively less important areas or far from the centre, did not receive adequate historical attention. Therefore, this work aims to offer a historical narrative of famines and scarcities which had distinct local variations. Fourthly, famines, so far, have been dealt with from several ideological perspectives, i.e., - exchange entitlement, food availability decline, Malthusian theory of surplus and productions etc. The present book does not intend to indulge into any particular viewpoint but to analyze the important aspects of famine-affected areas of colonial North Bengal during the period from 1866 to 1909 which has hitherto been overlooked by the modern scholars. The present study deals with the local events of famines and scarcities from the perspectives of environmental and ecological degradations which was further aggravated by the colonial state, market and changing social relations of production.

The book intends to examine in detail the pattern of peasant cultivation and the impact of rainfall, drought and colonial capitalism upon them within the specific area of North Bengal. The fluctuations in prices of crops and food grains which were triggered by the shortage of rainfall and colonial control of local markets during the time of scarcities or famines had revealed the critical character of colonial administration that had lacked any proper sense of local sufferings. This book also intends to examine the magnitude of unpredicted ecological disturbances which had been hazardous for the normal continuation of the economy or society in a particular region. Moreover, it attempts to demonstrate the impact of temporary ecological dislocations caused by shortage of rainfall or drought on productions, food prices and subsistence. Given this, the book also focuses on the importance of the understanding of diverse characteristics of the peasant society of colonial North Bengal which was markedly different from the other parts of Bengal.

The present book has been divided into four main chapters. The first chapter titled 'An Early History of Colonial Famine: North Bengal in 1769-70'includes a brief historical narrative of the Bengal Famine of 1770 with special reference to the impact of the famine in the districts of North Bengal. The second chapter titled 'Ecology and Population: Investigating Demographic Transformations in Colonial North Bengal' highlights the demographic transformations in relation with the ecological changes that had taken place in colonial North Bengal. The third chapter titled 'Rainfall, Crops and Colonialism: Famines in North Bengal, 1866-1891' deals with the background and impact of the 1873-74 Bengal-Bihar famine, and it also includes a brief description of the Bengal-Orissa famine of 1866 and the scarcity of 1884 and 1891 which had affected certain parts of North Bengal. The fourth chapter titled 'Famine, Relief and the Colonial State in North Bengal, 1896-1909' seeks to unearth the specific and distinctive aspects of the famine of 1896-97 in North Bengal and it also deals with the scarcity of 1908-09 which was limited to some particular areas of Northern Bengal.

However, the main objective of the above-mentioned chapters is to critically examine the ecological and environmental changes that took place in colonial North

Bengal in terms of variations in rainfall, short- and long-lasting drought and their subsequent impact on the human-nature relationship. The book investigates the nature and structure of agricultural production and subsistence which were considerably affected by the complex character of market, state and economy. Famines had brought into all these elements together in a single fold which was characterized by a continuous tension between market, politics and society.

REFERENCES

1. Rajat Datta, *Society, Economy and the Market: Commercialization in Rural Bengal, C.1760-1800,* Manohar, New Delhi, 2000, p. 238.
2. Madhav Gadgil, Ramchandra Guha, *This Fissured Land: An Ecological History of India,* Oxford University Press, New Delhi, first published 1992, thirteenth impression, 2010, p. 116.
3. Rajat Datta, Subsistence Crisis and Economic History: A Study of Eighteenth Century Bengal, in Ayesha Mukherjee (ed.), *A Cultural History of Famine Food Security and the Environment in India and Britain,* London and New York: Routledge, 2019, pp. 38-39.
4. G. W. Forrest, *The Famine in India,* Horace Cox, London, 1897, p. 16.
5. C.W. McMinn, *Famines: Truths, Half-Truths, Untruths,* Calcutta, 1902, p. 39.
6. Tirthankar Roy, *The Economic History of India, 1857-1947,* Oxford University Press, New Delhi, Second Edition, 2009, p. 362.
7. Rajat Datta, *Society, Economy and the Market,* p. 238.
8. Michelle Burge McAlpin, 'Dearth, Famine and Risk: The Changing Impact of Crop Failures in Western India, 1870–1920', *Journal of Economic History,* vol. 39, no. 1, March, 1979, p. 145.
9. David Arnold, *Famine: Social Crisis and Historical Change,* Blackwell, Oxford, 1988, p. 31.
10. Tirthankar Roy, *op. cit.,* p. 361.

11. Mike Davis, *Late Victorian Holocaust: El Nino Famines and the Making of the Third World*, London and New York: Verso, 2002, p. 246.

12. Ambirajan argues that due to the recurrence of famines during the 1860s the official perception had begun to change, and it was 'realized that population growth was a serious problem that merited close attention.' S. Ambirajan, 'Malthusian Population Theory and Indian Famine Policy in the Nineteenth Century', *Population Studies*, Vol. 30, No. 1 (Mar., 1976), p. 6.

13. Amartya Sen, *Poverty and Famines: An Essay on Entitlement and Deprivation*, Oxford University Press, New Delhi, Eleventh Impression, 2007, p. 2.

14. *Ibid.*, p. 3.

15. Ajit Kumar Ghose, 'Food Supply and Starvation: A Study of Famines with Reference to the Indian Sub-Continent', Oxford Economic Papers, New Series, Vol. 34, No. 2 (Jul., 1982), p. 383.

16. To quote Ghose, 'The severity of effects of either a decline in food production or a rise in the relative price of food depends on the structural characteristics of the rural economy concerned: the pattern of land distribution, the proportion of population dependent on exchange for acquiring food supplies, the nature of exchange relations and the degree of monetisation of the exchange relation.' *Ibid.*, pp. 383-284.

17. Sugata Bose, *Peasant Labour and Colonial Capital: Rural Bengal since 1770*, Cambridge University Press, Cambridge, 1993, p. 18.

18. David Hall-Mathews, Peasants Famines and the State in Colonial Western India, New York: Palgrave Macmillan, 2005, p. 1.

19. Rajat Datta, Society, Economy and the Market, p. 240.

20. Vinita Damodaran, 'Famine in Bengal: A Comparison of the 1770 Famine in Bengal and the 1897 Famine in Chhotanagpur,' The Medieval History Journal, 10, 1&2, 2007, p. 155.

21. B.M. Bhatia, 'Famine and Agricultural Labour in India: A Historical Perspective', Indian Journal of Industrial Relations, Apr., 1975, Vol. 10, No. 4 (Apr., 1975), p. 575.

22. *Ibid.*

23. Sugata Bose, *op. cit.*, p. 4.

24. Romesh Dutt, *Indian Famines: Their Causes and Prevention*, P. S. King & Son, London, 1901, p. 5.

25. Georgina Brewis, 'Fill Full the Mouth of Famine': Voluntary Action in Famine Relief in India 1896— 1901,' *Modern Asian Studies*, Vol. 44, No. 4 (July 2010), p. 888.

26. *Ibid.*, p. 907.

27. Mike Davis, *op.cit.*, p. 31.

28. Vinita Damodaran, 'Famine in a Forest Tract: Ecological Change and the Causes of the 1897 Famine in Chotanagpur, Northern India,' in Arun Bandopadhyay (ed.), *Nature Knowledge and Development: Critical Essays on the Environmental History of India, Primus Books*, New Delhi, 2016, pp. 109-142; Nirmal Kumar Mahato, 'Environmental Change and Chronic Famine in Manbhum, Bengal District, 1860-1910,' *Global Environment*, 6, 2011, pp. 68-94.

29. Braja Bandhu Bhatta, The Natural Calamities in Orissa in 19th century, New Delhi: Commonwealth Publishers, 1997; Anil Dhir and Ramesh Chandra Mohapatra (eds.), *The Great Orissa Famine 1866 (Na'anka Durbhikshya)*, Bhubneswar: Amadeus Press, 2017.

30. Jill Bender, 'The Imperial Politics of Famine: The 1873–74 Bengal Famine and Irish Parliamentary Nationalism,' Éire-Ireland, Volume 42:1&2, Spring/Summer 2007, pp. 132-156.

31. George Blyn, *Agricultural Trends in India, 1891-1947: Output, Availability and Productivity*, Philadelphia: University of California Press, 1966, p. 39.

32. Vinita Damodaran, 'Famine in a Forest Tract,' p. 129.

33. Michael Mann, 'Forestry and Famine in the Chambal-Jamna Doab, 1879-1919,' in Mahesh Rangarajan and K. Sivaramakrishnan (eds.), *India's Environmental History, Vol. 2: Colonialism, Modernity, and the Nation*, Permanent Black, Ranikhet, 2014, p. 445.

34. Vinita Damodaran, 'Famine in a Forest Tract,' p. 131.

35. Almost 250,000 tribals were recruited in the tea gardens of Assam from Chhotanagpur. For details see Sanjukta Das Gupta,

Accessing Nature: Agrarian Change, Forest Laws and their Impact on an Adivasi Economy in Colonial India, in Arun Bandopadhyay (ed.), *Nature Knowledge and Development: Critical Essays on the Environmental History of India*, Primus Books, New Delhi, 2016, pp. 98-99.

36. J. Donald Hughes, What Does Environmental History Teach? in Angela Mendonca, Ana Cunha, Ranjan Chakrabarty (eds.), *Natural Resources, Sustainability and Humanity: A Comprehensive View*, Springer, 2012, p. 11.

1

An Early History of Colonial Famine: North Bengal in 1769-70

The famine of 1770 had been a watershed in the history of famines in colonial Bengal as well as in India. Though there is a good deal of historical writings on the 1770 famine, many aspects of the famine still remain 'unknown and enigmatic.'[1] Considering the horror of the famine John Fiske once commented that the famine of 1770 had 'nearly exterminated the ancient civilization of Bengal.'[2] Hunter remarked that 'in the cold weather of 1769 Bengal was visited by a famine whose ravages two generations failed to repair.'[3] According to David Arnold, 'in terms of the enormous loss of life and the intensity and extent of human suffering involved, the Bengal famine of 1770 must count as one of the greatest catastrophes of the eighteenth century and, indeed, of modern times.'[4] The causes of the famine of 1770 had been attributed by the British officials to the 'exceptional drought and the consequent loss of the *aman* or autumn rice crop..'[5] The continuous failure of crops throughout the harvesting season of 1769-70 had created a condition of acute gain scarcity about which the Calcutta Council did not have any information.[6] After witnessing this sort of grain crisis, Mohammad Reza Khan commented that 'hitherto grain was scarce but this year [1770] it cannot be found at all.'[7]

The entire province of Bengal and its districts had been severely affected by this famine of 1770. According to Bose, 'the western and central Bengal districts of Nadia, Murshidabad, Midnapur, Birbhum, and Burdwan, Rajshahi and Dinajpur further north and most districts in adjoining Bihar were hardest hit by the famine.'[8] A brief description of the 1770 Bengal famine is given below

> "The crops of December, 1768, and August, 1769, were both scanty, and prices became very high; and throughout the month of October, 1769, hardly a drop of rain fell. The usual refreshing showers of January to May also failed in 1770, in which year, until late in May, scarcely any rain fell. The famine was felt in all the northern part of Bengal as early as November, 1769, but by the 4th of January, 1770, the daily deaths from starvation in Patna were up to fifty; and before the end of May, one hundred and fifty. The tanks were dried up, and the springs had ceased to reach the surface, and before the end of April, 1770, famine had spread desolation. In Murshidabad, at length, the dead were left uninterred; dogs, jackals, and vultures were the sole scavengers. Three millions of people were supposed to have perished. It is also said that within the first nine months of 1770, one-third of the entire population of lower Bengal perished for want of food."[9]

Hunter argued that in the early part of 1769 high prices were prevailing throughout the province due to the 'partial failure of the crops in 1768.' Despite of this, the scarcity, according to Hunter, had not been 'so severe as materially to affect the Government rental.'[10] However, in spite of the 'complaints and forebodings' of local officers, the authorities at headquarters reported that 'the land-tax had been rigorously enforced and the rains of 1769, although deficient in the northern districts, seemed for a time to promise relief.'[11] From Hunter 's remarks it is evident that rain was deficient in the northern districts which had felt the famine so severely. On the contrary, according to Hunter, rain was sufficient in the Delta and south-east Bengal. While comparing the succeeding years (i.e. 1771, 1772, and 1773) with that of the famine year (1769-70), Hunter had commented that the famine of 1770 was, therefore, 'a one year's famine,' caused by the general failure of the December harvest in 1769, and intensified by a partial failure of the crops of the previous year and the following spring.[12] In June 1770, the Resident at Darbar of Murshidabad noted that 'the scene of misery that intervened, and still continues, shocks humanity too much to bear description.'[13] In regards to the relief for the victims the Court of Directors asserted in November 1769 that 'We have taken and shall pursue every means in our power to relieve the miserable situation the poor inhabitants must be involved in from this dreadful calamity.'[14]

The 1770 famine, which arrived in Bengal from Bihar, had taken a great toll of one-third population of Bengal which included agricultural labourers, poor peasants, and artisans, etc. Purnia was the most severely affected tract where two lakhs of people perished in that district alone.[15] The districts of Nadia and Rajshahi were next two seriously affected areas in Bengal. Macaulay described the ecological conditions of the famine of 1770 in the following words:

> "In the summer of 1770, the rains failed; the earth was parched up; the tanks were empty; the river shrank within their beds; and a famine...filed the whole valley of the Ganges wit misery and death."[16]

In rural Bengal, Datta argues, the 'most harvest- and price-sensitive' social group was the textile producer, and one-third portion from this group, who were spinners and weavers, had died in Malda and Purnea during the 1770 famine.[17] In Rajshahi, a large section of the *chassars* (who reared silk worms) had died in 1770.[18] Nani Gopal Choudhury had estimated that in the district of Rajshahi, 'desertion and death together caused the disappearance of 66 percent of families: 47 per cent of this loss was due to mortality along.[19]

The famine had made a long-lasting impact in the sphere of changing ecological conditions. The colossal loss of human lives and an uncontrolled scenario of dispossession from agricultural land due to massive depopulation had further darkened the economic prospects of the Bengal province. The dispossession of the local landlords of Burdwan, Nadia and Rajshahi from their erstwhile property had thrown them into a vicious circle of debt.[20] After the draught a severe flood had occurred in the countryside of the pargana of Bhatoria of Rajshahi District.[21] This flood had swept agricultural fields where seeds were sown for the next harvest, and this produced great inconvenience for the people who were further affected by an extended crisis. In December 1770, the Supervisor of Rajshahi had reported a sharp increase in prices of rice which was later in 1771 had further reached to an abnormal rate.[22] Sinha argues that the famine had left its 'permanent' impact on government revenue in the district of Rajshahi, where from 1767 to 1770 the average land revenue collection was 27 lakhs and it was declined to 21.75 lakhs between 1770 and 1772.[23]

The areas of Rangpur district which were contiguous to the border of Purnia district was desolated by the famine. Though Rangpur, till May 1770, did not suffer much from the famine, in the months of August and September the district was completely ravaged by the famine. In August 1770, the price of rice in Dinajpur was six or seven seers per rupee, whereas in Rangpur, 'rice sold at from fifteen to twenty seers per rupee.'[24] However, the zamindari estate of Dinajpur held by Baidyanath was 'depopulated and ruined' by the famine which had made the zamindari lands as 'fallen' and 'waste' as a result of the 'want of seed and implements of cultivation.'[25] As part of relief measures rice was distributed free in Dinajpur and Rajmahal. Though at the initial stage, it was decided that ten rupees worth of rice should be distributed daily in Rangpur, in reality only five rupees worth of rice for charitable distribution was sanctioned by Mr. Becher, the Resident at the Darbar at Murshidabad.[26]

The famine of 1770 had for the first time, perhaps, initiated the political use (misuse?) of the ecological or climatological factors in order to justify the acts of imperial coercion that had continuously impoverished the population upto the fullest extent to the mercy of nature. The projection of acute shortage of rainfall or persistence of severe drought for long time over the excessive torture of the company officials to the pooper peasants had, in fact, established an unjust relationship between the political economy and the ecological factors that would have hardly justified the occurrence of the famine. Damodaran argues that there was a mutual dependency between the 'transport networks, market forces, and administrative policy' that had immensely contributed to transformation of a local scarcity in to a disastrous famine.[27] The private trade of the Company servants had a critical impact upon the intensification of the scarcities of grain. The entire administrative set up which was engaged in private trade had been accused and despite the Court of Director's investigation into this matter there was no satisfactory development in this regard.[28]

The continuous and consciousness planning of arguments by the Company officials and later by the Government officers had repeatedly emphasized the theory of draught or failure of rains in the province during the 1770. Nonetheless, almost after a century when George Campbell, the then Governor of Bengal had been trying to locate the cause of the 1770 famine, had found that in 1867 that 'the great misfortune of the last century was occasioned or very materially aggravated by…natural causes.'[29] Based on the statement of the Resident of Murshidabad, Campbell mentioned that in north Bengal the season of 1768-69 was 'bad.' On 17th August 1769, the Resident had reported that the "alarming want of rain which has prevailed throughout all the Upper parts of Bengal both the last and this season and particularly the latter, to a degree which has not been known in the memory of the oldest man."[30] On 26th August the Resident further added that

> "there is great reason to apprehend that in all the districts to the northward of Nuddea the crops of rice will be very short indeed. Since the season for rain began they have hardly had any, and if God does not soon bless this country with plentiful showers the most fatal consequences will ensue, —not only a reduction in the revenues, but a scene of misery and distress that is a constant attendant on famine. God, of his infinite goodness, avert the dreadful calamity."[31]

Due to the partial failure of crops high prices had prevailed during the early part of the 1769, but the servants of the Company were totally indifferent to towards this situation.[32] The northern districts which had usually exported rice to Calcutta had suffered a major setback in regards to the production of rice and as a result rice had become very scarce in Calcutta from the beginning of August 1769. From the end of January 1770, 'the evil was becoming very great'[33] in northern Bengal and from February onwards, the process of depopulation in Bihar had been continuing in a full swing. Apart from Rajshahi, the whole district of Rangpur had suffered seriously 'owing to the great scarcity of inhabitants.'[34] Along with Bihar, Dinajpur and the northern districts of Bengal had witnessed importation of rice from the other parts of the province. Rajshahi, however, was affected twice by the natural calamities. The drought of 1769 had been succeeded by the 1770 floods which inundated the low lands, where crops were sown with an expectation of a moderate rain. With the passage of time the situation in the district had become more critical. In 1771, the Supervisor of the district of Rajshahi had reported that 'numbers of ryots who have hitherto borne the first of characters among their neighbours pursue this last resource to procure themselves a subsistence.'[35]

The Government of the East India Company had extended a system of taqavi loan to the peasants, and among the districts of Bengal the northern districts had received a considerable amount as loan.

Table. 1.1

Grant of Taqavi during the famine of 1770

District	*Amount of Taqavi received (in rupees)*
Birbhum	20,000
Rajshahi	50,000
Nadia	30,000
Dinajpur	45,000
Purnia	69,047
Rangpur	35,000

Source: Nani Gopal Chaudhury, Cartier: Governor of Bengal, 1769-1772, p. 66.

Among other districts of Bengal proper the districts of northern Bengal had received the major Taqavi grants. Rajshahi, Dinajpur and Rangpur had received the most consistent relief in terms of taqavi, that signified the horrible condition of the peasantry and agricultural fields in this part of the country. However, taqavi did not ensure any amelioration in the condition of the peasants who were thrown out of the ancestral lands. Mr. Becher dictated that 'the Taqavi advanced to the ryots should be collected with an interest of two annas or 12½%.

There is no doubt that the excessive oppression by the Company officials had made the peasant-society most vulnerable to the climatic disorder. The increase in the collection of land revenue in 1770-71, i.e. after the famine year had demonstrated the fact that the Company did not show any slightest sympathy to the famine victims, and even continued to assert its domination over the poor people.[36] The small-pox epidemic which was coupled with the famine had resulted into the deaths of millions of people who were already under-nourished and devoid of any immunity to resist the epidemic. Thus, drought and epidemic wrought a havoc in the Bengal countryside which had altered the agricultural land into waste lands and killed millions of people.[37] In 1771, when agriculture was about to begin in the province it 'was discovered that the remnant of the population would not suffice to till the land [and] the areas affected by the famine continued to fall and were put out of tillage.'[38]

The relief operations carried out by the East India Company was inadequate.[39] Loveday commented that 'the methods actually adopted were unwise, unorganised, and ungenerous.'[40] The banning of exportation of rice from the affected areas and the remission of land tax was not successful enough to provide even any temporary relief to the distressed. Though the local officers were constantly urging for remissions of the land-tax and advances to the husbandmen, it received 'little practical effect.'[41] The state had also failed to 'detect localized falls in food availability.[42] The Company Government had issued taqqavi for the worst affected parts and the districts of Rajshahi, Dinajpur and Rangpur had received the highest per centage of taqqavi (except Purnia and Birbhum) that revealed the severity of distress in these districts.[43] However, in a year when thirty-five per cent of the whole population and fifty per cent of the cultivators were perished, not five per cent of the land-tax was remitted, and moreover, ten per cent was added to it for the subsequent year (1770-71).[44] Fiske commented that 'the relief came too late to avert depopulation' and the starving and shelterless people were migrating from 'one deserted village to another in a vain search for food.'[45] Hunter, while considering the relief measures as 'inhumanly inadequate' had admitted that in 1770 'the British Government knew very little about the country, and did still less for its inhabitants.'[46] Roy argues that the famine was the 'first major administrative challenge for the Company's state in Bengal, and to generations of writers, a sad comment on the chaotic, cynical, and mercenary way in which the state then functioned.'[47] Datta, on the other hand, comments that the Company had failed 'to provide any form of institutional relief' despite of having 'the cash reserves to do so.'[48]

The famine of 1770 had triggered the incidents of crimes in the rural Bengal. Social banditry in form of 'burning, plundering and ravaging' became wide spread. According to the government reports the border areas of Rajshahi witnessed an increased number of dacoity cases. In April 1771, the District Supervisor of Rajshahi had reported that – 'I receive advices from the parganas of the frequent firing of villages by people whose distress drives them to such acts of despair and villainy.'[49] He further stated that 'number of ryots, who have hitherto borne the best of characters amongst their neighbours, pursue this last desperate resource to procure themselves a subsistence.'[50] The Sanyasi-Fakir rebellion had been influenced to a great extent by the famine of 1770 which had provided a massive support base to 'vagabond' sannyasis who had 'infiltrated from the western part of India from beyond the territory of the Nawab of Oudh and entered Bengal through Purnia District in Bihar.[51] After crossing Purnia district, they moved towards Malda, Rajshahi and Rangpur districts. During the subsequent years of the Bengal famine of 1770 the numbers of the sannyasis and fakirs had increased to a great extent by 'a crowd of starving peasants, who had neither seed nor implements to recommence cultivation with, and the cold weather of 1772 brought them down upon the harvest fields of lower Bengal…'[52] The sannyasis and fakirs had raided villages after villages with their usual activities of 'begging, stealing and plundering.'[53] From Dinajpur reports were sent by the local officials that Sanyasis were 'plundering' in different parts of the district.[54] The entire region of north Bengal had been exposed to the Sanyasi and Fakir raiders from the borders of Tirhut, Morung, Cooch Behar. Sinha further stated that 'the progressive decline of North Bengal dates from the famine.'[55] Ghosh stated that northern Bengal in particular was infested by these banditti.[56] James Rennell, who was stationed at Belkuchy near Serajganj of Pabna in the month of February 1771 for the survey of Bengal province had narrated the following descriptions about the movement of the sannyasis and fakirs in different parts of north Bengal.

> "There is now in this part of the country a large body of Fakirs who are laying all the principal towns under contribution. They were yesterday at Lutchinumpur 4 coss from this place and after receiving two hundred rupees from the Gunge Daroga marched northward to Pucharya District [Pukharia pargana in the present district of Mymensingh]... They are about a thousand in number and tolerably well-armed; they came from the western provinces about a month ago and traversed the Dinajpur and Ghoraghat districts on the way ...I have met several of their detached parties which are indeed scattered over the whole province of Radshy (Rajshahi) and Ghoraghat (Dinajpur)."[57]

The local zamindars and rajas did not possess any considerable military power to oust the sanyasis from their estates. The Raja of Dinajpur reported that the fakirs were 'too great in number to be routed out' by the small party of zamindary army.[58] Therefore, the Company government had to deploy sepoys for the districts of Rajshahi, Dinajpur, and Rangpur in order to curb the activities of the sannyasis.

Fiske argued that the peasants who had lost their everything in the hands of the robbers had 'no alternative left but to become robbers themselves.'[59] Though there is a general conception that the peasants who were affected by the 1770 famine had joined in the ranks of fakirs and sannyasis, Bhattacharya, on the other hand, argues that there was 'no chances of any alliance with the peasantry because peasants had become the Fakirs' main victims.'[60] Bhattacharya further comments that though the peasants of Rangpur and Dinajpur had 'grievances' against the Company and the zamindars, the causes of those grievances were 'different from those of the Fakirs.'[61] Bhattacharya, however, eschews any possibility of 'direct impact' of the famine of 1770 on the 'gradual emergence of the fakirs' in the region of north Bengal.[62] Dasgupta states that the policies of economic exploitation which were initiated by the East India Company during the eighteenth century had 'intensively damaged the interests' of the peasants, the artisans and disbanded soldiers; and these groups had received support 'from the dispossessed old zamindars (like, Maharani Bhawani of Natore and Asaduzzaman Khan, a Nawab in Birbhum) and semi- autonomous chieftains (like, the Rajbanshi Rajas of Cooch-Behar and their relative Raikats of Baikunthapur or Jalpaiguri.'[63] This situation, according to Dasgupta, had become overtly 'desperate and antagonistic' after the advent of the 1770 Bengal famine.[64]

North Bengal had again suffered from further decay that was caused by the transfer of Diwani offices from Murshidabad to Calcutta in 1772 and this transfer had adversely affected the circulation of money which was usually much high in northern parts of Bengal beforc 1772.[65] Hunter had further asserted that 'before the commencement of 1771, one-third of a generation of peasants had been swept from the face of the earth and a whole generation of once rich families had been reduced to indigence.'[66] The old zamindaris of Burdwan, Nadia and Rajshahi had felt the same condition. Though the Maharani of Rajshahi was 'a lady of remarkable talent for public business' and had retained the control of her district, soon afterwards, being unable to pay the revenue to the Company 'was threatened with dispossession, the sale of her lands, and the withdrawal of her Government allowance.'[67]

Though the famine had aggravated the vulnerability of the poor people towards the climatic disorders such as drought and etc. and had transformed a vast region into a desolated place, the Company Government was not, however, anxious at all to the long-term consequences of the famine and depopulation. The Company officials were only concerned about their own economic interests. Nani Gopal Chaudhury comments that 'the account of the famine has found its place in the official records only to explain the Company's reduced income from commercial and revenue sources.'[68] The later writings of the colonial officials had exposed the devastations of 1770 famine merely from the administrative or governmental perspectives. In fact, Hunter had also considered the 1770 famine as a pre-history of the late-nineteenth century famines which were, according to him, handled more efficiently by the colonial administration than the previous one. It was said to believe that after the Bengal famine of 1770 'one-third of all Bengal, one of the most fruitful presidencies in India, lay "waste and silent" for twenty years.'[69] After the famine of 1770 Lord Cornwallis had started a policy of grain storing from the surplus of abundant years. However, there is no evidence that whether his successors had maintained such granaries. According to Loveday, 'public works were often, but not always, undertaken, and little or no attempt was made towards preparatory organisation.'[70] Despite of certain scattered famine-relief policies adopted by the Company administration 'there were no permanent famine officials, there were no codes, there were no regular reports on crops'[71] even till the end of first half of the nineteenth century. However, the Bengal famine of 1770 had become a template for the formulation of colonial administrative famine policies during the second half of the nineteenth century. Hunter in his *Annals of Rural Bengal* had simultaneously (sometimes even comparatively) studied the 1770 and the 1866 Orissa famine. While preparing the *Report* for the Bengal-Orissa famine of 1866, the Government in 1867, had emphasized the necessities to 'examine the records' of 1770 Bengal famine.[72]

REFERENCES

1. Tirthankar Roy, *Natural Disasters and Indian History*, New Delhi: Oxford University Press, 2014, p. 31.
2. John Fiske, *The Unseen World, and Other Essays*, Boston and Cambridge: Houghton, Mifflin and Company, 1876 (tenth edition), p. 192.
3. W. W. Hunter, *The Annals of Rural Bengal*, New York: Leypold and Holt, 1868, p. 19.
4. David Arnold, Hunger in the Garden of Plenty: The Bengal Famine of 1770, in Alessa Johns, *Dreadful Visitations: Confronting Natural Catastrophe in the Age of Enlightenment*, London and New York: Routledge, 2013, p. 86.
5. Ibid., p. 83.
6. Narendra Krishna Sinha, *The Economic History of Bengal: From Plassey to the Permanent Settlement*, Vol. II, Calcutta: Firma K. L. Mukhopadhyay, 1960, pp. 48-49.
7. Quoted in *Ibid.*, p. 49.
8. Sugata Bose, *Peasant Labour and Colonial Capital: Rural Bengal since 1770*, Cambridge University Press, Cambridge, 1993, p. 18.
9. Quoted in J. E. Scott, *In Famine Land: Observations and Experiences in India during the Great Drought of 1899-1900*, New York and London: Harper Brothers and Publishers, 1904, p. 3.
10. W. W. Hunter, *The Annals of Rural Bengal*, p. 20.
11. *Ibid.*, pp. 20-21.
12. *Ibid.*, p. 31.
13. L. S. O'Malley, *Bengal District Gazetteers: Rajshahi*, Calcutta: Bengal Secretariat Book Depot, 1916, p. 89.
14. Quoted in A. Loveday, *The History and Economics of Indian Famines*, London: G. Bell and Sons Ltd., 1914, p. 32.
15. Narendra Krishna Sinha, *op. cit.*, p. 50.
16. Quoted in Hemendra Prasad Ghose, The Famine of 1770, Calcutta: The Book Company Limited, no date, p. 41.
17. Rajat Datta, op. cit., p. 48.
18. Ibid. The reason behind the 'incredible mortality' of the chassar group was two-fold – firstly, due to the persistence of costly

silk-cocoons, the chassars did not have enough money to buy food; and secondly, chassars, who were highly specialized in this job, had become 'most harvest sensitive of all the affected social-strata and, not having enough food reserves to fall back up on, they died in large numbers.'

19. David Arnold, Hunger in the Garden of Plenty, p. 86.
20. Vinita Damodaran, 'Famine in Bengal: A Comparison of the 1770 Famine in Bengal and the 1897 Famine in Chhotanagpur,' The Medieval History Journal, 10, 1&2, 2007, pp. 154-155.
21. Narendra Krishna Sinha, *op. cit.*, p. 51.
22. L. S. O'Malley, *Bengal District Gazetteers: Rajshahi*, p. 89.
23. Narendra Krishna Sinha, *op. cit.*, p. 51.
24. Nani Gopal Chaudhury, *Cartier: Governor of Bengal, 1769-1772*, Calcutta: Firma K. L. Mukhopadhyay, 1960, p. 52.
25. Narendra Krishna Sinha, *op. cit.*, p. 54.
26. Nani Gopal Chaudhury, *op. cit.*, p. 61.
27. Vinita Damodaran, 'Famine in Bengal', p. 152.
28. Hemendra Prasad Ghose, *op. cit.*, p. 44.
29. George Campbell, 'The Famines which affected Bengal in the last Century,' in Further Report on the Famine in Bengal and Orissa in 1866 with Appendices, 1867, p. 21.
30. Quoted in *Ibid.*, p. 23.
31. Quoted in *Ibid.*
32. Hemendra Prasad Ghose, *op. cit.*, p. 37.
33. George Campbell, 'The Famines which affected Bengal in the last Century,' p. 25.
34. *Ibid.*, p. 29.
35. Quoted in Narendra Krishna Sinha, *op. cit.*, p. 64.
36. Vinita Damodaran, 'The East India Company, Famine and Ecological Conditions in Eighteenth-Century Bengal', in Vinita Damodaran et al (eds.), *The East India Company and the Natural World*, Palgrave Macmillan, 2015, p. 88.
37. *Ibid.*, pp. 88-89.
38. *Ibid.*, p. 89.
39. In Rangpur, John Gross was able to provide only Rs. 5 worth of rice among the indigent people 'even when the scarcity of

poor at this place still continuing very great from the scarcity of grain.' Quoted in Rajat Datta, *Society, Economy and the Market: Commercialization in Rural Bengal, C.1760-1800*, Manohar, New Delhi, 2000, p. 259.

40. A. Loveday, *op. cit.*, p. 32.
41. W.W. Hunter, *The Annals of Rural Bengal*, p. 39.
42. Tirthankar Roy, *op. cit.*, p. 29.
43. Cited in Rajat Datta, *op. cit.*, p. 260.
44. W. W. Hunter, *The Annals of Rural Bengal*, p. 39.
45. John Fiske, *op. cit.*, p. 195.
46. W. W. Hunter, The Annals of Rural Bengal, p. 40.
47. Tirthankar Roy, *Natural Disasters and Indian History*, pp. 32-33.
48. Rajat Datta, *Society, Economy and the Market*, p. 259.
49. L. S. O'Malley, *Bengal District Gazetteers: Rajshahi*, p. 89.
50. Ibid.
51. A. N. Chandra, *The Sannyasi Rebellion*, Calcutta: Ratna Prakashan, 1977, p. 38.
52. *Ibid.*, p. 32.
53. *Ibid.*
54. Narendra Krishna Sinha, *op. cit.*, p. 62.
55. *Ibid.*, p. 64.
56. Jamini Mohan Ghosh, *Sannyasi and Fakir Raiders in Bengal*, Calcutta: Bengal Secretariat Book Depot, 1930, p. 39.
57. Quoted in *Ibid.*, pp. 43-44.
58. A.N. Chandra, *The Sannyasi Rebellion*, p. 40.
59. John Fiske, *op. cit.*, pp. 200.
60. Ananda Bhattacharya, 'The Wandering Fakirs of Bengal: Heroes or Villains,' *South Asia Research*, Vol. 36(1), 2016, p. 4.
61. *Ibid.*
62. *Ibid.*, p. 7.
63. Atis Dasgupta, 'The Fakir and Sannyasi Rebellion,' *Social Scientist*, Jan., 1982, Vol. 10, No. 1 (Jan., 1982), p. 47.
64. Ibid.

65. Narendra Krishna Sinha, *op. cit.*, p. 64.
66. W. W. Hunter, *The Annals of Rural Bengal*, p. 56.
67. *Ibid.*, p. 58.
68. Nani Gopal Chaudhury, *op. cit.*, p. 31.
69. J. E. Scott, *op. cit.*, p. 3.
70. A. Loveday, *op. cit.*, p. 42.
71. *Ibid.*
72. Home Department, Public, No. 79 of 1867, Simla, the 10th May, 1867; in Remarks of Government on the report of the Commission appointed to enquire into the circumstances connected with the famine in Orissa and other parts of Bengal in 1866, with other papers relating to the famine, IOR/L/PJ/3/1100 No.99 : Mar 1867-Jul 1867.

2

Ecology and Population: Investigating Demographic Transformations in Colonial North Bengal

The colonial North Bengal was mainly comprised of eight districts, viz. – Darjeeling, Jalpaiguri, Dinajpur, Malda, Rajshahi, Rangpur, Bogra and Pabna. These eight districts had formed the Rajshahi Division which was placed under the official control of a Divisional Commissioner. The Princely State of Cooch Behar had been also considered as part of North Bengal due its contiguity and resemblance of population, land and climate with the neighbouring districts of the Rajshahi Division. W. W. Hunter in the *Statistical Account of Bengal* (vol. X) had placed the princely state with other neighbouring districts of Darjeeling and Jalpaiguri.[1] However, the districts of the Rajshahi Division had been formed throughtout the course of the nineteenth century and went through several internal changes in terms of administration and revenue collection operations.

Demography remains a crucial aspect of famine history. Demographic loss or mortality happened to be an important marker for analysing the severity of the famines. In fact, it is the mortality or demographic issues which had made a famine either as severe or as small. Famines which were caused by ecological dislocations and economic disruptions had induced migration of population from the affected region to the comparatively prosperous region. The migration of population was related with the changing pattern of land, production and consumption. Thus, ecology had a profound impact on the demographic transformations of the famine-affected region. On the other hand, large-scale influx of population to a particular place had made the region more vulnerable to the ecological disorders which further intensified the problem of crop failure and entitlement crisis. Dyson and Ó Gráda argue that 'famines often have demographic causes as well as consequences; and their consequences may be long-term as well as short-term.'[2]

In regards to the population of the North Bengal, the Census of 1901 had noted that 'North Bengal is the home of the Mech and Koch tribes, the last of the invaders from the north-east, whose nominal strength is still nearly a million and-a-half, in spite of the fact that large numbers have embraced Muhammadanism.'[3] The Census summarizes the demographic condition of North Bengal in the following words:

> "The relatively low density in Rajshahi is due partly to its containing a large portion of the Barind and partly to the presence of numerous marshes and lakes, including the Chalan *bil*, the largest sheet of inland water in Bengal. There is a belt of country running from north to south, through the centre of the district, where the population is as great as in almost any part of North Bengal. Malda also owes its low position to the Barind which extends over a great part of the district east of the Mahananda. In the alluvial tract west of that river, the population is generally dense, and in one police circle, Manikchak, there are no fewer than 935 persons to the square mile. Kuch Bihar is most populous on the Rangpur border and least so where it marches with the Western Duars. Dinajpur owns a share of the Barind, but its density is low throughout, and the most populous police circle in the

> district can boast of only 531 persons to the square mile. Jalpaiguri is even more sparsely populated. In only one police circle (Patgram, where there are a number of old families) does the population exceed 500, and in only three more does it exceed 400 to the square mile. The fewest inhabitants are in the Duars. Towards the west this tract has filled up rapidly owing to the extension of tea cultivation, but in the east, the population is still very sparse, and in Alipur it averages only 89 persons to the square mile. Darjeeling is throughout very thinly peopled. In the Terai the density is about the same as in Jalpaiguri, but it gradually diminishes towards the north, and in the head-quarters subdivision there are only 1 84 persons to the square mile."[4]

Northern Bengal was comprised of several aboriginal and emigrant tribes. There was variety of tribal population in colonial times in the districts of northern Bengal. From Darjeeling to Pabna the mosaic of several castes, tribes had provided a unique demographic character for the northern Bengal. Drought, scarcities or famines did not affect all communities in a same way, and there were also differences in the attitude of local populations to deal with the natural calamities. Most of the districts of North Bengal, which were constructed after the second half of the nineteenth century had witnessed a massive demographic transformation throughout the colonial period. There were several reasons which had contributed to this demographic shift. The subsequent portions of this chapter examine the process of demographic evolution in colonial North Bengal.

Figure. 2.1
Distribution of Population in North Bengal in 1901

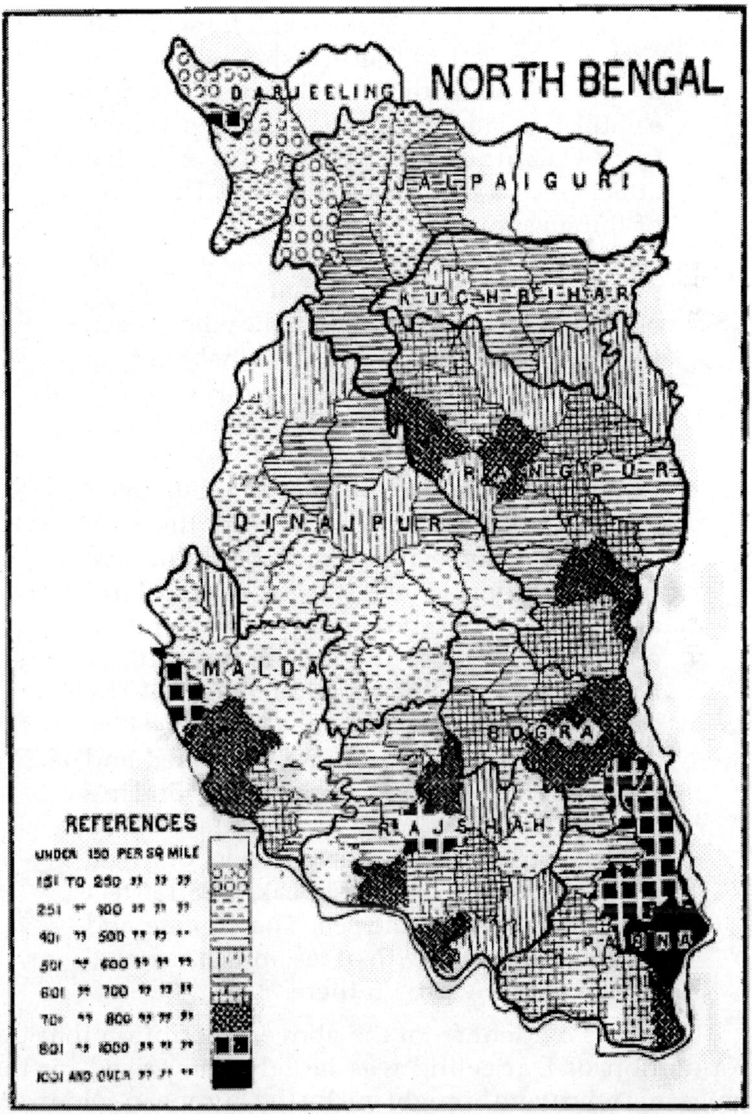

Source: E. A. Gait, *Census of India, 1901, vol. VI: Part I, the Report*, p. 20.

A. Campbell had depicted the emergence and formation of Darjeeling district as a hill-district or a sanatorium in the following manner:

> "Darjeeling, in lat. 27^0 north and long. 88^0 22′ east, was ceded to the British Government by the Raja of Sekim in 1835, to enable it to establish a sanatorium there for Europeans from Calcutta and Bengal.... The country attached was without inhabitants. This state of things soon altered. People flocked from all sides, and we rapidly acquired a thriving population. When I took charge there were not more than fifty families in the whole tract. In twelve years we had 10,000 inhabitants in it; and by an accession of territory, we had an increase of 36,000 in the Terai, or lowlands, at the base of the hills. In 1861, when I left Darjeeling, the total population was estimated at 60,000. The rapid progress of the new station was the result of free labour and free trade, regularly paid wages, a light land assessment, strict and prompt administration of justice, and close attention to the peculiar habits and customs of all classes. .....The scenery is unsurpassed anywhere in beauty and grandeur; a tract of finely wooded and variously shaped mountains extending northwards, till they terminate in a stupendous range of perpetual snow, of which Kunchinjunga, the highest peak, is 28,136 feet above the level of the sea. The climate and soil favour the growth of tea and chinchona, which are now grown there."[5]

Thus it is evident from the above description that the population of Darjeeling was largely comprised by the emigrants who were brought out by the European colonizers for facilitating trade in tea and other commercial purposes.

The transformation of Darjeeling from a land of 'without inhabitants' to a 'thriving population' can be attributed to the colonizers initiative of building a sanatorium there and to exploit the vast natural resources for their petty commercial interests. The hill stations of British India were regarded by the western observers as 'an island of Victorian values and symbols without a clientele.'[6] Imperial design behind the construction of sanatoriums or health-places in colonial India thus invites the scope for historical scrutiny of the colonial objective on the discourses of imperial practices which reinforced the distinction of this British enclave not only as a suitable place for colonial administrators, but also on the basis of a racial and spatial categorization that represented the sense of British superiority and difference spawned up from the fear of being degenerated.[7] Apart from this, alike many other hill stations or sanatorium around the Indian subcontinent, the construction of Darjeeling displayed the legacy of British perception 'as sites of colonial leisure and recreation; temperate places that represented socially, culturally and architecturally, derivations of metropolitan and imperial symbols of leisure' and in addition with an aim of its incorporation into the colonial economy.[8] O'Malley in his *Gazetteer* had remarked that 'The growth of the Darjeeling district affords the most remarkable instance of the expansion of population of which there [was] any record in Bengal.'[9]

Table 2.1

Growth of population in Darjeeling district, 1872-1941

Census	*No. of population*	*No. of increase*	*% of increase*
1871-72	94,717		——
1881	155,179	60,467	63%
1891	223,314	68,135	43.4%
1901	249,117	25,803	11.5%
1911	2,65,550	16,433	7%
1921	2,82,748	17,198	6%

1931	3,19,635	36,887	13%
1941	3,76,369	56,734	18%

Source: Arthur Jules Dash, *Bengal District Gazetteers: Darjeeling*, p. 49.

At close of the nineteenth century the population was returned as 249,117 in 1901 in comparison with the 94,717 in 1871-72. The population in 1901 was increased 2½ times greater than that of 1871-72.[10] The increase of population was due to the emigration of a large number of migrant people for the tea industry which made the district populous. In 1872 the number of tea estates in Darjeeling was only 74 with an area of 14,000 acres which was increased to 30,000 acres by the 153 tea estates in 1881; and in 1901 the tea estates were increased to 177 with an area of 45,000 acres.[11] The growth of agricultural tracts in the Terai region was also responsible for the increase of population in the district.[12] The total density of population in the district as a whole was 214 persons per square mile, whereas only in the Terai region there were 279 persons per square mile.[13] The development of communication through railways and roads were instrumental to encourage the people to migrate into the place. A large portion of population had migrated to the district from Nepal, Bihar and Sikkim, among the largest number of people came to the district from Nepal.[14] In the district of Darjeeling, Dash had mentioned that, there were 87 females to every 100 males according to the earlier gazetteer, whereas the 1941 census had recorded the male population as 1,99,891 against a female population of 1,76,478 i. e. just over 88 females for every 100 males.[15] The Nepalese, Lepchas, Limbus, Bhutias, and Rajbanshis were the principal inhabitants of the district with a considerable number of European population.

Figure 2.2.

Population Density in North Bengal in 1911

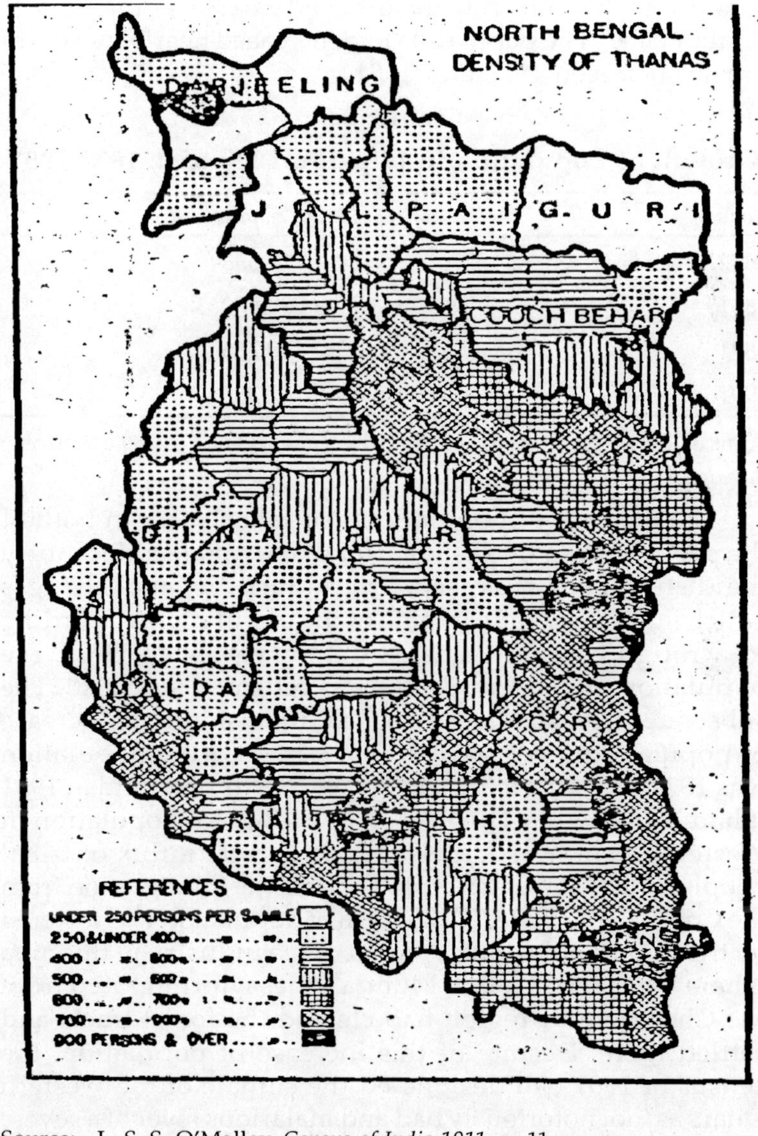

Source: . L. S. S. O'Malley, *Census of India 1911*, p. 11.

John F. Grunning had divided the district of Jalpaiguri into two 'well-defined' parts viz., – the permanently settled *parganas* which had formed the part of Rangpur, and the Western Duars which were annexed in 1865 at the time of Bhutan War.[16] The population had increased nearly two times greater between 1872 and 1901.

Table: 2.2

Growth of Population in Jalpaiguri District, 1872-1901

Census	*No. of population*
1872	417,855
1881	580,570
1891	680,736
1901	787,380

Source: John F. Grunning, *Eastern Bengal and Assam District Gazetteers: Jalpaiguri*, p. 30.

The increase of population had taken place in both of the parts. During the last quarter of the nineteenth century the district had witnessed several jurisdictional changes which influenced the estimate of the population. According to a rough estimate made by a survey in 1865-67, the population of Western Duars was returned as 49,620. The subsequent census had recorded a considerable increase of population in Western Duars – in 1881 the population was 182,687 which increased to 296,348 in 1891, and in 1901 it had increased to 410,606.[17] This growth of population in Western Duars was largely due to a great influx of tribal people from Chotanagpur plateau and the immigration from the Cooch Behar State. The growth of population was fostered by the remarkable development of tea industry in this area where the Santal, Oraon, Munda tribes who migrated from the Chotanagpur region had cleared the forest tracts and settled there. Despite of this increase of population, the census of 1901 had designated the climate of the Western Duars as 'not notoriously bad and malarious fever of a severe type' was prevalent which obstructed 'a natural increase of population.'[18] Apart from the migrated population, the district was largely inhabited by the Rajbanshis, Nasyas, and Sekhs as the aboriginal of that tract. Due to the peculiar nature of the soil, population was unevenly distributed in the district and in some areas the number of population was meagre.[19] Due to the precarious condition caused by the severe malarial fever, cholera and other diseases the death rate remained so high that the 'the Western Duars was accepted with resignation by the inhabitants, European and Indian alike...'[20]

The princely State of Cooch Behar had witnessed several transformations in terms of fluctuations in the number of population between 1872 and 1941.

Table: 2.3

Demographic fluctuations in the Cooch Behar State, 1872-1941

Census	*No. of total population*	*% of increase(+) decrease (-)*
1872	532,565	———
1881	602,624	13.15 (+)
1891	578,868	3.9 (-)
1901	556,116	4.1 (-)
1911	591,012	4.58 (+)
1921	590,599	0.07 (-)
1931	589,053	0.26 (-)
1941	638,703	8.43 (+)

Source: Extracted from Durgadas Mazumdar, *West Bengal District Gazetteer: Koch Behar*, 1977, p. 45.

The above table has shown decrease in population in 1891 and 1901 census. The deduction in 1891 was caused partly by the two epidemics of cholera and partly to the migration of people to the tea garden of Western Duars. The population had further reduced, as recorded by the 1901 census, by the prevalence of 'unhealthy climate' and the scarcity of food in 1897 when there was a widespread famine throughout the province.[21] There was again a decrease in population between 1911 and 1921 which was 0.07% and this was caused by the influenza epidemic. In 1931 there was also a further decrease of 0.26% which was resulted from the choler and small-pox epidemics that occurred in 1928 and 1929.[22] The census of 1911 had designated the princely state as 'thinly populated' where the maximum density was 552, and only Dinhata and Haldibari came with a moderate density.[23] Between 1891 and 1911 the number of females for every one thousand male had gradually decrease, whereas there was minor increase from 1911 to 1931.[24]

There were difficulties in obtaining accurate number for the Malda district prior to the census of 1872. Hunter had observed that the only immigrants into this District were a few hill-men from Chotanagpur who were mostly *Dhangars*, but there were also some Kols and Santhals.[25] Although there was general increase of population (5%) between 1872 and 1881 but there was a slight fall in the southern portion of the district of west of Mahananda, and this was caused by the malarial attack during the second half of the decade.[26] But there was an increase of 14.5% between 1881 and 1891, as a result of opening of the *barind* tract by the Santhals who contributed to the increase of population in the southern portion of the district.[27] The immigration of Santhals into the district had continued for the next decade (1901) when the population was increased by 8.5% and this was further increased by 1911 to 13.5% due to the constant inflow of the Santhals.[28] The areas which were suffered from droughts and famines were the high winter rice lands of the barind and parts of the Shibganj, Kaliachak and Kharba thanas.[29]

District of Dinajpur had witnessed the immigration of seasonal labourers from the neighbouring tracts from where a large number of tribal population had migrated into the district. Hunter was of the opinion that at the time of harvesting labourers had migrated to Dinajpur from neighbouring Districts as reapers who used to get 4 *annas* a day for their work.[30] Day-labourers had also come from Rajmahal to the large river side marts, from January to March, to husk rice for the grain merchants and *Dhangar* coolies also used to come regularly every year to Dinajpur to work on the roads, or to clear jungle for the zamindars.[31] Apart from the migrated people there were large numbers of aboriginal and semi-aboriginal people who lived in this district. Koches or Rajbanshis who were principally agriculturists had also inhabited this land. Hunter had mentioned the description of the Assistant Magistrate of Dinajpur regarding this group of people in the following manner:

> "The Koch and Palis or Paliyas, as they are indifferently called, are a people peculiar to this part of the country, and are distinguished from all other Bengalis by their broad faces, flat noses, and projecting cheekbones, as also by their appearance and different style of dress. They profess to be Hindus; but while they follow the Hindu religion in the main, they also practise some ceremonies borrowed from Musalmans and others, which are apparently remnants of an older superstition.... The Palis are subdivided into three classes - the Sadhu, Babu, and Desi Palis."[32]

Prior to the census of 1872 the slow rate of population growth had been observed and this was due to the prevalence of malarial fever, 'for which this district has as evil a reputation as its neighbour Rangpur.'[33] In 1872 it was reported that deaths occurred in Dinajpur was excessively high than that of the other districts in the Division and in 1876 the fever mortality had reached to the 22.05 per mile of the total population of the district.[34] There was slight increase in population in 1891 (2.7%) than the earlier decade and this increased had continued for the next couple of decades.[35] The census of 1911 had noticed unfavourable conditions for the increase of density in the district and this was due to the unhealthy climate and 'the south [was] covered by the high undulating ridges of the Barind, in which cultivation [was] either impossible or unprofitable.'[36]

For Hunter, Rangpur which was the most populous district in the Rajshahi Division contained nearly one person for every acre and the most thickly settled parts of the district were the tracts on both side of the Tista, which divided the District from north-west to south-east.[37] The first Census (1872) had reported 2,149,972 number of population which in 1881 Census had been diminished to 2,097,964, and it again decreased to 2,065,464 by 1891.[38] Due to the prolonged prevalence of malarial fever the district had lost 4 percent of its population between the years 1872 and 1891. Although before 1881 the malarial fever was limited in the *thanas* of Mithapukur and Pirganj which located at the centre of the district, but a general deterioration of the condition had been noticed from 1891 in the *thanas* east to district and north of them; and this time the malarial fever was accompanied with frequent cases of cholera that collectively increased death-rate in the district.[39] The contagion for cholera was caused, as apprehended by the colonial administration, by the coolies who were migrating to Assam tea gardens via the district of Rangpur and on the other hand, the malarial prevalence and severity was caused by the obstruction of the old drainage channels in the south and west of the Tista, and the overall prevalence of water-logged conditions of the district.[40] Despite of long-continued unhealthiness, the 'very fertile soil' of Rangpur was praised in the census of 1901 for producing 'a far greater population than Dinajpur to the west, Kuch Bihar and Jalpaiguri to the north or Goalpara in Assam to the east.'[41] The only places where there were less than 500 persons to the square mile were two unhealthy and ill-drained police circles in the south-central part of the district on the bank of the old Karatoya and a tract along the eastern boundary which included in its nominal area the bed and sandy *chars* of the Brahmaputra.[42] In the Report of the Survey and Settlements, Arthur Coulton Hartley had remarked that 'before 1910' the data and information regarding the prevalence of diseases and their impact was not reliable and mentioning the improvement in the public health since the 1920s onwards he stated that 'on account of the prevalence of malaria, it still cannot be reckoned as one of the healthy district of Bengal, it is no longer notorious.'[43]

Table. 2.4

Yearly death-rate per mile of population in Rangpur district

Year	*Death-rate (per mile)*
1911-20	31.59
1921-30	27.00
1931	25.23
1932	20.72
1933	28.05
1934	27.11
1935	27.55

Source: Arthur Coulton Hartley, *Final Report of the Rangpur Survey and Settlement Operations, 1931-38,* (1940), p. 7.

Although the table has shown a decline in the death-rates but at the same time these were static and the years were going on without any check in death-rates which were principally caused by the malarial fever that was 'more pronounced in the south-west than in any other area.'[44]

The growth-rate of population in the district of Rajshahi had been recorded unevenly in different parts. From 1872 to 1891 the *thanas* to the north and west of the district had shown increased number of population, whereas the central and southern portion of the district had witnessed decrease in population.[45] In fact, it was remarked that 'no district in

Bengal [had] such a bad record' than the district of Rajshahi, since it had made 'no advance' in population growth.[46]

Table: 2.5

Growth of population in Rajshahi, 1872-1911

Census	*Total number of population*	*% of increase (+) & decrease (-)*
1872	1,421,865	———
1881	1,449,033	+ 1.9
1891	1,437,859	-0.8
1901	1,460,584	+ 1.6
1911	1,480,587	+ 1.4

Source: L. S. S. O'Malley, *Bengal District Gazetteers: Rajshahi*, p. 49.

It can be noticed that population had decreased in 1891 by 0.8 percent and till 1901 the central and southern thanas had suffered a loss of 12.8 percent of population due to malarial attack in the district, whereas in contrary to this population increased by 25.6 percent in Barind and by 59.3 percent in the fertile tracts of Naogaon and Panchupur in the Naogaon subdivision.[47] The relatively low density in Rajshahi, as identified by the census of 1901, was due partly to its containing a large portion of the Barind and partly to the presence of numerous marshes and lakes, including the Chalan bil, the largest sheet of inland water in Bengal.[48] Despite of continuous prevalence of fever, population rate had was increased in 1911 census by 1.4 per cent, which included the increased number of Muslim population in comparison with the Hindus who had lost 3 per cent of their population.[49] The census of 1921 had returned with a total population of 1,489,675 (573 per square mile) and increase of population since 1872 was one thousand per annum.[50] The fluctuation of population in some *thanas* of the district between 1872 and 1921 was as follows:

Table: 2.6

Variations in Population in *thanas* of Rajshahi, 1872-1921

Thana	*Population in*		*Variationper cent*
	1872	*1921*	
Godagari	34,683	59,771	+ 72
Puthia	143,087	79,932	-44
Charghat and Lalpur	206,766	102,927	-50
Manda	92,328	144,392	+56
Nator	139,652	107,458	-23
Baraigram	127,941	89,673	-29
Boalia	110,307	99,926	-9
Tanor	91,032	92,948	+2
Bagmara	128,687	125,397	-2

Source: W. H. Nelson, *Final Report on the Survey and Settlement Operations in the District of Rajshahi, 1912-1922*, (1923), p. 20.

The above table has shown a steady decline in population in Nator subdivision, and Charghat and Puthia *thanas,* which was due to the decrease in the means of subsistence of people caused by the decline in silk industry or by the deterioration of fertility power of land; and these problem were equally instrumental in the *thanas* of Boalia, Tanor and Bagmara.[51] The reason for the decrease of population in Nator subdivision, and Charghat and Puthia thanas was the 'bad climate' which had been in 'a serious change for the worse in the climate operating' during the 80s of the nineteenth century.[52] This change for the worse could also be seen in the drainage system which subsequently affected public health. Although the Atrai from the north, and the Narad and the Baral from the Ganges were formerly active streams in this region but Narad had dried up entirely, and the Atrai and the Baral were in a decadent position.[53] The slow but constant depopulation of some parts of the country had contributed to the increase of jungle and fallow land which coupled with the malarial mosquitoes caused 'further disease and depopulation.'[54] However, the Barind tract was the developed part of the district where immigration of considerable number of Santhals had taken place along with the addition of other aboriginals, both of whom had migrated into the district for agricultural employment.[55]

The decades between 1872 and 1901 had observed a constant increase of population in the district of Bogra.

Table. 2.7

Growth of Population in Bogra, 1872-1901

Census	*Total no. of population*	*Density per square mile*	*Percentage of increase*
1872	689,467	459	——
1881	734,358	490	6.6
1891	817,494	563	14.8
1901	854,533	629	11.7

Source: Extracted from J. N. Gupta, *District Gazetteers of Eastern Bengal and Assam: Bogra*, pp. 27-28.

There was continuous increase of percentage and density population between 1872 and 1901. Although it was believed that the increase between 1881 and 1891 was due to the expansion of Eastern Bengal State Railway from Sara to Siliguri in 1878, but Mr. Lyon, the Collector of Bogra was of the opinion that since there was 'scarcely any migration either inwards or outwards', therefore, the number of population in the district 'increased by births alone.'[56] The tract between the Karatoya and Daokoha where jute had been grown most abundantly was the most densely populated part of the district.[57] Bogra had received a considerable immigration of people from its neighbouring district Pabna, Nadia, Saran, Chotanagpur plateau, and the United Province.[58]

The population of the district of Pabna had increased between 1872 and 1881 by 8.3 percent, which increased in 1891 by 3.85 percent and this was further increased by 4.3 per cent in 1901 census.[59] The population would have been much greater if there had not been emigration of a large number of people from the district to the districts of Rangpur and Goalpara where the people could find 'cheap and fertile' lands for settlement and agriculture.[60] In the census of 1901, Pabna stood first in respect of density of population and this was mainly due to the rich jute fields of the Sirajganj Subdivision. It was also probable that the actual area was greater than would appear from the figures based on the survey, and that in some parts the district had gained by alluvion which could be seen in the Shahzadpur thana where the minimum area held a density of 1,235 to the square mile.[61] The years between 1911 and 1921 had witnessed 'unfavourable' conditions as a result of prevalence of malaria and influenza which carried away more than one percent of total population during 1918 and 1919.[62] Pabna had the highest density of population in northern Bengal which was 828 persons per square mile and Sirajganj subdivision was the most thickly populated part of the district.[63]

Apart from the birth or death-factors the population of northern Bengal had been largely influenced by the process of inter-district migration. For northern Bengal chief impetus had come from the two factors- viz. immigration of Santhals from the Santhal pargana or the Chotanagpur region, and the seasonal migration of people from the neighbouring districts to a particular district especially during the time of jute cultivation which involved a great number of labourers. In fact this was an important reason to argue that the number of people shown in the district census might not be the permanent number of population, especially for the case of the group of people who frequently migrated from one district to another in search of occupation and subsistence; thus while collecting the number of people for the census data the time of a year emerged as most crucial factor. The Nandigram *thana* of Nator subdivision of Rajshahi district had received population from the district of Bogra and the population of Badalgachhi had been enlarged by the Oraon tribal people. Haraprasad Chattopadhyay has shown that the Atrai police station had received jute traders and labourers till 1929 due to the rise in price of jute; and the police station of Biral and Raiganj of Dinajpur had become populated by the labourers from other districts when the jute industry was greatly prospered, but the immigrant labourers moved away from the police stations before the census was taken.[64] It has been already noticed that the district of Jalpaiguri and Darjeeling had witnessed a great number of tribal people in accordance with the development of tea industry in those districts. Inter-district and intra-district migration among the districts of northern Bengal was very much common in this region which caused a constant fluctuation of population. Bhatiyas from the district of Mymensingh, Pabna,and Bogra had immigrated into the *char* lands of Nageswari, Bhurangamari, and Rahumari in the district of Rangpur and settled there; on the other hand, a number of villages in Shariakandi of Bogra had been abandoned by their people among whom some had migrated into Mymensingh, and others fixed with the *thanas* of Panchbibi, Khetlal, and Jaipurhat of the Bogra district.[65] The *char* lands of Pabna and Malda had attracted a large number of people from their neighbouring district for the fertile agricultural fields. There was also migration between the princely state of Cooch Behar and the districts of Bengal.[66]

Table. 2.8

Variations in Population in the Rajshahi Division, 1872-1921

District	*1921*	*1911*	*1901*	*1891*	*1881*	*1872*
Rajshahi	1,489,675	1,480,587	1,460,584	1,437,859	1,449,033	1,421,865
Dinajpur	1,705,353	1,687,863	1,566,845	1,482,355	1,442,320	1,429,900
Jalpaiguri	936,261	902,660	786,326	679,623	579,373	416,781
Darjeeling	282,748	265,550	240,117	223,314	153,646	91,996
Rangpur	2,507,854	2,385,330	3,164,115	2,065,249	2,097,553	2,153,061

of water' which intensified ecological vulnerabilities during the time of its shortage.

Though most of the district gazetteers of North Bengal districts had mentioned that the districts of North Bengal were comparatively free from any threat of famine, the account of subsequent sufferings from the drought and famines had revealed the opposite one. The official correspondences, which are mentioned in the subsequent chapters, have reflected that the districts of Rajshahi Division had been suffered from the menace of local drought and widespread famine as well. North Bengal districts had been frequently mentioned as 'secured from famine' or 'unlikely to famine.' However, the objective of this book is to challenge this official narrative which did not pay any serious attention to the plight of people of this region. It is mentioned several times in the official narratives that famines were caused by failure in local rainfalls, though enough evidences were there which revealed that administrative failure and artificial crisis had heightened the tensions of famines. The demographic dimension of famines in colonial North Bengal had direct relation with the ecology and market-economy of this region, because crop failure and grain-crisis had been intensified through a common dialogue between rainfall and colonialism. The regional or local variation of population had responded differently for this region from the other regions of Bengal and India as well. Hence, it is an imperative to investigate the popular responses towards the famines and scarcities which had occurred during the period of study.

REFERENCES

1. W. W. Hunter, *A Statistical Account of Bengal, Vol. X: Districts of Darjiling and Jalpaiguri, and State of Kuch Behar,* London: Trubner & Co., 1876.

2. Tim Dyson and Cormac Ó Gráda, 'Famine Demography: An Introduction,' Working Paper Series, Centre for Economic Research, WP01/25, October 2001, Department of Economics, University College Dublin.

3. E. A. Gait, *Census of India*, vol. VI: Part I, the Report, Calcutta: Bengal Secretariat Press, 1902, p. 15.
4. *Ibid.*, p. 20.
5. A. Campbell, 'On the Tribes around Darjeeling,' *Transactions of the Ethnological Society of London*, Vol. 7, No. (1869), pp. 145-46.
6. Judith T. Kenny, Climate, Race, and Imperial Authority: The Symbolic Landscape of the British Hill Station in India, *Annals of the Association of American Geographers*, Vol. 85, No. 4, Dec., 1995, p. 694.
7. *Ibid.*, p. 699 and 700.
8. Nandini Bhattacharya, Leisure, Economy and Colonial Urbanism: Darjeeling, 1835–1930, Urban History, August 1, 2013, 40(3), pp. 442-43.
9. L.S.S. O'Malley, *Bengal District Gazetteers: Darjeeling*, p. 43.
10. *Ibid.*, p. 44.
11. *Ibid.*
12. For a detail discussion of demographic transformation in the Terai region during the colonial period see Sudip Khasnobish, *Socio-economic and Political Transition of Darjeeling Terai (1864-1994)*, Unpublished Ph.D dissertation, University of North Bengal, February 2016, ch. II.
13. L.S.S.O'Malley, *Bengal District Gazetteers: Darjeeling*, p. 47.
14. In the census of 1891, it was found that 88,000 people were born in Nepal against the total population of 223,314. The 1931 census had recorded that 59,016 people were born in Nepal against the total population of 319,635. Arthur Jules Dash, *op. cit.*, p. 50.
15. *Ibid.*, p. 51.
16. The first attempt to record the number of population was conducted in the year 1858-59 at the time of the Revenue Survey of Rangpur when it was appeared from a rough estimate that the population of the permanently settled areas of Jalpaiguri was 189,067 which was considered as 'too low' in 1870 by the Deputy Commissioner of the District. John F. Grunning, op. cit., p. 30.
17. *Ibid.*, p. 31.
18. *Ibid.*, p. 32.

19. *Final Report on the Survey and Settlement Operations in the Jalpaiguri District, 1906-1916*, The Bengal Secretariat Book Depot, Calcutta, 1919, pp. 10-11.
20. *Ibid.*, p. 15.
21. Durgadas Mazumdar, *op. cit.*, p. 45.
22. *Ibid.*
23. L. S. S. O'Malley, *Census of India 1911*, Vol. V, p. 12.
24. Durgadas Mazumdar, *op. cit.*, p. 45.
25. W. W. Hunter, *A Statistical Account of Bengal, Vol. VII: Districts of Malda, Rangpur and Dinajpur*, p. 41.
26. The total number of population in 1872 was 677,328. G. E. Lambourn, *Bengal District Gazetteers: Malda*, Calcutta: Bengal Secretariat Book Depot, 1918, p. 27.
27. *Ibid.*
28. *Ibid.*, pp. 27-28.
29. G. E. Lambourn, *op. cit.*, p. 56.
30. W. W. Hunter, *A Statistical Account of Bengal, Vol. VII: Districts of Malda, Rangpur and Dinajpur*, p. 376.
31. *Ibid.*
32. *Ibid.*, p. 380.
33. F. W. Strong, *op. cit.*, p. 31.
34. *Ibid.*
35. The Census of 1901 had reported an increase of 5.3 percent with a total number of population of 1,567,080 which was increased in 1911 by 7.72 percent with a total population of 1,687,863. This increase was due to the immigration of Santhals in the southern thanas who were brought to clear the jungle tracts of the district and thereby contributed to the expansion of agricultural frontier. *Ibid.*
36. The Balurghat subdivision had only 380 persons per square mile. L. S. S. O'Malley, *Census of India 1911*, Vol. V, pp. 12-13.
37. W. W. Hunter, *A Statistical Account of Bengal, Vol. VII: Districts of Malda, Rangpur and Dinajpur*, p. 207.
38. J. A. Vas, *op. cit.*, p. 34.
39. *Ibid.*
40. *Ibid.*

41. The density of population was little less than that of Bogra and was almost the same as that of Mymensingh which was located on the south-east. E. A. Gait, *op. cit.*, p. 20.
42. *Ibid.*
43. Arthur Coulton Hartley, *op. cit.*, p. 7.
44. Ibid., p. 8.
45. L. S. S. O'Malley, *Bengal District Gazetteers: Rajshahi*, p. 49.
46. *Ibid.*
47. *Ibid.*
48. E. A. Gait, *op. cit.*, p. 20.
49. *Ibid.*
50. W. H. Nelson, *Final Report on the Survey and Settlement Operations in the District of Rajshahi, 1912-1922*, Bengal Secretariat Book Depot, Calcutta, 1923, p. 20.
51. *Ibid.*, p. 21.
52. *Ibid.*
53. Ibid.
54. The expansion of Eastern Bengal Railway embankments along the lines of the rivers had obstructed the natural drainage and created a favourable condition for the malarial mosquitoes. *Ibid.*
55. L. S. S. O'Malley, *Bengal District Gazetteers: Rajshahi*, p. 51.
56. J. N. Gupta, *District Gazetteers of Eastern Bengal and Assam: Bogra*, p. 28.
57. *Ibid.*, p. 29.
58. *Ibid.*, p. 30.
59. L. S. O'Malley, *Bengal District Gazetteers: Pabna*, p. 29.
60. *Ibid.*, p. 29 and 31.
61. E. A. Gait, *op. cit.*, p. 19.
62. The census of 1921 had shown a decrease of 39,092 persons which represented 27 percent of the population. There was overall deduction of population throughout the Pabna district except for the thanas of Raiganj and Taras. L. S. O'Malley, *Bengal District Gazetteers: Pabna*, pp. 29-30.
63. *Ibid.*, p. 30.

64. Haraprasad Chattopadhyay, *Internal Migration in India: A Case Study of Bengal*, K. P. Bagchi & Co., Calcutta, 1987, pp. 80-81.
65. *Ibid.*, p. 81.
66. It was recorded in the census of 1931 (Vol. V, Part I) that 61,000 persons born in British Bengal immigrated into the State of Cooch Behar, while 29,000 persons born in the States of Cooch Behar and Tripura had migrated to the British Bengal. Cited in Ibid. For more details see, A. E. Porter, *Census of India, 1931, Vol. V. Bengal & Sikkim, Part I – Report*, Calcutta Publication Branch, Calcutta, 1933, p. 104.
67. Ratnalekha Ray, *Change in Bengal Agrarian Society, c.1760-1850*, Manohar, New Delhi, 1979, p. 174.
68. *Ibid.*, p. 190.
69. Sugata Bose, *Peasant Labour and Colonial Capital: Rural Bengal since 1770*, Cambridge University Press, Cambridge, 1993, p. 121. For a detail analysis on the 'jotedars' also see Sugata Bose, *Agrarian Bengal: Economy, Social Structure and Politics, 1919-1947*, Cambridge University Press, Cambridge, digital version, 2008, pp. 3-33.
70. The cultivated area in Rangpur had increased by 15 percent in the early 1870s in comparison with that in 1809. Sugata Bose, *Peasant Labour and Colonial Capital*, p. 23.
71. Cited in *Ibid.*, p. 32.
72. A. E. Porter, *Census of India, 1931*, p. 10.
73. In the year 1930-1931 a cyclone had visited Gaibandha subdivision in Rangpur district and an earthquake had caused great damage to property in Cooch Behar and Rangpur district. *Ibid.*
74. *Ibid.*, p. 11.
75. S. C. Majumdar, *Rivers of the Bengal Delta*, University of Calcutta, Calcutta, 1942, p. 5.

3

Rainfall, Crops and Colonialism: Famines in North Bengal, 1866-1891

The second half of the nineteenth century had witnessed a series of famines in Bengal as well as in India. There were three general reasons for the occurrence of these famines viz. – shortage of rainfall, crop failure and the condition of market and economy which was regulated by the colonial state and private agencies. Apart from the large-scale famines, North Bengal had also witnessed some scarcities which were caused by the failure of local rainfall and price-rise. This chapter examines the relationship between rainfall and crop failure in North Bengal where colonial control of market and economy can be understood distinctively in terms of ecological dislocations and regional variations of agriculture, trade and subsistence. The Bengal-Orissa famine of 1866 was the first large-scale famine of the second half of the nineteenth century. A large area of Bengal and Orissa had suffered from the famine of 1866. Though the Bengal-Orissa famine of 1866 mostly ravaged the areas of Orissa and lower Bengal, it had also affected some parts of northern Bengal. Later, along with Bihar, the districts of Rajshahi Division of colonial Bengal was also affected during the Bengal-Bihar famine of 1873-74. Thus, the districts of northern Bengal had to go through a series of drought and scarcities between 1866 and 1874, which was further extended in 1891. Among these, the famine of 1873-1874 had caused great inconvenience for the people of this region. In fact, in comparison with the other previous famines, the districts of northern Bengal, this time, was most severely hit by the rainfall deficiency and crop failure. Though the chapter mainly deals with the background and impact of the 1873-74 Bengal-Bihar famine, it also includes a brief description of the Bengal-Orissa famine of 1866 and the scarcity of 1884 and 1891 which had affected considerable areas of northern Bengal.

I. North Bengal in the Bengal-Orissa Famine (1866)

Before going into the discussion about Bengal-Bihar famine of 1873–74 it is necessary to look into the famine-affected areas of northern Bengal during the famine of 1866 because during these eight years i.e. between 1866 and 1874 northern districts of Bengal had to go through a major crisis in regard to the production and prices of agricultural crops. This part of the chapter does not intend to discuss the famine-condition of the districts of Orissa or the lower districts of Bengal. This part of the chapter only concentrates on the impact of the 1866 famine upon the districts of northern Bengal, because this helps us to understand about the changing ecological situations in this part of the country and will also introduce the region in terms of famine and scarcities that had occurred since the second half of the nineteenth century. The famine of 1866 was created by several seasons of erratic rainfall and the situation was further deteriorated by the continuous unwillingness of the local administration to import food. The Bengal-Orissa famine of 1866 began 'in the classic fashion of a double failure of crops in the 1865 season.'[1] However, Roy argues, the government this time had taken a long time to declare the condition as famine 'until it was too late.'[2] The colonial administration, Roy further comments, had only concentrated on the limited areas of coastal Orissa because the 'interior uplands were unknown terrain, difficult to access.'[3] Thus, it is an imperative to explore the famine conditions that prevailed in the district of Rajshahi in 1866. W. W. Hunter has summarized the famine condition of the Rajshahi Division in the following manner[4] –

Table: 3.1

Famine condition of Rajshahi Division in 1866

Total Population	Agricultural Population	Labourers and Poorer Craftsmen	Highest Price of Rice per maund in 1866	Famine Prices Rice per maund; District Average.	Famine Warnings. Rice per maund in January; District Average.
8, 893, 738	5, 384, 868	1, 761, 654	Av. Rs. 4-10	Av. Rs. 4 - 4	Av. Rs. 2-10

Source: W. W. Hunter, *Famine Aspects of Bengal Districts*, p.10. Collected from the Tabulated Famine Warnings.

Malda, Dinajpur and Rangpur did not have to suffer much (in comparison with the severity of famine prevailed in the districts of Orissa) from this famine though there was a sharp rise in the prices of food grain, specially rice. In the district of Malda, there was a serious failure of the *aman* crop which was coupled with the great rise in prices in January and February of 1866. This accelerated the situation towards a famine. Though the District mainly depended on the *aman* or winter rice crop, the *aus* or autumn crop could not even make up for the total loss of the former. According to the report of the Collector of Malda district "...during the famine of 1866 the price of rice rose to 10 seers a rupee, or 4 rupees a maund ; and that of paddy to 18 seers a rupee, or Rs. 2-4 per maund."[5] The overall agricultural scenario of the district of Malda in 1866 was as follows –

Table: 3.2

Crop condition in the district of Malda, 1866

Total Land Cultivated (in acre)	Crops Cultivated Land (in acre)	Outturn of Rice (Rs./bigha)	Outturn of Pulses and other Crops) (Rs./bigha)	Collective Outturn of Rice and winter Crops (Rs./bigha)
426, 583	Rice-250,000 Wheat-25,000 Other Food Grains-10,000	Normal Land-15-18; Inferior Land-10-15	Rs.7- Rs. 10	Rs. 20 – Rs.25

Source: W. W. Hunter, *Famine Aspects of Bengal Districts*, pp. 119-20.

Hunter's account, however, had not displayed the actual total number of agricultural and labour population since the Census Report of 1872 failed to provide any authentic data about the Muslims 'who live[d] by agriculture, and of the aboriginal and semi-aboriginal castes living by cultivation'. On the other hand, the Census remained silent about the agricultural and labouring women of this district during the time of famine. The aboriginal and semi-aboriginal tribes of Malda were mainly cultivators but on the approach of famine they gave up their fields in search for hired labour, and were thus thrown on the labouring population.[6] The famine had contributed to the development of additional system of communication in the district. Since river communication in the district was abundant at all seasons of the year, the Collector of the district suggested to build a 'good metalled' road to 'connect English Bazar and other towns with the Ferry that crosses the Ganges opposite Rajmahal.'[7] The Collector had also proposed to build a similar road which would run to meet the new line of rail to Darjeeling.[8] Hunter in his *The Annals of Rural Bengal* had presented a comparative study between the famine of 1770 and 1866 inspite of existence of 'very little evidence' for comparison. In regards to the causes of the 1770 and 1866 famine, Hunter argued that in both cases, the immediate cause of the dearth was the premature cessation of the autumnal rains, resulting in the general failure of the December harvest and the partial failure of the spring crops.[9] At the same time, Hunter had admitted that 'in both cases, the Government failed to perfectly appreciate, or to deal with the true character of the calamity until the suffering amounted to actual starvation.'[10]

In Dinajpur (stretched between Champaran district on the west and Rangpur on the east), though the *aman* or winter rice did not fall short, still the price of best cleaned rice was Rs. 4-7 per maund and for common rice, it was Rs. 4-1-6 per maund. However, in 1871 it had returned to its ordinary rates that prevailed before the famine.[11] The increase in agricultural land caused by the large scale reclamation by the Santhals, alike Malda, was affected in Dinajpur due to the non-availability of the necessary credit.[12] But the scarcity in this district was confined to a comparatively small area and it was suggested by the Government not to adopt any special measures for the relief of the distress in this district.[13] In Rangpur the unusual prices during 1866 caused considerable inconvenience in the District, but the scarcity fortunately never rose to a famine. At the beginning of November 1865, just before the winter harvest, the price of rice had risen to the maximum; the cost of ordinary rice was eight seers per rupee, while the price of very cheapest rice was as dear as 9.5 seers. Though these prices, however, lasted for a short time, i.e. up to the gathering in of the new crop but with such rates prevailing, the winter crops were very scanty to feed the people, and the possibility to substitute it by the spring crop was also very poor.[14] Anticipating the approaching of famine in the district the Collector suggested for the import of grain from the other neighbouring districts so that '[T]he State purchases might induce neighbouring Districts to pour in supplies.' At the same time it was apprehended that as a result of excessive amount of importation 'prices would fall, and the confidence of the merchants might be shaken, and private enterprise brought to a stop.'[15] There was increasing fear in the official circle that if there would be 'no import at all, the scarcity might turn into famine even for the provident portion of the community, and irretrievable disaster might ensue.'[16] The continuous decrease in the wages of labour and the absence of any quick transport further worsened the situation. The years from 1864 to 1866 had witnessed a general collapse of stocks that disclosed considerable and rapid decline in the average quantity of rice obtained for one rupee at the major grain markets of the rice producing districts of north Bengal.

Table: 3.3

Variations in food-grain prices from 1864 to 1866 in Northern Bengal

Districts	*September 1864*	*September 1865*	*September 1866*
	Seer	*Seer*	*Seer*
Malda	30	19	11
Dinajpur	27	21	9¾
Rangpur	27	22	11

Source: *Document 17. Famine Report: Famine in Behar and Sonthal Parganas, 1866. Papers and correspondence, including the report of the Famine Commission and the Minutes of the Lieutenant Governor of Bengal and the Governor General.*[17]

In Rangpur, though famine had not reached to severe extent, the prevalence of high prices of crops in the district produced 'demand from other district.'[18] During the end of the 1866 (in November), prices of crops had reached to highest level before the gathering of winter rice harvest.[19] In the Gazetteer it was concluded that 'the scarcity never amounted to famine or rendered it necessary to invoke Government aid.'[20] The princely state of Cooch Behar had to suffer slightly from the 1866 drought and scarcity which, according to Hunter, 'did not amount to absolute famine' in the state.[21] Therefore, neither the state nor the colonial government had to adopt any relief measures for Cooch Behar. However, a very severe drought, caused by the absence of local rainfall had occurred in 1854, which considerably affected the prosperity of the people of the princely state. The drought had resulted in the general failure of the rice crops, and caused the condition of 'partial famine.'[22] On the other hand, according to Hunter, the drought of 1854 had amounted to a 'famine', though the highest prices that prevailed in 1854 were lower than that of 1866.[23] Since the Maharaja of Cooch Behar was a minor in 1854 and was residing at the Court of Wards Institution at Calcutta, the Chief Minister of the State imported large quantities of grain from Sirajganj and other places, and sold it at cost price to the people.[24] Rice had been also importing continually during the next three months and was distributed over the all parts of the state.[25]

II. Rainfall, Crops and Colonialism: North Bengal in the Bengal-Bihar Famine

After the Bengal-Orissa famine of 1866 the northern districts of Bengal had fallen into another severe scarcity of food crops which eventually lead to a famine in 1873-74. The 1873-74 Bengal-Bihar famine had affected a vast area of Bengal, Bihar and Nepal. "The Bengal-Bihar famine of 1873-74" as C. E. Buckland puts it "began while Sir G. Campbell was Lieutenant-Governor and came to an end after Sir R. Temple had succeeded him"[26] and in this famine northern districts of Bengal had to suffer exclusively in comparison with the other districts of Bengal.

From the early government accounts (February 1874) it is noticeable that a vast portion of eastern and northern India was affected by the shortage of rainfall which created severe distress. It is stated that:

> "The portion of Bengal in which severe Famine began to show itself so carly as the end of February, is the northern tract of Chumparan, Tirhoot and Bhaugulpore, between the Gunduk on the east and the Kosee on the west. Further to the east North Purneah and Western Dinagepore are severely distressed....in the depressed rice tract between a point point forty miles north of the Ganges and Nepal that famine in its worst form prevails over a population estimated...by Sir George Campbell at 2,300,000."[27]

The 1873-74 famine did not appear suddenly - the meteorological conditions over the past two years made the situations ripe for the impending famine. During the three successive years, from 1871 to 1873, the rainfall in

Bengal had been irregular. Though the rainfall was fairly good in 1871, but it did not help to bring good production of crops. In 1872, inspite of insufficiency there was proportionate distribution of rainfall. But the year 1873, was 'dry almost beyond precedent' and '[T]o the North of the Ganges ...... the rain was far below the average.'[28] The crop failure of 1873 due to drought and its subsequent impact on agriculture has been aptly put forward by George Campbell, the then Lieutenant-Governor, (on 22nd October, 1873) in the following manner:

> "in Bihar and North Bengal the rains, late in coming, had been so heavy as to do great injury to the *bhadoi* crop, and they had stopped so prematurely that the winter rice was almost all lost, and there was great fear that the ground would be too dry to admit of the *rabi* being sown. In East and Central Bengal the crops would be poor, but not extremely so: in Orissa alone they were good."[29]

But as the days of October, 1873 were passing by and no rain came, apprehension increased. When a considerable portion of October had passed without rain the Lieutenant Governor ordered a circular on the 13th October which read that the crop and price-current returns regularly submitted should be supplemented by further reports giving fuller details of the food supplies of the country. The Lieutenant Government stated that:

> "The reports we have from Northern and Central Bengal and the whole of Behar are as bad as they can be;...There is an area north of the Ganges; comprising most of the Rajshahye Division, Purnea, and North Tirhoot, in which the rain has been extraordinarily short, and in which I fear, nothing can now save us from great dearness and distress. If the next two or three weeks should pass without good rain, the

> consequences in these districts would be painful..."[30]

H. L. Johnson, the Private Secretary in the General and Revenue Department of Bengal had described the considerable shortage of rainfall which created severe distress in vast tract of Bihar and northern Bengal and admitted that in these parts of the country rains were not only 'very late to commence and very early to cease' but in quantity it was 'below the average in amount to an extraordinary degree.'[31] According to him the most severely affected areas were located 'in the tracts north of the Ganges and near the Himalayas, which were usually rice producing countries, the north-east of Behar, and the north of Bengal, Dinajpore, Rungpore, and almost the whole of the Rajshahye Division.'[32] George Campbell, the then Lieutenant Governor of Bengal had narrated the advent of the famine in 1873 in the following manner:

> The rainy season of 1873 commenced late and rather scanty, but during July and August the rain was sufficient for agricultural operations, ... after that the rains failed more suddenly and completely than had been known in the present century, and the effect on the main rice crops over great tracts was most disastrous... When September passed with scarcely any rain the situation became serious, and as October advanced without a drop of the final rainfall usually expected at that season, the reports from all sides became alarming in the highest degree. ... I had ... the extreme difficulty of making a sure forecast, especially where a statistical information was so very imperfect in Bengal. ... There were still slight hopes of an unusually late fall of rain, but nothing came; and in the first half of November the prospects became very black indeed. ... there was an excessive

> failure of the rice crop in Behar and parts of Bengal north of the Ganges, a short crop in a wider area; ... the prospects for the spring crops in Behar were very bad... owing to the failure of the latter rains, the ground was so dry that the seed could not possibly germinate."[33]

Richard Temple in his Minute had narrated the issue of deficient rainfall in the following manner:

> "In Bengal and Bihar, after a season of extra ordinary heat during May and June of 1873, the rain did not begin till date, that is in July, and even then was scanty. It lasted more and less, but never abundantly, till the end of August, when it for the most part ceased prematurely."[34]

The *Report of the Indian Famine Commission 1878-80* had summarized the shortage of rainfall in the following manner:

> "The monsoon of 1873 was not abnormal during the 3 months, June, July and August, but in northern Bengal it ceased prematurely in September; and much of the winter rice crop, which ripens in November, was consequently lost."[35]

Meantime the reports from the Commissioners made the atmosphere more alarming. The Commissioner of Patna wrote that there was no rain, nor sign of rain. The Commissioner of Rajshahi reported a panic in the district of Bogra, where rice had risen from 24½ to 12½ seers to the rupee within two days. It fell, however, to 18 seers within two or three days afterwards. The Commissioner of Rajshahi added – 'now I fear rain would do little good, and there is no probability of any further fall.' On the 22nd October, the Lieutenant Governor wrote to the Secretary to the Government of India that:

Table 3.4

Comparative deficit of rainfall in 1873 in the Rajshahi Division (Extracted)

Dist.	*Station*	*1873.*	*Avg.*	*Deficit*	*Fall to end of April*	*Fall to end of June*	*Fall to end of Aug.*	*Fall in Sept.*	*Total fall to end of Sept*	*Fall since Sept.*
Dinajpur	Dinajpur	43.53	84.59	41	1.96	22.33	41.59	1.62	43.21	.32
Malda	Malda	27.02	53.88	26.9	3.23	7.01	21.14	4.96	26.10	.82
Rajshahi	Boalia	32.14	61.71	29.6	6.31	10.53	28.29	2.57	31.86	.28
	Natore	43.88	63	19	9.73	14.76	37.41	5.98	43.49	.39
Rangpur	Rangpur	44.64	88.19	43.5	6.44	23.73	41.69	2.57	44.26	.38
	Bhawaniganj	47.99	95	47	7.87	20.38	39.77	7.35	47.12	.87
	Titalia	83.52	95	11.5	4.55	38.83	68.19	14.53	82.72	.80
Bogra	Bogra	37.12	88.41	51.3	8.94	13.32	33.25	3.49	36.74	.38
Pabna	Pabna	43.26	65	22	3.09	17.40	37.79	4.02	42.81	.45
	Sirajganj	35.46	95	59.5	.....	13.28	30.40	4.23	34.63	.83

Source: Extract from the Proceedings of the Government of India in the Department of Agriculture, Revenue, and Commerce, No. 813, - dated Calcutta, the 6th March, 1874, WBSA.

> "In parts of [northern Bengal and north-east Bihar] usually moist tract the rainfall [had] hardly exceeded that which is usual in the driest parts of North Western Provinces. It is in this tract that the greatest failure has taken place...."[36]

The difficulties of Government in regards to the scarcity was not absolutely confined to the British territory and British subjects. The strip of Nepal territory, known as the Terai, lying between the Himalaya and the distressed north Bengal districts, a rice growing tract, had been suffered from the failure of the rains.[37] However, the Lieutenant Governor was 'most anxious' for the Bihar and North Bengal region.[38]

It is evident from the above table that Sirajganj, Bogra, Bhawaniganj, Rangpur and Dinajpur had witnessed the acute shortage of rainfall and the percentage of deficiency from the average for these areas were 59.5, 51.3, 47, 43.5, and 41 respectively.[39] These places had been suffered from almost half the percentage of rainfall than the average rainfall. The considerable deficiency in rainfall had adversely affected the rate of crop production in the field. However, the failure of rice had been attributed to the widespread cultivation of jute and other non-food crops which had ultimately helped to transform the nature of agricultural land. George Campbell had himself stated that 'the difficulty [was] not to use our land, but to find land for all that [was] desired to grow without interfering with the food of the population. The demand for jute seem[ed] to go on increasing without limit – the cry [was] that it [was] displacing rice to a dangerous extent.'[40] The uncontrolled process of commercialization of agriculture thus adversely affected the existed pattern of agricultural production in Bengal where sudden shortage of rainfall caused great inconvenience for the poor peasants. While the failure of rains massively affected the rice production, the peasants did not have any stock from the previous seasons due to their absolute dependency over the jute and other profitable non-food crops.

In the districts of Dinajpur, Rangpur, Bogra, and parts of Rajshahi, and Malda of the Rajshahi Division the whole yield of all food crops of 1873-74 was estimated to be less than three-eighths of the yield of an ordinary average crop, and relief works on a more or less extended scale would be required soon. The Government had sent a steamer and flats to ply on the Ganges from Kooshtea to Rajshahi, and had ordered a small light-draught steamer, with flats, to ply on the inland waters of Rajshahi. He had further directed the formation of bullock trains on certain traffic routes in Rajshahi for the carriage of railway material and of food grains to depots.[41] Apart from this various minor road works, have been sanctioned in different districts. In regard to the food supply of the distressed districts the Viceroy had laid down the general rule that the Government should trust to the trade and to the improved means of communication for the natural flow of food from other parts of India to make up the deficit in Bihar and Northern Bengal. The Viceroy had authorised the Lieutenant Governor to arrange for supplying and storing food at centres of relief works where many labourers were likely to be gathered together, and where local supplies might be insufficient to bear any extra strain.[42]

The *Report of the Indian Famine Commission 1878-80* had summarized the famine condition and subsequent relief works in the following manner:

> "The Bengal Government, from inquiries instituted for the purpose, was led to believe that the inevitable effect of this loss would be to involve the inhabitants of a large part of the province in a severe famine; it accordingly set about making preparations with the utmost energy to carry out relief measures on a scale and with a thoroughness which had never been equalled before. The principles adopted by the Government were very different from those accepted on any

> former similar occasion. It was considered that the operations of private trade could not be relied on, and therefore that it would be necessary to accept the responsibility of providing the distressed districts with the whole quantity of food likely to be required. After elaborate estimates had been framed, it was decided, with the approval of the Government of India and the Secretary of State, to import 480,000 tons of rice; and the greater part of this stock was purchased for the Government in Burma, sent up-country by railway, and distributed to depots scattered over the famine area by the agency of Government officers. The estimates provided against every possible contingency, the failure of contractors, murrain among the cattle, the recurrence of drought in the ensuing monsoon. Relief was administered mainly in the form of employment on works and of gratuitous assistance to the infirm; but under rules which in their details were very different from those previously followed. Tests were not to be stringently enforced in localities where the distress was excessive and widespread. In place of the self-acting tests which on previous occasions had been held to be useful and to some extent necessary, reliance was placed on personal knowledge, on the part of the relieving officer, of the applicant's condition and want.[43]

A 'large special establishment' of inspecting officers was appointed, and the famine-affected areas were subdivided among them with an anticipation that with the help of the resident *zamindars* and leading *raiyats*, 'they might obtain such personal knowledge of the condition of every village and its inhabitants.'[44] It had been further stated that about 340,000 tons of grain were disposed of in the relief operations, 'a quantity sufficient to provide sustenance for not less than 3,000,000 people for 7 months.'[45] Rice had been imported from Burma to Calcutta 'with entire efficiency and punctuality' by the vessels of the British India Steam Navigation Company. Apart from this, where private trade was exhausted and failed to supply the people shops were established at a later period for the sale of Government grain.[46] However, this time the Government 'had a treasury full beyond all precedent' and a large quantity of 'available cash'[47] had denoted the successful and organized collection of land revenue during the previous years of the famine. However, the Government had to face great difficulties for the transport of supplying rice in the remotest corners of the affected districts especially during the supplies of large quantity of grains, but the problem had been solved by the indigo planters who were under a contract with the Government.[48] This practise had generated much criticism against the Government which promoted the exercise of the feudal authorities of the planters in such a critical time.

George Campbell had stated that 'The supply of funds to meet famine on a large scale rested wholly with the Government of India, so that I could have done little without their sanction.'[49] Apart from the execution of the provision of work and supply of food for the labourers, Campbell had argued for the prohibition of the export of rice from the affected areas for which the '...Viceroy in Council was expressly empowered to take such action, and native opinion was all in favour of such a course.'[50] Campbell's suggestion had triggered a debate in the official circle and the idea of 'prohibition of export' was negated by the British administration. Campbell, however, was very much clear in his arguments that he cogently put forward in support of the prohibition of export. Campbell's 'first proposal was to prohibit the export of food grains from all India', because he believed that 'at that time (in October) it was not improbable that the famine would have been very much greater than has...proved to be the case' and 'throughout almost the whole of Bengal proper there was universal fear of an extreme failure of the rice crops.'[51] Campbell had justified his position by showing the following figures of export which was carried out during and previous the famine years –

> "The previous year, 1872-73, was of plenty, in which the exports much exceeded the average, - the comparison, therefore, is hardly fair, - but comparing these two years, a return prepared for the Government of India shows that from 1st October 1873, to 28th February, 1874, 173, 161 tons of food grains were exported from Bengal against 241, 618 tons in the corresponding period of the previous year. The reduction is only a little more than one-fourth – about 28 per cent. ..... the export from Bengal from 1st November to end of March was a little over 172, 000 tons....against this export we may set a still larger import made by Government."[52]

In the final discourse, 'Her Majesty's Government approved the decision of the Government to meet the emergency by the purchase and import of food rather by prohibition of export, and so it was settled.'[53] However, it was not until February that the Government imports had outnumbered its exports and even at the end of February the imports were scarcely more than half the exports.[54] For the northern districts, especially, Campbell stated that 'throughout the previous months [from October 1873 to February 1874] the grain supply of the country was very seriously diminished by exports, and the flow of grain being seawards, the flow north to the distressed districts was prevented.'[55] With regard to the execution of relief-works, Sir G. Campbell's, the then Lieutenant Governor of Bengal (1873), view was that- 'to render effectual aid to the people, it is of all things most necessary that work should be offered in good time, so that the existence of public works may be known to the people at large, and those who stand in need of work may find their way to the work and be suitably provided for, before the greatest stress comes.' [56]

In order to administer the relief activities for all the affected areas of Bengal and Bihar the Government had formed a Central Relief Committee and the officers of the this committee were given executive control over the relief operations of all the Local Committees.[57] It was also mentioned that the functions of the Central Committee should be limited to the collection and distribution of funds and the receipt of reports.[58] The duty of superintending the operations of Relief Committees rests with the sub-divisional and district officers under the general instructions of Commissioners of Divisions. The Relief Committees had been authorised by the instructions to adopt any measures necessary to meet sudden and severe distress and the same authority was given to the local officers under similar circumstances.[59] Local officers were also empowered with 'best of their power' to 'act promptly' in a situation of 'sudden danger'.[60] It is to be noted here that the famine of 1873-74 had introduced a new template for the famine-relief operations in Bengal. In fact, organization and execution of famine-relief works had now been accentuated directly and responsibly for the first time in Bengal as well as in India. To quote Richard Temple, who succeeded Campbell:

> "Lord Northbrook had, in the first place, to consider the question whether the Government should undertake the responsibility for counteracting the effects of this drought, and for averting the famine which would otherwise result. He decided that it should, although such a task had never yet been accomplished in India. During the former famines of this century, so much mortality had occurred despite the efforts put forth by the State, that loss of life had come to be regarded as inevitable. Nevertheless, it was announced in the Gazette that a

> widespread famine was anticipated, that much was expected of the people in the way of self-help and from the trade in respect of enterprise, but that the Government would interpose to do whatever could not otherwise be done in order that none should perish who might possibly be saved." [61]

Since the private enterprise was not capable enough to meet the situation, Government had decided to import large quantity of food-grains from the outside part of northern Bengal. At the same time, it is to be noted that at the very outset of the famine the government had admitted its incapability to 'adequately deal with' the famine and 'overtake it'; and further acknowledged that the government could only 'partially mitigate' the impact of this 'very severe and very widespreading' famine.[62]

Over the greater part of the Bengal proper there would be, it was hoped, from half to three quarters of a full average crop, while in North Bengal and Behar (containing a population of 26 millions) the yield of the food crops was estimated to be from one-quarter to one-third of full average years.[63] It was hoped that northern Bengal, which was ordinarily an exporting tract might have considerable stocks of previous years, and it was decided that from the other exporting districts (Sylhet, Backergunj, and Orissa) considerable old stocks would have to be brought to the market. In the Patna, Bhagalpur, and Rajshahi Divisions the late rice crop, the main staple of the country, was said to be as bad as it had been anticipated by the Government. Adding further distress to this there had been no rain during the last week of November, 1873. A small parcel of rice (only 1300 maunds) was loaded on the Government steamers transferred for service in the Rajshahi Division where Government had to pay three rupees a maund, or very nearly the rate then prevailing in Calcutta.[64] It must be noted here that the colonial administration was observing 'a healthy private trade [which] was going on between Eastern Bengal and Rajshahi in small boats, from which rice was eagerly brought by the residents along the rivers.'[65]

The erratic rainfall of 1873 in north Bengal resulted in a large-scale loss of crops. In 1873, the rainfall in Malda was 27.26 inches, or half of the average (i.e. 53.88 inches).[66] In Malda, the monthly distribution of rainfall for the year 1873 was as below:

Table: 3.5

Monthly Distribution of Rainfall in Malda in 1873 (in inches)

January	February	March	April	May	June	July	August	September	October	November	December	Total Rainfall
0.45	...	0.29	1.19	0.06	4.36	7.08	7.76	4.91	0.92	...	0.24	27.26

Source: A. P. MacDonnell, *Report on the Food Grain Supply and Statistical Review of the Relief Operations in the Distressed Districts of Behar and Bengal During the famine of 1873-74*, Calcutta, 1876, p. 251. (Henceforth *Report on the Food Grain Supply*).

As a result of this erratic rainfall the outturn of *aus* or autumn rice was very poor and it returned on an average only a six-anna crop, or less than half of that of an ordinary year and the *aman* or winter lowland rice was short of half an average.[67] The proportion of the consumption of food grains of the people, while the prevailing ratio was seven-eighths of rice and one-eighth of all other sorts of grain, had declined drastically due to the damage of five-eighths or three-fourths of those crops in 1873.[68] The failure in the harvest consequently affected the markets. In January 1874 the price of rice had increased to more than double to the normal price in that month and the prices continued to rise and in April they reached to 10½ seers for the rupee. This situation was further worsened by the declining rate of import of food grains from Dinajpur, as this region was also affected by natural irregularities.

Table: 3.6

Cost of paddy and ordinary rice in different parts of Malda

Part of the District	*Place*	*Cost of Paddy (seers per rupee)*	*Cost of Ordinary rice(seers per rupee)*
Central part	Mangalbari & Balia Nawabganj	19	10½
North-East part	Bamangola	18	13
	Gazole	21	13
North-West part	Chanchal	——	10
	Tulsiganj and Abadpur	——	10½
	Samsi	——	10¼
	Fatepur Hyatpur	18	12
South-West part	Shibganj, Kansat & Turtipur	——	11½ - 12
South-East	Rohanpur & Gomastapur	21	15

Source: Narrative of scarcity and relief in the Malda district for the Fortnight ending March 7th, 1874.[69]

It is evident from the above table that paddy had been always costly than the ordinary rice and in many parts of the district paddy had even vanished from the market which had helped to increase the price of paddy. Government had to intervene into this situation by extending relief measures to the victims of Malda district. The relief statistics are mentioned below (all figures are in *tons*) –

Table: 3.7

Relief Statistics for the district of Malda, 1874

Total Rice Stored	*For Charitable Relief*	*For Cash*	*For Wages*	*For Advanced Loan*
3, 946	1, 315	1, 253	243	907

Source: G. E. Lambourn, *Bengal District Gazetteers, Malda*, Calcutta, 1918, p. 56.

Apart from the distribution of rice, government had also speeded up the relief measures through the distribution of money directly to the distress people. The costs of relief have been mentioned below (all figures are in rupees):

Table: 3.8

Statement of Government Expenditure in the District of Malda in 1874

Charitable Relief	*Wages for Relief Work*	*Advance for Loan*
26, 951	1, 06, 762	48, 450

Source: G. E. Lambourn, *Bengal District Gazetteers, Malda*, p. 56.

As a result of the distribution of money to affected people, according to the government estimate, – "[T]he number of persons charitably relieved rose from 1, 036 in the middle of April, to 6, 340 in the middle of May, and 13, 009 in the middle of July, but fell to 4, 458 in the beginning of September, and to 469 in the first week of October."[70] This data shows the comparative improvement in the plight of the distressed and their reducing number displays the subsequent recovery of the region within a short span of time. Chanchal was situated in the most severely distressed part of Malda. Early in the season grain was imported for the relief of tenants. Relief works were opened this part and as many as 2, 000 persons being employed daily on roads and tanks.[71] Apart from this, a considerable number of populations was engaged in repairing of roads and digging tanks and there were total 31,938 persons who had participated in these works.[72]

Table: 3.9

Statement showing total number of persons employed on road and relief works in Malda during the fortnight ending 7th March 1874

Areas of relief works	*Roads*	*Men*	*Women*	*Children*	*Total*
	District roads	8138	1819	258	10215
	Municipal roads & tanks	625	271	34	930

North-western tract	On nine relief roads	8616	1825	448	10889
	On six tanks	4456	2518	211	7185
Eastern tract	On two relief roads	1264	—	186	1450
South-eastern & central tracts	On three roads	679	504	86	1269
	Total	23,778	6937	1223	31938

Source: Narrative of scarcity and relief in the Malda district for the Fortnight ending March 7th, 1874.

Eight centres for distribution of gratuitous relief were opened and other relief operations also were arranged at the expense of the Chanchal estate.[73] Though governmental relief in form of distributing rice against cash, wage-payment, charitable-relief and advance for loan had been extended to the victims, this could not provide any long-term relief because they were insufficient for a large portion of people.

Dinajpur had to suffer most seriously from the shortage of rainfall. The average rainfall in the district from 1868 to 1872 was as followed:

Table: 3.10

Average Monthly Rainfall in the District of Dinajpur from 1868 to 1872 (in inches)

January	February	March	April	May	June	July	August	September	October	November	December	Total
0.57	0.78	1.28	1.52	5.08	23.88	17.12	15.40	13.13	5.61	.....	0.05	84.48

Source: A. P. MacDonnell, *Report on the Food Grain Supply*, p. 223.

In 1872, though the rainfall was 5½ inches under the average, the harvests did not fall into any trouble. In 1873 the rainfall was noticeably short from the average (84.88 inches); it was only 43½ inches, i.e. more than half of the normal. The September-October rains which were much essential for the winter rice crop were almost in a vanishing condition. The table below shows the monthly rainfall of the year 1873 in Dinajpur:

Table: 3.11

Monthly Distribution of Rainfall in Dinajpur in 1873 (in inches)

January	February	March	April	May	June	July	August	September	October	November	December	Total
0.50	0.28	0.61	0.66	0.41	18.27	8.24	12.62	1.62	...	....	0.32	43.53

ource: A. P. MacDonnell, *Report on the Food Grain Supply*, p. 224.

As a result of the total deficiency in rainfall in the early months of rainy season, as the Collector of the district, Mr. Robinson had mentioned, the early rice and other rainy season crops 'were in the best parts one-fourth and generally one-eighth of an average crop, while in many parts the outturn was *nil*'.[74] On the failure of the winter rice, he further observed that 'crop would certainly not yield more than three-eighths of an average crop in any part, in most parts not one-fourth of the average, and in very large tracts nothing at all.'[75] The outturn of the autumn crop in 1873 was 9, 308 tons and for winter rice crops it was 1, 24, 462 tons which were too insufficient to meet the total deficiency of 4, 38, 000 tons of food grain.[76] In January 1874 the produce of the rice harvest raised to 1, 48, 310 tons and the total supply in grain which the district drew from the local sources from January to September (1874) was 1, 50, 000 tons that was about six months' supply at ordinary rates of consumption.[77] On the other hand rice export from the district was much greater than the import quantity. In 1873 the quantity of rice exported from the district was 10, 93, 520 maunds while the quantity of import was 650 maunds; and in 1874 the quantity of imported rice was only 1, 121 mound whereas against the quantity of 20, 059 mounds of export. The entire system of import and export had been operated exclusively through the river traffic. This tendency, however, resulted in the increase of price-rice and by January it was two and a half times as dear as it usually was in that month. The district of Dinajpur had witnessed a fluctuation of prices of common rice throughout the year of 1874. The table below shows the monthly price of common rice in 1874.

Table: 3.12

Monthly Price of Common Rice in 1874 (all figures are in *seers* for one rupee)

January	February	March	April	May	June	July	August	September	October	November	December
12.5	13.8	12.1	9.5	8.3	8.9	10.4	12.5	16	19	24.9	28

Source: A. P. MacDonnell, *Report on the Food Grain Supply,* p. 226.

The government had collected information from the local officers as to the extent of the scarcity and subsequently preparations had been made to import large stocks of rice from Burma and elsewhere. As a result of the breakdown of the ordinary machinery of the grain trade relief funds were opened. From April 1874 onwards, relief works were commenced in the severely affected areas of Kaliaganj, Raiganj, Hemtabad, Pirganj, Ranisankoil and Thakurgaon *thanas* and government depots for the sale of grain at reasonable rates were opened at Raiganj and many other important places.[78] The relief works had been conducted mainly through public works like- construction of new roads, the repair of the old ones and digging of tanks. 12 lakhs maunds of food-grain had been sanctioned by Richard Temple to meet the distress of the district which was, according to Temple, mostly suffered during the period between 15th May and 15th August, 1874.[79] The daily number of labourers employed in this relief works reached nearly 95, 000 in May 1874 and by the end of the year the money spent by the government on the relief amounted to nearly Rs. 24, 00, 000 including the value of rice paid as wages and distributed as cost-free relief.[80]

Table: 3.13
Statement of Grain and Cash Expenditure by the Government in Dinajpur in 1874

	Charitable Relief	*Wages of Labour*	*Advanced on Loan*
Grain (tons)	2, 732	2, 934	12, 533
Cash (rupee)	37, 633	11, 61, 492	23, 300

Source: A. P. MacDonnell, *Report on the Food Grain Supply*, p. 227.

On the basis of the outcome of the sales and advances of grain and money, MacDonnell had assumed that each 20 seers of grain relieved an individual for a month and each thirty *annas* another individual for a similar period and in aggregate the number of people relieved by these measures during these days were 14, 71, 059.[81] Distribution of money and grain had, however, helped to ameliorate the condition of people, though for a very small number and for a shorter period of time. The zamindars of Dinajpur had also contributed according to their own way by extending cultivated areas in the district. The famine of 1873-74 encouraged the zamindars 'to bring colonies of Santhal tribes from the Santhal parganas to clear huge Barind tract covered by jungle.'[82] As a result, the cultivated area of the district was increased one third by the beginning of the twentieth century.[83] For the reclamation of jungles the zamindars used to provide capital as advance and they obtained the return of this loan by enhancing the rent of this new cultivable land. In Rangpur, the case was little different. Here the reclamation process was carried out under the *jotedars'* enterprise and the result was that the zamindars could obtain only a smaller portion of the profit produced by the increased rent of the land.[84]

However, the reason for the most severe sufferings of the peasants and tenants of Dinajpur was inherent in the pattern of land holding of this district. Referring to the Buchanan Hamilton's survey of Dinajpur district in 1808, Ray and Ray argue that only 6 per cent of the cultivating population held 36.5 per cent of the land leased by raiyats from the zamindars, whereas 52.1 per cent of the agricultural labour did not possess any land.[85] These landless labourers had to work either as sharecroppers or as agricultural labourers under the zamindars.[86] This section of population of Dinajpur had to suffer most seriously because they did not have any access to the production of land on which they worked and at the time of scarcity of food-grain they had no means to collect food either from the market or from their previous year's savings, if any. Thus, the landless poor agricultural labour had become most vulnerable to the climatic disorder and required government or private relief to overcome the situation.

The distressed peasant and common people of the district of Dinajpur had received a considerable amount of help from their local landlords and zamindars in form of gratuitous relief, maintenance of 'poor-houses', providing cash and grain as advance etc. Srimati Sham Mohini of Dinajpur, who was locally known as the Maharani had owned large estates (with a rental of £ 40,000) in the distressed portions of the Dinajpur district. The Maharani had abstained from collecting rents from her tenants during the year of scarcity and distributed to her tenants about £ 5,000 worth of rice and seed grain.[87] She had also taken initiatives for digging tanks in her estate, donated land free of charge to the villages for their tanks, maintained a relief house where about 90,000 persons received relief since the onset of the famine and also took the responsibility for the payment of all advances of grain made by the Government to her ryots.[88] Babu Khetra Mohon Sing, the Maharani's agent, had 'efficiently' managed the charitable activities made by the Maharani and had also provided 'great assistance to the relief officers, especially by collecting carts, at a critical juncture of the transport operations...'[89] Several other zamindar and wealthy people had contributed to the relief works in the district. Babu Radha Govind Roy Saheb of Dinajpur had started a private poor-house where gratuitous relief was given and he assisted the government relief officers 'whenever and in whatever was he asked.'[90] Babu Shetab Chand Lahoree, resident of Murshidabad, but zamindar in Dinajpur, deputed a special agent to administer relief measures on his estates.[91] Babu Shyama Sankar Roy was also involved in the relief-works in the district of Dinajpur. He 'imported grain for his people, opened relief works, maintained two relief houses throughout the famine, made large advances to his ryots for food, and materially assisted the relief officers of Government.'[92] Apart from the zamindars or landlords, several other wealthy natives of the district of Dinajpur had contributed enormously to the relief works during the period between February and early weeks of March. They were mostly involved in providing engagement of a good number of labourers in repairing of roads in several parts of the district. Babu Purna Chandra Gupta, at Goraghat, had provided employment for 1200 to 1300 persons daily; Babu Hara Kali Mukherjee, who started work between Kaliaganj thana and Malda Road received 1400 persons at public work (including 200 women).[93]

Cultivation of land or agriculture as a whole had possessed some exceptional characteristics in the district of Rangpur. The minimum increase in cultivation in Rangpur between Buchanan's time and 1872-73 could be attributed partly to the effects of recurring fever that resulted in the considerable decline of the population and partly to a 'considerable deterioration' in the productive powers of land in some parts of the district.[94] Gopal Chandra Dass, the Special Deputy Collector of Rangpur, had observed that the holding size of 50 per cent of the cultivators was below seven or eight *bighas* (i.e. less than three acres) of land and they were capable of using only one plough and a pair of bullocks.[95] The plight of the more poor peasants was too horrible to obtain their bare subsistence. Even in the pre-famine period, during the latter half of 1871, the ryots started to shift from their old land which they cultivated and frequently abandoned one and take another holding.[96] Due to the lack of any permanent establishment in land a large section of peasants could not secure occupancy rights which caused an atmosphere of uncertainty and inconsistency in agricultural production. On the other hand, the rates of rent in Rangpur, a district of large absentee landlords, had already reached to its height and it could not afford any further enhancement.[97] Indicating to the surprising difference between rental and revenue, being respectively Rs. 86, 89, 750 and 9, 74, 088, MacDonnell remarked, '[i]n no other district of Bengal where condition has been reviewed is there such a great disproportion between the revenue and rental as in Rungpore.'[98] All these factors together had made the whole agricultural sector of the district so easily vulnerable to any climatic disorder.

In Rangpur, there was not only serious deficiency in the rainfall in 1873 but it was also very unseasonably distributed. In every month the rainfall was noticeably under the normal quantity. In May there was no rain, in July it was only one-third of the average fall and it came to an abrupt end in the month of September when an ample rainfall was in utmost necessity for the maturity of the winter crop of the year.[99]

Table: 3.14

Monthly Distribution of Rainfall in the District of Rangpur in 1873 (in inches)

January	February	March	April	May	June	July	August	September	October	November	December	Total
0.05	0.24	1.10	6.54	0.97	12.91	5.88	13.23	4.90	0.16	...	0.54	46.32

Source: A. P. MacDonnell, *Report on the Food Grain Supply*, p. 237.

The impact of rainfall felt differently in the different parts of the district. The rainfall was also unevenly distributed throughout the district. The rainfall was comparatively heavier in the east, along the line of Brahmaputra and this region produced the best harvest within the district - half of the average which was parallel to the production of the eastern part's low-lying lands. There was shortage of rain also in the southern and western parts of the district but the central part suffered the worse by having a total loss to one-eighth or three-sixteenths of an average harvest.[100] The district was so hard hit by the shortage of rainfall that at the harvesting time in January 1874, the average produce of the whole district was of three annas or one-fifth of an average crop. The total outturn of autumn (*aus*) and winter crops (*aman*) in 1873 was 201, 318 tons with the total deficiency of 573, 000 tons of an ordinary year while in January 1874, the food-supply of Rangpur derived from all internal sources was 209, 000 tons.[101] This deficiency, however, was countered by the end of the winter season of 1874 with an overall outturn that yielded a full average harvest.

Table: 3.15

Prices of Common Rice and Wheat in Rangpur in 1874 (in *seers*)

January	February	March	April	May	June	July	August	September	October	November	December	Total
0.05	0.24	1.10	6.54	0.97	12.91	5.88	13.23	4.90	0.16	...	0.54	46.32

Source: A. P. MacDonnell, *Report on the Food Grain Supply*, p. 239.

In the beginning of 1874 the price of common rice, which was the staple article of diet of all classes, was two and one-third times than the usual price in that month. The continuous import of rice from Cooch Behar, Assam and Dacca was not capable enough to minimize the price and in April the trade had collapsed due to 'a general failure of the supplies in the market throughout the district.'[102] As a result of this, prices at the headquarters market raised to 5-8-0 maund which was nearly four times than the usual rates at that time of the year and in the remote areas they rose to Rs. 6. The high prices of grains produced a lot of distress to the poorer people who by no means had any scope to purchase grains during this time of scarcity and the crisis reached to such an extent that a man, as it was reported, had to sale his wife for Rs. 10.[103]

In order to prevent this famine situation, as Hunter remarked, the Collector of the District considered to make arrangements for '[e]their the food must be taken to the people, or the people to the food; and in that practice both courses would have to be followed.'[104] At the same time it was realized that this would not have been possible without the improvement in the exiting communication system.[105] Hence, the construction of new and repair of old roads formed the major part of relief-work initiated by the Government in this area for the labouring and cultivating classes. The Northern Bengal State Railway which had been started earlier now expected to cover all areas of the district. But the greatest relief had been provided by the nature itself when sufficient rain during the rest of the months enormously contributed for the betterment of the condition. Government, thus, needed to provide minimum expenditure for the relief operations in contrast to the intensity of crises prevailed in the district.

Table: 3.16

Statement of Grain and Cash Expenditure in the District of Rangpur in 1874

	Charitable Relief	*Wages of Labour*	*Advance on Loan*
Grain (tons)	1, 517	922	1, 823
Cash (rupee)	1, 54, 975	4, 50, 909	1, 75, 934.

Source: A. P. MacDonnell, *Report on the Food Grain Supply*, p. 241.

This nominal help of the state was complemented by private charity on which the common people had to mostly rely on. Relief centres were opened by Rai Lachmipat Bahadur who was known for his 'liberality and benevolence' as 'specially recognized by the Government', and his private charity helped to raise the confidence of the people in the early months of 1874.[106] Apart from Rai Lachmipat Bahadur, 'landed proprietors and wealthy classes of Rangpur' came forward to help 'their tenantry in their hour of need.'[107] Babu Ramani Mahon Roy Chaudhury of Rangpur had also maintained a relief-house on his estates, imported grain, and sold it at cheap rates to his ryots during 1874.[108] In addition to this, the relief provided by the Government relieved '760, 889 individuals, or 35 per cent of the population,...for the period of one month.'[109]

The situation became worse in the May of 1874. Richard Temple stated that:

> "The month of May had now set in, and the famine had thoroughly declared itself. Employment, agricultural and other, was at a standstill, and there were no wages for the poor to earn. No supplies of grain were brought out and the corn markets were all closed. The Government, before opening its stores, waited to the latest safe day, in order to afford every possible chance to the trade. Its officers were however obliged to sell their grain in vast quantities, the prices being fixed at what were regarded as famine rates. Still starvation stared the people in the face, unless the Government should give them employment and pay their wages in grain."[110]

Among the districts of northern Bengal particularly Malda, Dinajpur and Rangpur where the deficiency of rainfall and price-rise were more prominent, were the worst sufferer of the famine of 1873-74. These parts were mostly depended on the winter rice crop which had managed to overcome the scarcities of the famine period and the much-desired rainfall during the winter and a favourable cold weather harvest delivered a great relief to the distressed. Southern and northern districts of Bengal showed a considerable difference in regard to the quantity of crop failures. In the former areas (southern districts) Government had merely to supplement the food supply of the districts through private trade or by supplying a small quantity of grain as a precautionary measure, whereas it had to undertake the responsibility to feed a large portion of population for the later (northern districts) and for this purpose it had to import into the three districts nearly 83 lakhs of maunds of grain.[111]

Large scale imports had been continuing from the upper-Bihar and other surrounding places. The Luckeeserai consignments for the South of the Monghyr District had been sent. The Rajmahal consignments laden on 500 carts were sent to the Northern Bengal Railway, and Major Lindsay, the Superintending Engineer, had reported that some of it had already reached Parbatipur, the place of storage.[112] Lindsay had reported that engineers were deputed along the line from Durwani in the north of the Rangpur District down to the swampy lands in the Rajshahi District where work had already begun. It was stated that since there was no great demand for employment, all the able bodied Boona coolies (the "navvies" of this part of India) who were working on local roads would have to be transferred to the railway works, while the local roads would be kept for the destitute of the districts.[113] In Northern Chumparan, parts of Rangpur, Eastern Rajshahi, and South-eastern Purnia food had already been scarce. Despite of 'sincere' effort in order to obtain information regarding the stocks held, the administration could hardly acquire any information from the people who were 'suspiciousness... in regard to such inquiries.'[114]

However, the general outcome of the opinions given by the local officers was that the stocks held were 'small, not more than equal to a three months' supply' and this was corroborated by the fact that the new rice was in some places already coming into consumption. As parts of relief works various new roads had been marked out, and work had been commenced both upon new roads and upon the repairs of old roads. In parts of Saran, Monghyr, Purnia, Rajshahi, and Rangpur the demand for employment was higher than in ordinary years.[115] Places of storage for Government grain had been selected, and the constructions of storage houses had been commenced during middle of December 1873. It can be noticed here that the Government had made considerable delay in constructing storage houses or distribution of government grain among the sufferers, and on the other hand, no actual relief operations had been commenced, nor had any preparatory arrangements been made, except in Malda. The prevalence of cholera at Gualundo and on the banks of the Meghna made it desirable to avoid the Calcutta and Gualundo route. On the other hand, Government grains from Madras and Burma had continued to come in and further shipments from Saigon, Burma, and Madras had been advised. But the despatches to the Rajshahi Division were not going on so rapidly from Gualundo and Koosthea; and in this circumstances Government had decided to send more Bengal rice from Calcutta by a steamer and two flats for Kaliaganj and Chilmari on the mouth of the Tista.[116] Thus, it can be stated that in northern Bengal a great amount of grain-relief had been carried out through river routes by river boats, barges and steamers. This was made possible with the help of land transport by carts and country carriage where river streams did not support.[117] However, a portion of this water carriage had been stationed at those points on the Ganges where the several main rivers and their tributaries met with the great river.

Table: 3.17

Number of steamers, barges and river boats used for carrying relief-grain

	Steamers	*Barges*	*River boats*
At Godagaree for the Mahanadi river system of Malda and Purneah	4	5	1, 000
At the Burral river for the Atrai river system of Dinajpur and Bogra	3	3	750

Source: Minute by the Hon'ble Sir Richard Temple, K. C. S. I., Lieutenant Governor of Bengal, dated the 31st October 1874, MSS EUR F486/21.

Government had decided to promote emigration from the distressed tracts and in response to that a good number of emigrants had started for the Assam tea gardens via

Durbhanga, Nathpur, Titalya, Jalpaiguri, and Dhubri.[118] The Government of India had also set aside the sum of five lakhs of rupees to promote a system of State emigration to British Burma.[119] The terms offered were a three year's agreement on wages, of which the minimum was guaranteed to be - for men, Rs. 10 each, for women, Rs. 6, and for children of between 10 and for 16 years of age, Rs. 3.[120] A superintendent of State Emigration had been appointed, and instructions had been given to the district officers to make the terms widely known not only to labourers but to influential local men, who were invited to assist in including emigrants to come forward. Apart from the appointment of a superintendent of State Emigration, District Officers were provided with a power to exercise discretion in selecting persons likely to prove useful colonists.[121] Aged, sick, and infirm people would not be sent 'unless their infirmity [was] one temporarily caused by privation, and likely to pass away with proper care.'[122] It was hoped that this experiment would prove to be an advantageous one for the British Burma, where the demand for labourers and colonists was nearly increasing.

In Bogra, the scarcity of 1874 had produced a greater failure of the crops due to the premature cessation of the rains.[123] It was stated that the Government had already informed the people 'two or three months before the winter crop was cut, so that the peasantry were alive to the danger that was imminent, and accordingly preserved for their own consumption whatever grain they were able to save by artificial irrigation or other means.'[124] It must be noted here that the government had not taken into the consideration about the economic condition of the poor peasants who could not afford the cost of 'artificial irrigation' at the time of drought or scarcity. About the middle of the March, Sir Richard Temple, the Famine Commissioner, visited the district and marched through some of the worst parts of it, and recorded in his minute-

> "I consider, having regard to all the circumstances, that 240,000 mans ought to be provided for this district, of which 50,000 mans have been already ordered, leaving190,000 mans remaining. Out of the 50,000 mans ordered, 20,000 mans have arrived. No time should be lost in bringing up fresh supplies, as the amount in hand is small as compared with the extent of possible distress."[125]

In the months of April and May the scarcity became more intense and the situation had aggravated more in the backward parts of the districts, especially in the police division of Panchbibi and the western jungle tracts of Sherpur. The condition of Bogra had been narrated by the Collector of the district on 1st June 1874 in the following manner:

> "I have travelled a good deal in the interior during the fortnight and from ocular observation I am in a position to say that in no place which I visited was the condition of the country or the people such as to cause very great anxiety; although, undoubtedly, the great price of food must have inflicted hardship and some hunger on the very poor. The price of food everywhere is high, as will be seen from` the following quotations, which represent almost accurately the bazaar rates down to this day, giving the number of pakka seer per rupee at which rice was selling during the last fortnight:-Bogra town, 9½ to 10 ½ seers; Dhupchanchia, 10½ seers; Panchbibi, 9 seers, Khetlal, 10½ seers; Sherpur, 7½ seers; Sibganj, 9 to10½ seers. Notwithstanding the great dearness, which must cause pinching to very many, I cannot say that I anywhere observed upon the persons of the people signs of hunger or of

> deficient sustenance. Men, women and children have an appearance of being sufficiently nourished. Everywhere the village bazaars were adequately supplied with food, although at very high rates. Wherever I have been, I have found the people, with few exceptions, in there usual state, although it is universally said that if Government had given no help there would have been great distress. Nowhere have I observed any general depression. There is certainly no difficulty in getting food for anyone who has money to buy it. The very poor must be straitened, but measures for their relief are in full operation, and they have not been slow to take advantage of them."[126]

There is no doubt that there was a considerable difference between the 'observations' of the Collector of the district and the Famine Commissioner. While on the one hand the Famine Commissioner had suggested for 'fresh supplies' in the district, on the other hand the Collector had talked about the 'men, women and children' who were appeared to him as 'sufficiently nourished.' These differences of opinion in the long run had badly influenced the making of any uniform famine-relief policy for the district. Hunter had stated that 'even in the low-lying lands the crops [were] for the most part destroyed.'[127] Babu Govinda Kanta Bidyabhusan, the Deputy Collector who visited the eastern part of the district had reported that 'in *thana* Sibganj the *aus* crop did not yield an average crop in consequence of the want of the usual supply of the rain; and varied from a quarter to a half; and the general appearance of the crops ... [was] discouraging.'[128] Moreover, as a result of the shortage of rainfall in some parts of Bogra complaints had been raised about the scarcity of drinking water which was, however, happened to be one of the greatest needs of rural Bengal and the chief cause of the bowel complaints of most of the population.

From the month of December, the situation began to change in many parts of the district. Though this change was brought by the use of irrigation, the situation was not favourable for all parts of the district.[129] The thanas of Adamdighi, Badalgachhi, and the south-west of Bogra had witnessed a good crops whereas the thanas of Khetlal and Panchbibi had been provided with 'bad account of the crops', because 'in these parts the people had not been able to effect irrigation.'[130] Apart from this it was also reported that the failure of the crops in the east and south of the district was more prominent than to the west.[131] So far the execution of relief action in the district was concerned, it was believed that 'no part of Government action during the famine was attended with better results than the manner in which the whole country was kept informed of the actual and possible extent of the failure in each district.'[132] Since the local production was not sufficient for the local people, pulses were imported into the district. Government had to think about large scale importation of grains and maximum accommodation of labour recruitment in the tracts where crops had failed. Seven relief roads, including feeder roads were planned to distribute the reliefs as well as for the inclusion of labourers through public works.[133] Even till the month of March 1874, the prices rose abnormally high and the Government thought of establishing storehouses for rice. During the month of April and May the scarcity seemed to be increasing and in June it was worst.[134] Most surprisingly, it was not known that how did the Collector on the 27th July become able to report that the scarcity was substantially at an end.

On the 28th December, 1873 there was a little rainfall on Bihar and one or two parts of the Rajshahi Division. Although the letters from the Relief Commissioner's Camp in Dinajpur had confirmed of 'rain doing good, and of more rain being expected', on the whole the spring crop did not greatly improve the condition of purely rice tracts, like Northern Tirhut, Soopole, Dinajpur, and Bogra.[135] In Rangpur the prices were from 15 to 11¼ seers per rupee. At the same time, at two places on the Ganges the upward trade was registered – 'at Gualando at the junction of the Ganges and Brahmaputra, and at Sahebganj, where the hills of Western Bengal about on the river.'[136] This upward trade had included moderate amount of rice and pulses which came chiefly from Murshidabad and Rajshahi. On the other hand, 85,000 maunds had been despatched from the stations of Koosthea and Goalundo on the Eastern Bengal Railway to other places in the Rajshahi Division. Both in Bihar and Rajshahi the local officers seemed to be more and more disposed to trust to carts rather than boats for carriage to places off the very great rivers.[137] In the districts of Saran, Monghyr, Tirhut, Bhagalpur, and Dinajpur considerable bodies of men were employed on relief works which demonstrated the critical conditions prevailed in those districts and the great majority of the people had belonged from the ordinary labouring classes.[138] Foods in exchange of works were obtaining by the people either from petty dealers who set up shops there, or at neighbouring markets. The Government had proposed that while roads and waterways would be constructed as part of relief works from the district funds and from such additional grants as the Government would make time to time; tanks and other landed improvements should have to be undertaken by the landlords themselves from the advances.[139]

So far the amount of private importations in the districts of northern Bengal was concerned, the local officers had unanimously admitted that their amount was decreased. As a result, cooperative associations had been formed at Murshidabad and Puthia (located in Rajshahi District) for importing grain and selling it at cost price. Though some zamindars of the Rajshahi Division asked the Government to import rice for their estates and sell it to them at cost price, the Lieutenant Governor considered that it would be better to refer the zamindars to dealers in the Calcutta market. However, the Lieutenant Governor had assured them that 'the govt transport officers and appliances would give every help in forwarding any grain they might to its destination.[140] Maharani Surnomai of Cossimbazar, who owned estates in Murshidabad, Dinajpur, Rajshahi, Rangpur, Pabna, and Nuddea, had come forward to help the tenants and aided the Government relief officers 'in every possible way.'[141] Maharani Surnomai had imported grain and distributed it in her villages, remitted or suspended the rent of distressed ryots, and 'made herself responsible for the repayment of Government advances.'[142]

Government had now started special measures for recruiting a large number of populations for the railway works. The Officiating Secretary of the Statistical Department (Govt. of Bengal) had proposed to the Superintending Engineer of the Northern Bengal (State) Railway that railway works should maintain 'as much as possible for the able-bodied workmen' who would work 'by the piece', whereas the 'less able' labour would work on the feeder roads on a daily basis.[143] The arrangements for sending grain to Malda, Rajshahi, Dinajpur, and the Northern Bengal Railway works were all part of one scheme.[144] Grain was sent by the Eastern Bengal Railway to Koosthea, from there it was taken by Government steamer and flat and dropped at Dhaparee, Rampur Boalia, and Godagaree. From Godagaree it was carried by boat to Malda and Raiganj; from Malda and other parts on the Mahanadi it moved by cart to Gazole; and from Raiganj the Khurba depot was supplied.[145] Some 5,000 maunds were sent from Rajmahal by cart to Dinajpur, despite of the fact that the route was 'tedious and costly'. Almost 20,000 maunds had been supplied by using the river route of the Oorasagur, Baral, and Atrai river to Goalundo, though the rivers were low and boats of the upper draught were few. Major Lindsay was of the opinion that the route from Rampur Boalia and Dhapari could be used, partly by land and partly by inland steamers. The district of Bogra had been supplied with grain purchased in Eastern Bengal and it was sent up the Brahmaputra through local boats. For Rangpur grain from Eastern Bengal and Calcutta was sent to Kaliaganj and Chilmari at the mouth of the Tista, both by boat and by steamer. Part of the trade had been carried

Figure 3.1. Extension of Bengal-Bihar Famine, 1873–74

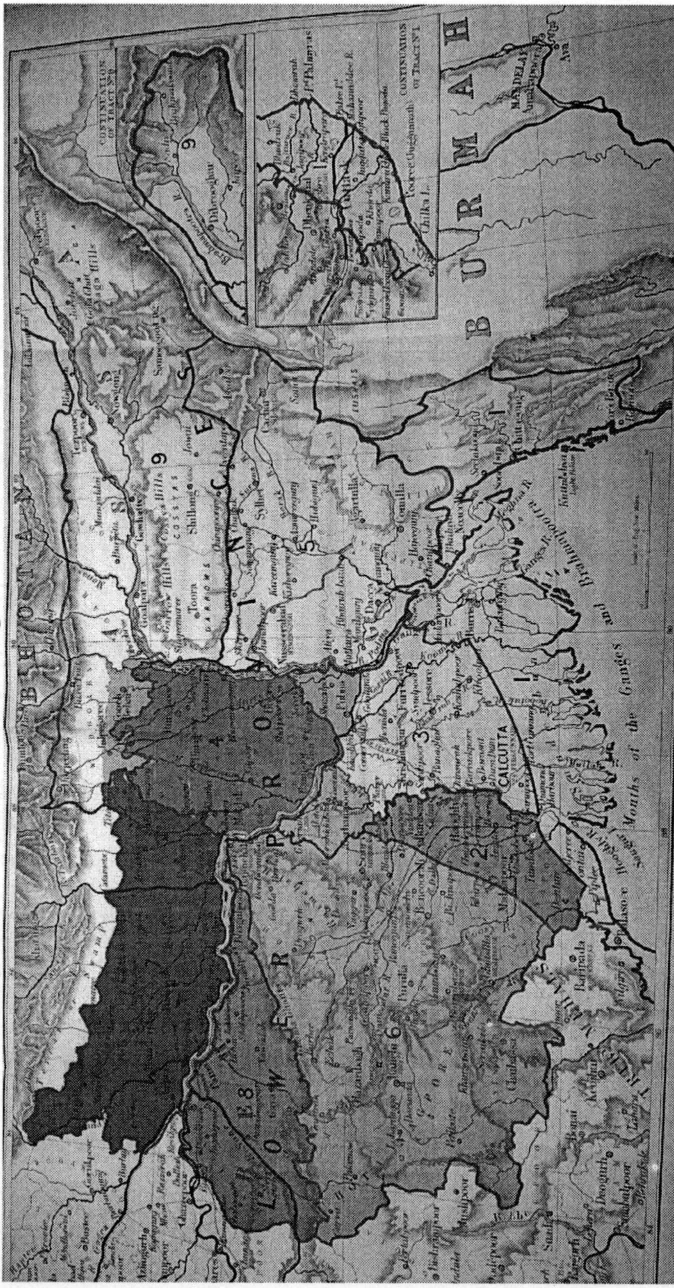

Source: Correspondence between the Government of India and the Secretary of State in Council relative to the Famine in Bengal, Part I, Her Majesty's Stationary Office, London, 1874. (British Library)

up to the Tista in boats to the *ghats* opposite and above Rangpur, and rest of the part had been carted to the store houses in the interior from Kaliaganj.[146]

Hunter was of the opinion that the famine of 1874 was felt more severely by the district of Rajshahi. [147]For the district of Rajshahi, the year 1873 was ended with a deficient rainfall. The average rainfall in the Nator subdivision was 61 inches annually, but in 1873 only 43 inches had fell; and in Sadar subdivision there was a deficiency of 27 inches in a normal fall of 59 inches. Out of the normal fall of 18 inches in September and October in Nator, only 6 inches fell in 1873; while in Sadar sub-division the normal fall during those months, had fell short by 13 inches.[148] The deficient rainfall resulted in an extensive failure of rice crops in the district and the *Barind* tract was the most severely affected area of the district where the outturn of *aman* rice (winter rice) was estimated only 3 *annas*, while elsewhere it was 6 to 7 *annas*.[149] The failure of crops had eventually led to the rise of prices of food grains to an abnormal level. In January 1874, the price of rice was twelve seers for the rupee which was more than twice in comparison with the normal rates. During the month of May and June there was sudden rise of the prices and in July it was reported that 'several persons so emaciated that they could scarcely walk and a large number of children [was] in a very reduced condition.'[150] However, the absence of any deaths caused by starvation had been attributed by the Collector to the availability of governmental relief and that was why the Collector had unequivocally acknowledged government's success in distributing relief among the victims. According to the Collector, 'had it not been for the relief afforded, there would have been many deaths from starvation.'[151] This could be evident from the increased number of people who received gratuitous relief. The number of people who received gratuitous relief in the middle of April was 1500 whereas at the end of July it increased to 59, 000. But from the August the situation had changed and by the end of August the number was reduced to 40,000 and by the end of September it was 8000.[152] W.H.

D'Oyly, the Collector of Rajshahi had provided the following account of Government grain which was expended for the purpose of charitable relief in the district from July to November 1874.

Table: 3.18

Expenditure of Government grain from July to November, 1874 in Rajshahi District

	Mds.	*Rs.*
Government grain actually expended in Charitable relief up to the end of July 1874	36,812	1,06,714
Estimated expenditure of Government grain in charitable relief from 1st August up to November 1874	34,590	98,828
Total	71,402	2,05,542

Source: From W.H. D'Oyly, EsQ., the Collector of Rajshjahi, to the Commissioner of Rajshahi Division. (No. 281C, dated Boalia, the 17th October 1874), WBSA.

In the district of Pabna, the rice production had been half of the average and the pulses were five-sixth of an ordinary year.[153] During the month of May 1874, peasants of few parts of Sirajganj subdivision had suffered from want of food. So far the causes of shortage of rice-production was concerned, it can be said that as a result of extension of jute cultivation a great portion of rice producing land had been converted to jute-land which had not only affected the rice production but also produced a condition when people got deprived of local supply and exposed to the export of rice from the outside area.[154] Though Hunter had praised the conversion of rice-land into jute-land by highlighting that 'the jute might succeed when the rice failed, and the rayat would then have something wherewith to purchase food', he had clearly overlooked the basic fact that in a situation of an overall scarcity of production the peasant could not buy rice despite of having more money. Nonetheless, the Government had organized relief operations through the local authorities in form of charitable relief, and also provided cooked and uncooked food to the people who were unable to work. The recipients of charitable relief mostly were the 'widows with families, sick labourers, old men without children.'[155] The total cost of the charitable relief in 1874 was Rs. 83,000; and the amount spent on roads and relief works was Rs. 28, 000. Apart from these Rs. 76, 000 was spent on money and grain as advance to the cultivators through their landlords, 'from whom security was taken for the repayment of the loans.'[156]

The famine affected areas of Bihar and north Bengal had witnessed a large-scale import of food-grains during the month of January 1874. A total of 19,25,000 maunds of food-grains had been contributed from different parts of Bengal as well as in India. For Bihar, the food-grains had been imported directly from the North-West Provinces and the Central Provinces, and for north Bengal food grains were imported from the districts of eastern Bengal. The following table has shown the amount of food-grains poured into the famine-stricken areas on January 1874:

Table: 3.19

Food-grains imported to the famine-affected areas in January 1874

	Maunds
From the North-West Provinces and the Central Provinces direct into the Bihar Districts	4,44,000
From the Eastern Bengal direct into the Northern Bengal Districts	80,000
From Calcutta, either Bengal, or Orissa, or Saigon, or Burmah, or Madras rice	14,01,000
Total	19,25,000

Source: *Eighth Special Narrative of the Draught from the 1st to the 15th January 1874.*

From various reports and notices the Government had

come to know about the status of 'the local officers' arrangements and preparations' and in accordance with that the Government had decided further to maintain a weekly supply to the Patna, Bhagalpur and Rajshahi Division.[157] Moreover, the local officers were advised to work on the better functioning of the local transport of grain. As the Government did not 'trust' the private trade for the north of Champaran, for Dinajpur, and part of Purnia in terms of their efficacy and promptness, local officers were entrusted to make necessary arrangements for the transport of grain.

Table: 3.20

Weekly import of food-grain to the affected areas

Patna Division	1,69,000 maunds weekly
Bhagalpore Division	1,05,000 maunds weekly
Rajshahi Division	60,000 maunds weekly

Source: *Eighth Special Narrative of the Draught from the 1st to the 15th January 1874.*

The difficulties in the way of rapid transport were much greater in the Rajshahi Division. Boat transport in shallow inland waters was very slow during the winter season and as a result the local officers had started to open cart routes on a large scale, and to organise a large number of carts and bullocks. The failure of the water routes had convinced the Lieutenant Governor about the great need of the Northern Bengal Railway.[158] Still the Government had taken some special measures to improve facilities for transporting grains. The Government river- steamer viz. Koladyne had been sent to help the Tista at Koosthea. Since the Tista was 'proved too weak for the duty required of her', and native boats took from 12 to 15 days to go up-stream from Koosthea to Godagare, it was expected that with the help of the Koladyne the work of crossing grain from Koosthea to the river-side depots in the Rajshahi District would proceed more rapidly.[159] The tracts in which distress was most imminent were the eastern part of Purnia, the northern part of Malda, and all the north-western half of Dinajpur. The Rajshahi Division was not, however, dependent on water carriage only, into the north and centre of Dinajpur grain was being carried by seven routs, namely

(a) by the East Indian Railway to Caragola, then by the Darjeeling road to Dengra Ghat and by cart across into Dinajpur;
(b) by the East Indian Railway to Rajmahal, and then by cart from the right bank of the Ganges to Malda and Dinajpur;
(c) by steamer from Koosthea to Godagari, and then by boat up the Mahanadi to Raiganj;
(d) to Godagari as before, and then by cart up to the old Darjeeling road to Dinajpur;
(e) from Koosthea by steamer to Rampur-Boalia, then by cart to the upper Atrai and by small boats up the river;
(f) from Koosthea to Dhapari, and then by cart to the Atrai above Natore and onward both by cart and by boat; and
(g) by the Oorasagur, Baral, and Atrai rivers to Nowgong, and then by cart or by very small boats to the north of the district.[160]

In Dinajpur, a district where intense famine conditions had prevailed only 14,000 labourers were employed besides the labourers on the Northern Bengal Railway. The 'practical result' of the comparisons instituted by Colonel Nicolls was that in North Bihar, wages were low and labourers were bringing in their women and children to the roads; while in the Rajshahi Division wages were high, and it was quite contrary to usage for labourers to bring their women and children to work.[161] It must be noted here that the Government had adopted two different policies for two different areas, despite of having adequate knowledge about the extent of distress in this part of the country. Although Major Lindsay reported that the river Atrai would be navigable during February and March of 1874 but the Commissioner, Mr. Molony, was of the opinion that this river route was to be extremely tedious and uncertain and a boat could only make one trip into the Upper Atrai in the season.[162] Military officers for relief works were sent by the Government of India - Major Ker, of the Quarter-Master General's Department, and Captain Grant was sent to the Rajshahi Division. However, the Government declared that as the distressed parts of Rangpur, Bogra, Malda, and Rajshahi were near to the Brahmaputra and the Ganges, so these areas could be supplied with certainty.[163] On the other hand, as Dinajpur was the most depressed district of all – it had required from 600,000 to 10,00,000 maunds (37, 000 tons) and so far the latest reports were concerned only from 35,000 to 40,000 maunds a week were moving forward to the district.[164]

The supply of food grain was still insufficient in all the large marts, except in north Bihar, and at some places in the interior of the Rajshahi Division. The Magistrate of Rangpur had reported the condition of the people to be worse, and a police officer who was employed on inspection reported severe distress leading to the sale of wives and children.[165] The Commissioner's report showed that the Government had constituted six relief sub-divisions in Dinajpur district. In Malda district only one relief subdivision besides the district head-quarters had been opened. But in the worst tract of the district seven relief centres were in operation, where from 140 to 200 people were relieved daily.[166] The Magistrate of Rangpur had reported about the following relief centres and persons relieved in these centres:

Table: 3.21

Number of relief centres and persons relieved in Rangpur

Relief Centres	*Persons relieved*
Pyraband	400
Meetapuker	231
Pirgunj	76
Govindganj	34
Kamdair Hat	Unknown
Gaibanda	39
Sunderganj	150
Kaliagunj outpost	16
Naldanga	120
Luckhipur	80
Total	1,146

Source: Twelfth Special Narrative of the Drought from the 20th February to the 15th March 1874

The Commissioner of Cooch Behar had reported that in the protected state of Cooch Behar and in the young Raja's zamindaries, situated in the Rangpur District, there was much scarcity. The reason for the scarcity was that rents could not be collected by tenure holders due to a considerable crop-failure and there was severe distress prevailing among the old and infirm.[167] In the early months of 1874, there was some sporadic distress in Cooch Behar, which was relieved from the State treasury; but in the month of May very severe distress broke out in the Cooch Behar zamindaries which were located in the district of Jalpaiguri.[168] In these circumstances, the Commissioner of Cooch Behar had imported and stored grain from the revenues of Cooch Behar and had opened relief works, and arranged for indoor works for the women and infirm.[169] However, with the help from the state-treasury the government had spend rupees

2 lakhs, that 'was taken out of the invested capital which was accumulated during the minority of the present Raja.'[170]

The scarcity of food-grain caused by the 1873-74 famine had triggered the increase of incidents of crime in the princely state of Cooch Behar which was almost double than the previous years. In 1874-75 there was total eleven cases of dacoity which was only five in 1870-71.[171] Not only in Cooch Behar, other parts of Bengal had also witnessed increasing number of crimes during the famine year.

Table: 3.22

Crimes in northern Bengal districts in December 1873

District	*December 1873*				*Total crimes for December*		
	Dacoity	*Robbery*	*Theft*	*House-breaking*	*1873*	*1872*	*1871*
Malda	....	....	30	34	64	54	45
Rajshahi	....	17	2	20	39	26	20
Rungpur	2	...	46	33	81	53	33
Dinajpur	7	1	39	55	102	71	38

Source: Resolution. Scarcity and Relief Department., Calcutta, the 20th January 1874.

The above table shows a continuous increase of crimes in the districts of Malda, Rajshahi, Rangpur and Dinajpur between 1871 and 1873. Dinajpur had witnessed the highest number crimes than the other districts. However, house-breaking and theft were the most common features of crimes which occurred in December 1873.[172] However, these incidents of crimes, it was stated, 'did not seem to alarm the district officers.'[173] But in Rangpur a serious case of robbery of grain from carts had occurred.[174] In course of time as the famine got intensified in the districts of northern Bengal, occurrence of crimes was also simultaneously increased during the early months of 1874. An account of crime for the month of February shows an upward trend in crime rates in all parts of northern Bengal.

Table: 3.23

Comparative return of crime in the distressed districts for the month of February 1874

District	*Crimes committed during February 1874*				*Total for Feb. 1874*	*Total for Feb. 1873*	*Total forFeb. 1872*
	Dacoity	*Robbery*	*Theft*	*House-breaking*			
Dinajpur	5	2	49	63	119	58	54
Malda	2	2	47	45	96	21	30
Rajshahi	---	---	103	106	229	109	149
Rangpur	1	2	41	33	77	66	59
Bogra	---	---	61	44	105	48	47

Source: Extracted from Enclosure No. 6 to the Thirteenth Special Narrative

From the above table, we may say that the incidents of crime had been overwhelmingly increased in the month of February 1874 than the previous years in the affected districts of north Bengal. Among other districts, Rajshahi was the most notorious district in terms of occurrence of crimes, like – theft and house-breaking.[175] Except Rangpur, The crime-rates was almost double in most of the affected districts of north Bengal than the immediate preceding year; however, for Malda, it was increased to four times in 1874 than that of 1873. This increase in the crime rates was a clear indication to the growing intensity of the famine in these tracts. In March, the incidents of crimes were comparatively low than the February.[176] One probable reason might be that since the end of February the government had started to ensure a steady import of rice from the outside areas which helped the affected people to procure grain in a comparatively cheap rate. However, on the other hand, Mukherjee shows that there was a steady rise in the crime-curve since 1871, and among the all five divisions of Bengal, Rajshahi had the sharpest rise in the cognisable crime between 1869 and 1874.[177]

Table: 3.24

Total cognisable crime in Rajshahi Division, 1864-1874 (selected years)

Year	*Number of crimes (in thousands)*
1864	7.7
1865	7.6
1866	8.4
1867	6.9
1870	7.1
1871	7.8
1872	13.8
1873	15.7
1874	16.4

Source: *Bengal Police Annual Administration Reports*, 1864-1874.[178]

From the above table, in can be stated that the famine years i. e. 1866-67 and 1873-74 had witnessed a considerable increase in cognisable crimes, and crime-rates became double between the two famine years, between 1866 and 1874. Therefore, scarcity had a profound impact on the occurrence of crimes in the districts of Rajshahi Division.

In Malda, Rajshahi, and Bogra, and especially in Rangpur, private trade in grain was rapid but rice from eastern Bengal was being carried largely into the districts through the Brahmaputra. The Magistrate of Rangpur wrote:

> "The rice which is brought for sale is nearly all imported; very little of it is home produce. The southern part of the district is mainly supplied by boats from Dacca and Sirajganj, the west from ... Dinajpur and Bogra, and the north and east from Cooch Behar and Jalpaiguuri."[179]

The Government, however, possessed no statistics of the private importations, which reached the distress districts by many rivers and channels. From Rangpur it was further reported that 'in some parts there .... and at the relief houses there were a considerable number of people suffering from disease and starvation combined.'[180] In these circumstances, the Government of India had agreed to help Dinajpur and other districts by ordering selected native officers of the army to work as Assistant Superintendent of Relief Circles in the famine-affected districts.[181] In addition to this Richard Temple put the grain requirements of Dinajpur at 12 00,000 maunds, 'a quantity somewhat in excess of the estimate framed by the local officers and the Bengal Government.'[182] In regard to the transport of grain in the different district of Rajshahi Division, it was stated that –

> "The pack-bullock and cart routes from Hyatpur and Manick Chuck (opposite Rajmehal) into North Dinajpur and Malda are already carrying between them 4, 000 maunds a day, which is beyond the highest estimate previously made of their capabilities. From Godagari and Rampur Boalia daily despatches up to 8, 000 and 9, 000 maunds are being made into Dinajpur and Malda besides about 2, 000 maunds, a day which the Northern Bengal Railway works are receiving via Dhapari and Baral river. The Bogra district is transporting to its stores and onward into South-East Dinajpur all the grain it receives. Rungpur has hitherto sent on about 2, 500 maunds a day from its depot at Kaliaganj on the Brahmaputra. If the total allotment of this district should now be increased, the transporting power will no doubt be expanded."[183]

It is evident from the above statement that river and cart routes were used to transport the grain in different parts of north Bengal. This amount of grain, it was expected, would significantly help to normalize the prices of rice in the affected tracts.

Table: 3.25

Selling price of rice in the districts of Rajshahi Division

District	*Number of seers of common rice sold for a rupee*			
	On 31st Jan	*On 28th Feb.*	*On 14th March*	*On 28th March*
Dinajpur	13¼	14	12¾	10¾
Malda	11¾	12	12	9½
Rangpur	11¼	11¼	11[!	11½

Source: Fourteenth Special Narrative of the Drought from the 20th March to the 2nd April 1874.

It is evident from the above table that in course of the time though the rate of common rice in Dinajpur and Malda gradually became low, but the high prices were still stagnant in the district of Rangpur. The numbers of work-people on the Northern Bengal Railway were increasing, about the 15th March there were 9, 000 labourers on the railway bank, besides about 3,000 on the feeder roads and the earth-works completed was equal to a bank 24 miles long and 4 feet high.[184] The Engineer-in-Chief was very anxious to complete the railway bank from Jalpaiguri down to the Ganges this season, and he had arranged to import labourers from other distressed districts. The Magistrate of Bogra had been instructed to send over for work-upon the railway any distressed people of his district who might be willing to take work away from their homes.[185] This massive recruitment of workers, however, had showed the increasing intensity of famine in this tract.

The Lieutenant Governor's reports based on his tour of several north Bengal districts during this time were very 'favourable and creditable' to the Commissioners and Additional Commissioners who made it possible for Richard 'to express himself as thoroughly satisfied with the conduct of the Rajshahi officers and with the forwardness of their preparations.'[186] In Rajshahi, silk crop faced a great loss and the accounts from Rangpur were also less favourable.

Near Sadullapur and Govindganj of Rangpur the village inspection has disclosed "greater distress than was anticipated." The district report informed that:

> "In the tract lying west of the Kurotya the state of the villages is wretched beyond description; the people have sold everything they possessed, and are now solely dependent on Govt. Many have sold their plough cattle, the last thing which a Bengalee ryot parts.... a man had sold the roof over his head. Many ryots have deserted the place altogether and gone Bogra and elsewhere..... the people seem to be most grateful for the relief works.....Everyone is to be found on the road; the women are now coming readily, bringing their children with them. All are most anxious to get Govt rice. The want of water is felt nearly as keenly as the want of food...A few cases of cholera, with one death, have occurred among the coolies."[187]

Scarcity of water was also a matter which even aggravated the sufferings of the people. Scarcity of water had instigated the people to draw water from polluted sources and this caused widespread cholera several districts of the Rajshahi Division. However, relief arrangements were organized for the distressed people. The number of people who received charitable relief of all kinds according to the latest returns from the districts was as follows:

Table: 3.26

Number of people received charitable relief in Rajshahi Division from the 3rd to the 16th April, 1874

District	*No. of people*
Dinajpur	4,464
Malda	931
Rajshahi	185
Bogra	583
Rungpur	6,827

Source: Fifteenth Special Narrative of the Drought from the 3rd to the 16th April, 1874.

Exports from the affected districts had been proved disastrous for the administration because it had intensified the famine condition in the affected tracts. There were many instances which proved the unplanned exports as harmful for the affected areas. Although some supplies had been reached to the riverside districts such as Malda, Rajshahi, Pabna, Bogra, and parts of Rangpur; but no relief worth estimate had come to Dinajpur, which has the broadest area of distress in all North-Eastern Bengal. In this situation, the Dinajpur marts had already supplied all their own to their neighbourhood and export largely to Rajshahi and Pabna.[188] However, massive export of rice from the eastern tract of Dinajpur, although had good crops, to the neighbouring tract of Rangpur, which was in distress, had made the former area a distressed one.[189] Thus, it can be noticed that an average producing area had become a deficit area as a result of governmental policy of indiscriminate export from the area. In the Cooch Behar Division though there was but slight failure of crop (chiefly in a locality to the south of Jalpaiguri), but grain was exported rapidly to parts of Purnia and Dinajpur.[190] Then in the Jalpaiguri district there arose panic in the grain markets regarding the amount of depletion of stocks and the quantity of grains stored by the dealers in their stocks.[191] The Rangpur and Bogra districts had obtained much of their food supply for many weeks from Mymensing across the Brahmaputra. The original allotments of rice for the five districts of Rajshahi, Dinajpur, Rangpur, Bogra, and Malda, has been mentioned below:

Table: 3.27

Amount of allotment of rice in the Rajshahi Division between 12th to 25th June, 1874

District	*Qnt. of rice (Mds.)*
Dinajpur	12,00,000
Rangpur	3,00,000
Bogra	2,40,000
Malda	1,50,000
Rajshahi	1,00,000
Railway works	1,00,000
Total	20,90,000 (=76,849 tons.)

Source: Twentieth Special Narrative of the Drought from the 12th to the 25th June 1874.

In Rajshahi and parts of Pabna, difficulties arose chiefly from a deficient supply of food grains, owing to the falling off in importations, and in order to counter this situation sanction had been given for the sale of Government rice in those places where the deficiency was serious. Due to the shortage of the executive machinery in Bengal, the Government had endeavoured to set up 'large special machinery' to deal with the famine. However, local zamindars and rajas had adopted some initiatives in order to deal with this situation. Srimati Sarat Sundari Debi of Puthia who was locally called as Rani held estates in the Rajshahi and Rangpur districts. At the beginning of the distress in 1874, she came forward with large subscriptions and maintained relief-houses at her own cost where 3,500 people were fed daily.[192] She had also extended advance in cash and grain to her ryots and supplied large funds to a local association for importing grain.[193] Babu Haranath Choudhury of Dubulhati (in Rajshahi) maintained a relief house where more than 1, 000 destitute poor were fed daily, and he had also advanced money and food to not only the ryots of his own estate, but also of other estates.[194] Raja Promonath Roy of Dighaputhia, who owned extensive estates in the Bogra and Rajshahi Districts, had conducted considerable relief works at his own cost, maintained four relief houses, at which about 1,400 people were fed daily, and advanced money and seed grain to the ryots.[195]

The great bulk of the relief operations in that district of Jalpaiguri had been carried on spontaneously at the cost of the Cooch Behar State under the guidance of Sir W. J. Herschel, Bart., the Commissioner of the Cooch Behar Division through a combination of Government officials and the zamindari agency of the distressed tract of Boda.[196] The district was not expected to be badly distressed, and was not therefore classified as a distressed district. The relief had been organized and an improvised system of accounts and superintendence was in full operation when a panic occurred which threatened to reduce the rest of the district to famine.[197] C. Bernard, the Officiating Secretary of the Government of Bengal, Scarcity and Relief Department had stated that distress was at first confined entirely to the Chuklajat estates held by the Raja of Cooch Behar, and all relief operations (inclusive of grain importations) were conducted at the cost of the Cooch Behar State.[198] In the month of May distress suddenly threatened the rest of the district. In order to avert the situation, about 41,000 maunds of Government rice were poured rapidly into the district outside of the Cooch Behar estates and another a sum of about Rs. 25,000 had been spent from Government funds almost entirely on carriage.[199] The entire cost of the famine-relief in the Jalpaiguri district and in the Chuklajat estates (as the zamindaris belonging to Cooch Behar State) were about 4½ lakhs, of which 3 lakhs had been spent by the Cooch Behar State and 1 lakh represented the value of 41,000 maunds was supplied by the Government, and Rs. 25,000 was the cash outlay of Government.[200] Despite of these circumstances it was believed that since the district of Jalpaiguri was 'bounded on the north throughout its entire length by the lofty range of the Himalayas, it [was] very probable that either the local rainfall, or the supply of water brought down by the rivers and streams would be affected by even the severest drought...'[201]

However, for Dinajpur which was the worst sufferer of the famine in Bengal, the Officiating Secretary of the Scarcity and Relief Department had informed about the 'collection of advances directly from the ryots by a Government establishment, without the aid or intervention of the zamindars' as contemplated by the Relief Commissioner of the District of Dinajpur.[202] The Lieutenant-Governor had sanctioned temporarily for six months the agreements as proposed by the Commissioner for beginning the collection of the advances at the end of April, the position should be reconsidered that whether such 'large establishment' would be retained or not 'through the rainy season.'[203] The Relief Commissioner of the District was entrusted with the 'discretion as to how far [he would] direct the employment of zemindars on the work of realizing advances' was instructed to 'make proposals for realization of advances in other districts.'[204] However, no cash advances had been made in this district to the traders for purchase of grain.[205] The *haimanti* i. e. late rice crop yielded a full crop in many parts of the district and the surplus stock of the Government had almost been disposed of. There was a widespread belief among the government officers that a good outturn of haimanti crop would help the zamindars to realize the advances made by the government through them.[206]

In Malda the amount of grain advanced was only a little over 25,000 maunds. The Collector of the District proposed to employ Baboo Ishan Chunder Sen as a Special Deputy Collector on a consolidated allowance of Rs. 200 a month, with two pyadas on Rs. 5 each a month, for the collection of the advances.[207] Apart from him, Inspectors, Mohurir

Table: 3.28

Relief-woks in the Rajshahi Division till November 1874

Famine Districts	No. of relief centres	Amount of grain actually stored	Amount of grain in transit	Daily avg. no. of persons employed on relief works			Rate of wages expressed in money and grain	No. of persons receiving gratuitous relief	Amount of grain consumed
				By P.W.D	By Circle Officers	Total			
Murshidabad	10	4, 281	......	1,008	1,138	2,146	2½ annas worth of grain per 100 cubic feet.	3,630	3,393
Rajshahi	9	4,175	....	376	269	645		261	2,905
Pabna	2	1,195	......	....	....	....	½ seer rice, 1 chittack dal, with salt and oil	1,458	1,014
Total	21	9,651	....	1,384	1,407	2,791		5,349	7,321

Source: Progs. no. 132, *Proceedings of the Lieutenant Governor of Bengal, Scarcity and Relief Department*, January, 1875, WBSA.[214]

were also appointed to assist him and expedite the collection.[208] Being the Manager of Chunchal estate Mr. Raily was expected to realise all advances made to his own ryots along with the other ryots to whom he also made advances in that relief circle. In the month of December the reaping of the great winter rice crop was conducted and it was reported that rice was 'very plentiful in the district.'[209] There were few cases of cholera reported in Kaliachak, Shibganj, and Gazole *thanas* of the Malda district.[210] In Bogra the advances amounted to 73,000 maunds, and a Sub-Deputy

Collector, Mohurir, Inspectors were appointed since a larger establishment would be necessary.[211] Regarding the collection of advances W. Robinson, the Relief Commissioner of the Rajshahi Division had anticipated that a very large proportion could be realised in full after the harvesting of the winter rice crop, which was the main staple in all four districts. [212] This idea, however, received the sanction of the Lieutenant Governor of Bengal who shared the same view 'that a second instalment may be collected in April 1875 in those parts of the country which yield a cold-weather crop.'[213]

The maintenance of relief centres in the districts of Murshidabad, Rajshahi and Pabna even in the November 1874 had reflected the fact that the famine was not ended yet. Moreover, people had been also offered regular works of employment, cash, grain and gratuitous relief to deal with the distress. Government, from this time onwards, was also busy in realizing the advances from the zamindars that they made on behalf of the government. Thus, the famine had continued till the end of 1874 and throughout this long span of one year (1873-74), the people of the districts of north Bengal had witnessed unprecedented subsistence crisis. The government expenditure for the several heads of relief works during 1873-74 is mentioned below:

Table: 3.29

Statement of District wise Government Expenditure (in cash) in 1873-74

District	*Charitable Relief*	*Wages for Relief Work*	*Advance for loan*
Malda	26, 951	1, 06, 762	48, 450
Dinajpur	37, 633	11, 61, 492	23, 300
Rangpur	1, 54, 975	4, 50, 909	1, 75, 934
Murshidabad	2, 38, 000	70, 795	26, 031
Rajshahi	46, 998	51, 841	1, 33, 872
Bogra	56, 440	2, 58, 111	53, 998
Pabna	12, 211	22, 456	66, 519

Source: Tabulated from A. P. MacDonnell, *op. cit.*, p. 51, 227, 241, 269, 280, 290 and 297.

Water routes were used for the movement of grain wherever it was possible, but the dryness of the season hindered navigation. Steam ferries were established to cross the grain over to the north of the Ganges, and steamers were bought or built in north Bengal. Moreover, over-all 41 steamers ordered from England and about 7,000 country boats and canoes were employed on the ferries and the water routes.[215] Another important step to overcome the shortage of production was the import of food grains from the better yielded areas. But as imports collapsed in the April of 1874, Government's plan of import was affected due to the nature and extent of the shortage in the districts concerned. In 1873-74 the crop failure was so intense in nature in comparison with the 1865-66 periods that private trade was almost incapable to meet the deficiency. Furthermore, it contradicted Government's own perception that high prices would obviously entice supplies from surplus to deficient zones. In 1866 private trade in the famine areas was stuck at several points by the physical difficulties of transport and communication; and in addition to this the underlying problem of exchange failure and the persistence of existing trade pattern made it almost impossible to cut through the prevailing lines of inflow and outflow or to repair a system of imports in the face of a crisis for normally surplus district.[216] On the other hand inspite of having normal quantity of production; exports from the affected districts, sometime, increased to such a magnitude that the balance was reversed and famine rates continued in the district.[217] The Government measure of public works did not serve the purpose of their own because the peasants or artisans were not trained to do such work and ultimately this could not help to bring out any permanent solution of the improvement of the communication system. But at one extent it had been admitted by the Government that '...methods of relief administration were devised during the Behar[-Bengal] famine, upon which subsequent experience has only improved."[218] Finally it was believed that:

> "It was also a subject of great satisfaction and congratulation that the event proved that the people were by no means pauperised and demoralised by the liberal relief given. When the rainy season of 1874 commenced in due course, very large numbers of the people receiving relief voluntarily went off to their own fields; before long they had almost wholly disappeared. The new crop was cultivated, and- the famine ' came to an end. The advances made to the cultivators were eventually recovered with wonderful punctuality..."[219]

Sir Richard Temple was of the opinion that: 'Thus the famine of 1874 was over; the deaths from starvation were so few compared to the many millions concerned, that practically there had been no loss of life.'[220] He further stated that: 'this disaster affected 20 millions of people in a greater or less degree.'[221] But regarding the mortality in the famine periods (1873-74) Romesh Dutt was of the opinion that"...there was no loss of life from this famine."[222] It had been observed in the '*Census of Bengal, 1881*' that "[t]he Bengal famine of 1873 was fortunately not attended with any great loss of life, so that persons have been found to deny the occurrence of any famine at all in the strict sense of the word."[223] The deficient rainfall of 1873-74 was substituted in 1875-76 with the increase in average rainfall and this caused an outstanding harvest of autumn crops. The production of winter crops was also great in the districts of northern Bengal with the exceptions of Dinajpur and Rangpur where the rainfall in 1875 was respectively half of the average and thirty per cent short of the average.[224]

Table: 3.30

Rainfall in 1875 in the Districts of Malda, Rangpur and Dinajpur (in inches)

Districts	*Rainfall in 1875*	*Average Rainfall*
Malda	54.40	53.33
Rangpur	60.45	83.93
Dinajpur	43.60	78.92

Source: *Document 12. Annual Report 1875-76: Weather, crops, and Prices of Bengal.*[225]

Shortage of rainfall, once again, contributed to the rise of prices in Dinajpur and Rangpur. In 1875, the price of rice gradually rose from April to July and though reduced for the time being after the harvesting of the *aus* or *bhadoi* crop, it was increasing gradually from October to December and fell again in January and February; and this reduction was caused by the major production of the autumn or *haimanti* crop.[226] But this crisis had not been regarded as very serious to call for a Government intervention. An agrarian crisis caused by a shortage of production eventually turned into a famine due to the failure in exchange relations. With the introduction of railways and the successive diffusion of market economy into the agricultural field in the latter half of the nineteenth century, the effect of crop failure was less intense, but more widespread in nature. A famine or acute dearth now came more frequently in the form of a noticeable rise in prices which generally caused suffering over a wider area as in 1873-74 in Bengal rather than a severe hunger, starvation and mortality confined merely to the famine area.

III. Scarcity of 1884 and 1891

The south-west monsoon rains of 1884 were ill-distributed and insufficient in greater part of the province of Bengal. A prolonged break occurred during August in North Bengal, Behar and Chota Nagpur. However, it was developed into a favourable rain in September and October over most of the province, but the crops were generally below the average, and a more or less pronounced failure of the winter rice crop was reported in November to have occurred in the Sadar and Nawada subdivisions of Gaya, the Behar sub-division of Patna, the Sadar sub-division of Darbhanga; in parts of Nuddea and Murshidabad; and in parts of the Burdwan, Birbhum and Bogra districts.[227] The prolonged cessation of the rains in August alarmed the local Government, and inquiries were instituted in all divisions as to the state of the crops and the condition of the people, but with the copious rainfall of September and October these anxieties were greatly. Hence, it was considered that distress would at the most be now confined to strictly limited areas in the above mentioned districts and would nowhere be very severe.[228] Accordingly in November, further and more minute enquiries were directed to be instituted in those areas in order to determine the following factors – number and location of villages likely to be actually affected, the classes of people in each village likely to need relief, the best means of affording it and the probable cost.[229] Special attention was also suggested for stimulating private charity and enlisting the co-operation of local residents of influence and public spirit in meeting such distress as might be expected to occur. The total State expenditure on relief in the province amounted to 3½ lakhs of which Rs. 2,41, 900 were for loans and advances, and the rest chiefly for gratuitous relief.[230]

The district of Dinajpur had again fallen into a scarcity in 1891-92.[231] The rains were very deficient in the months of September and October 1891 in parts of Bengal, especially in Behar and districts lying north of the Ganges. The *bhadoi* or early rain crop was generally a full average, and the districts where this crop was largely sown enjoyed a comparative immunity from distress in spite of the failure of the succeeding winter and spring crops. The general good harvests of 1890 were another helping fact. The winter rice crop of 1891 in the affected parts of Behar was nowhere above 50 per cent of an average crop and in the most affected parts it was considerably less.[232] On the high lands the crop in many parts of Darbhanga and Muzaffarpur totally failed. In the cold weather no rain fell till February, and the *rabi* crop was exceedingly bad in all districts.[233] The total area affected in Dinajpur was 1,030 acres where 447,000 numbers of people were affected by this scarcity. It was believed that since the districts were well stocked and trade was active, therefore, no anxiety was at any time felt as to food supplies. Prices of the chief staple grains were high, rice being at 11 and 12 seers and wheat at 12 and 13 seers the rupee throughout the scarcity; but the commoner grains of the early rain crop were procurable at 16 to 20 seers, and this had a great effect in limiting distress.[234] In order to counter this situation of scarcity, for the district of Dinajpur, Rs. 27,000 was spent on charitable relief from the district funds which was, according to some other estimates, Rs. 23, 076; for establishments and other charges Rs. 3,582; and for loans and advances Rs. 5838.[235] The distinctive features of the relief-works of 1891-92 scarcity was the substitution of piece-work or rather payment by results for task work for all able-bodied labourers, and these comprised the immense majority of the relief workers. The workers who were engaged with the relief-works had been classified into three categories – (a.) persons who were paid by piece-work, (b.) persons who were paid by task-work, and (c.) persons paid by daily wage. [236] After the prices became moderate and uniform over the whole distressed area then it was thought to fix a uniform wage-rate in all districts in Behar and North Bengal to avoid the danger of emigration from the neighbourhood of home to a district where a labour could receive a higher wage.

REFERENCES

1. Tirthankar Roy, *Natural Disasters and Indian History*, New Delhi: Oxford University Press, 2014, p. 44.
2. *Ibid.*, p. 46.
3. *Ibid.*, p. 45.

4. In his study, in order to calculate the weights, money and prices Hunter has made these according to his own convenience in the following manner respectively – "To convert the weights ...... multiply the seers by 2 to find the pounds, and the maunds by 82 to find the pounds — i.e., 2 lbs. = 1 seer; 82 lbs. = 1 maund", "[A] rupee for all practical purposes in small calculations may be taken as two shillings ; and an anna as three-halfpence, or l-16th of a rupee", "[T]he rate of rice is expressed either by so many rupees and annas the maund, or more commonly by so many seers per rupee." W.W. Hunter, *Famine Aspects of Bengal Districts,* Trubner & Co., London, 1874, p. xii.
5. *Ibid.*, p. 119.
6. *Ibid.*, p. 122.
7. W. W. Hunter, *A Statistical Account of Bengal Vol. VII: Districts of Malda, Dinajpur and Rangpur*, Trubner & Co., London, 1876, pp. 92-3.
8. *Ibid.*
9. W.W. Hunter, *The Annals of Rural Bengal,* New York: Leypold and Holt, 1868, pp. 41-42.
10. *Ibid.*, p. 42.
11. W. W. Hunter, *Famine Aspects of Bengal Districts,* p. 115.
12. B. Chaudhury, 'Eastern India', in Daharma Kumar (ed.), *The Cambridge Economic History of India,* Vol. II: c. 1757-2003 (henceforth CEHI), Orient Blackswan, New Delhi, 2008, p. 160 and 309.
13. F. W. Strong, *Eastern Bengal District Gazetteers,* Dinajpur, Allahabad, Pioneer Press, 1912, p. 65.
14. W. W. Hunter, *Famine Aspects of Bengal Districts,* p. 97.
15. *Ibid.*
16. *Ibid.*, pp. 97-8. Though Hunter has taken into account the number of populations, engaged in agriculture and the people worked as labour in the above-mentioned districts as highlighted by the Census of 1872, but he did not show any specific implications of these population statistics during the famine year of 1866.
17. Amiya Kumar Bagchi and Arun Bandopadhyay, (eds.)., *Documents on Economic History of British Rule in India, 1858-1947: Eastern India in the Late Nineteenth Century,* Part I: 1860s-

1870s, Manohar, New Delhi, 2009, p. 283.

18. J. A. Vas, *Eastern Bengal and Assam District Gazetteers: Rangpur*, Pioneer Press, Allahabad, 1911, p. 70.
19. *Ibid*. The price of ordinary rice had reached to eight seers per rupee and the cheapest rice had reached to nine-and-half seers per rupee.
20. *Ibid*.
21. W. W. Hunter, *A Statistical Account of Bengal, Vol. X: Districts of Darjiling, and Jalpaiguri and State of Kuch Behar*, Trubner & Co., London, 1876, p. 395.
22. Harendra Narayan Chaudhury, *The Cooch Behar State and its Land Revenue Settlements*, The Cooch Behar State Press, Cooch Behar, 1903, p. 79.
23. Hunter, *A Statistical Account of Bengal, Vol.X: Districts of Darjiling, and Jalpaiguri and State of Kuch Behar*, p. 395.
24. Harendra Narayan Chaudhury, *op. cit.*, p. 79.
25. *Ibid*.
26. C. E. Buckland, *Bengal under the Lieutenant Governors: A Narrative of the Principal Events and Public Measures during Their Periods of Office from 1854 to 1898*, Vol. I, S. K. Lahiri & Co., Calcutta, 1901, p. 555.
27. A Fortnight in the Famine Country of Bengal, March 1874, Serampore Press, Serampore, 1874, p. 1. The account of famine which was compiled in this Fortnight description was first published in the *Friend of India* newspaper on 19th and 26th March, 1874.
28. Document 10. Annual Report 1873-74: Land Settlements, production and distribution, weather and crops, land revenues of Bengal in Amiya Kumar Bagchi and Arun Bandopadhyay, (eds.) *op. cit.*, p. 156.
29. C. E. Buckland, *Bengal under the Lieutenant Governors: A Narrative of the Principal Events and Public Measures during Their Periods of Office from 1854 to 1898*, Vol. II, S. K. Lahiri & Co., Calcutta, 1901, p. 577.
30. 'First Special Narrative of the Drought to the 14th November 1873,' Special Narratives of the Drought in Bengal and Bihar, 1873-74, Papers. *Bengal Famine*, Mss Eur F86/127: 1874.

31. 'From H. L. Johnson, Esq. Private Secretary, for Secretary to the Government of Bengal, in the General and Revenue Department, to the Secretary to the Government of India in the Department of Agriculture, Revenue, and Commerce' in Correspondence between the Government of India and the Secretary of State in Council relative to the Famine in Bengal, Part I, Her Majesty's Stationary Office, London, 1874. (Hereafter Correspondence between the Government of India and the Secretary of State in Council) (Asian and African Studies, British Library).
32. *Ibid.*
33. George Campbell, *Memoirs of My Indian Career,* Vol. II, Macmillan & Co., London, 1893, pp. 320-322.
34. Minute by the Hon'ble Sir Richard Temple, K. C. S. I., Lieutenant Governor of Bengal, dated the 31st October 1874, MSS EUR F486/21.
35. Cited in C. E. Buckland, Bengal under the Lieutenant Governors: A Narrative of the Principal Events and Public Measures during Their Periods of Office from 1854 to 1898, Vol. II, S. K. Lahiri & Co., Calcutta, 1901, pp. 556-557.
36. 'First Special Narrative of the Drought to the 14th November 1873'.
37. Minute by the Hon'ble Sir Richard Temple, K. C. S. I., Lieutenant Governor of Bengal, dated the 31st October 1874, MSS EUR F486/21.
38. 'Special Narrative of the Drought of 1873 from 15th November to 21st November 1873,' Correspondence between the Government of India and the Secretary of State in Council, Part I.
39. Extract from the Proceedings of the Government of India in the Department of Agriculture, Revenue, and Commerce, No. 813, - dated Calcutta, the 6th March, 1874. Papers. Bengal Famine. MSS EUR F86/125: 1873-1874.
40. George Campbell, Note on the Question of Prohibiting the Export of Food during Famine, London: G. Phipps, Printer, 13 & 14, Tothill Street, Westminster, 1874, p. 11; in Offprints of articles by Sir George Campbell on famine administration, anthropology and land tenure. Also report of House of Lords debate on the Bengal famine, from The Mail, Apr 27, 1874. Mss Eur E349/17: 1874-1886.

41. Extract from the Proceedings of the Government of India in the Department of Agriculture, Revenue, and Commerce, No. 813, - dated Calcutta, the 6th March, 1874.

42. *Ibid.*

43. Cited in C. E. Buckland, *op. cit.*, Vol. I, pp. 556-557.

44. Ibid.

45. "The famine area was estimated at 40,000 sq: miles, and the population affected at 17 millions. Of these 735,000 were employed on works for 9 months, 450,000 received gratuitous relief daily for 6 months, and 3,200,000 bought grain at low rates enough to support them for 7 months, or received advances of grain or cash, large part of which was repaid to the Government." *Ibid.*, p. 557.

46. George Campbell, *Memoirs of My Indian Career,* Vol. II, p. 328.

47. Richard Temple, *op. cit.*, p. 396.

48. This system was mostly prevailed in Bihar where indigo was not managed on usual mercantile principles, rather they had received estates from zamindars who leased out lands to the planters. The planters through this process enjoyed some feudal power which had been exercised to get the carts and bullocks of the ryots at the planters' disposal for the carriage of indigo and other purposes. Now these carts and bullocks were exercised for carrying the grains to the distressed districts upon terms very advantageous to themselves. There was no doubt that the terms of their contracts had provided them with the increased rates from the Government rates which was enormously in excess of those which they paid the ryots. George Campbell, *Memoirs of My Indian Career,* Vol. I, p. 329.

49 George Campbell, *Memoirs of My Indian Career,* Vol. II, p. 322.

50. *Ibid.*

51. George Campbell, *Note on the Question of Prohibiting the Export of Food during Famine*, pp. 5-6.

52. *Ibid.*, p. 7.

53. George Campbell, *Memoirs of My Indian Career,* Vol. II, p. 323.

54. George Campbell, *Note on the Question of Prohibiting the Export of Food during Famine*, p. 8.

55. *Ibid.*

56. C. E. Buckland, *op. cit.*, vol. II. p. 577.

57. From the Officiating Secretary to the Government of Bengal in the Statistical Department to the Commissioners of the Patna, Bhagalpur, and Rajshahi Divisions, and to the Magistrates and Collectors of Distressed Districts, No. 1308 – S. R., Calcutta, the 8th March, 1874. Papers. Bengal Famine. MSS EUR F86/125: 1873-1874.
58. *Ibid.*
59. Extract from the Proceedings of the Government of India in the Department of Agriculture, Revenue, and Commerce, No. 813, - dated Calcutta, the 6th March, 1874. Papers. Bengal Famine. MSS EUR F86/125: 1873-1874.
60. *Ibid.*
61. Richard Temple, *Men and Events of My Time in India,* John Murray, London, 1882, p. 394.
62. From C. Barnard, Esq. Officiating Secretary to the Government of Bengal, to the Secretary to the Government of India, with the Governor General, No. 3379 dated 10th November 1873; in Correspondence between the Government of India and the Secretary of State in Council, Part I.
63. Second Special Narrative of the Drought from the 15th to the 21st November 1873, Mss Eur F86/127 : 1874.
64. Third Special Narrative of the Drought from the 22nd to the 28th November 1873, Mss Eur F86/127: 1874.
65. *Ibid.*
66. Amiya Kumar Bagchi and Arun Bandopadhyay (eds.), *op. cit.*, p. 157.
67. A. P. MacDonnell, *Report on the Food Grain Supply and Statistical Review of the Relief Operations in the Distressed Districts of Behar and Bengal During the famine of 1873-74,* Bengal Secretariat Press, Calcutta, 1876, p. 251.
68. Ibid., p. 252.
69. Further Correspondence between the Government of India and the Secretary of State in Council, Part III.
70. G. E. Lambourn, Bengal District Gazetteers: Malda, Bengal Secretariat Book Depot, Calcutta, 1918, p. 51.
71. Minute by the Hon'ble Sir Richard Temple, K. C. S. I., Lieutenant Governor of Bengal, dated the 31st October 1874, MSS EUR F486/21.

72. Narrative of scarcity and relief in the Malda district for the Fortnight ending March 7th, 1874, Further Correspondence between the Government of India and the Secretary of State in Council, Part III.
73. Minute by the Hon'ble Sir Richard Temple, K. C. S. I., Lieutenant Governor of Bengal, dated the 31st October 1874.
74. A. P. MacDonnell, *op. cit.*, p. 224.
75. *Ibid.*
76. *Ibid.*, p. 225.
77. *Ibid.*
78. F. W. Strong, *op. cit.*, p. 66.
79. Minute No. 46, by the Honourable Sir Richard Temple, K. C. S. I., dated Dinagepore, 11th March 1874, Further Correspondence between the Government of India and the Secretary of State in Council, Part III.
80. F. W. Strong, *op. cit.*, p. 66.
81. A. P. MacDonnell, *op. cit.*, p. 226.
82. Ratnalekha Ray, *Change in Bengal Agrarian Society c. 1760-1850*, Manohar, New Delhi, 1979, p. 197.
83. *Ibid.*
84. *Ibid.*
85. Ratna Ray and Rajat Ray, 'Zamindars and Jotedars: A Study of Rural Politics in Bengal,' *Modern Asian Studies*, Vol. 9, No. 1 (1975), p. 84.
86. *Ibid.*
87. Minute by the Hon'ble Sir Richard Temple, K. C. S. I., Lieutenant Governor of Bengal, dated the 31st October 1874, MSS EUR F486/21.
88. *Ibid.*
89. *Ibid.*
90. *Ibid.*
91. Lahoree had conducted several relief works, provided advance grain to his ryots, maintained a charitable relief house at his own expense throughout, and also abstained from insisting the peasants for paying rent. *Ibid.*
92. *Ibid.*

93. From E. E. Lowis, Esq., Officiating Magistrate of Dinajpur, to the Secretary to the Government of Bengal, Scarcity and Relief Department, No. 304 – S. R., dated Dinajpur, the 9th March 1874, in Further Correspondence between the Government of India and the Secretary of State in Council, Part III.

94. B. Chaudhury, op. cit., p. 304.

95. The condition of the distressed group, who formed 35 per cent of the agricultural labour population, as recorded by Dass, had no land or implement of their own and they survived by the *bhagai* or *batai* (a very negligible part of the produce) i.e. on others' mercy. Gopal Chandra Dass, Report of the Statistics of Rangpur for the year, 1872-73 (Calcutta, 1874), p. 85.

96. B. Chaudhury, *op. cit.*, p. 305.

97. Asoke Sen and Others, *Perspective in Social Science Vol.2: Three Studies on the Agrarian Structure in Bengal, 1850-1947*, Calcutta, 1982, p. 31.

98. A. P. MacDonnell, *op. cit.*, p. 234.

99. *Ibid.*, p. 237.

100. *Ibid.*

101. *Ibid.*, p. 238.

102. *Ibid.*, p. 239. The grain import had shattered because of induced rice of prices in Assam and Cooch Behar which resisted export of rice from these areas and on the other hand there was a joint effort of local grain dealers to boost up prices to an extreme point. p. 240.

103. Glazier's Further Notes on the Rangpur Records, p. 48 cited in J. A. Vas, *Eastern Bengal and Assam District Gazetteers: Rangpur, 1911*, p. 71.

104. W. W. Hunter, *A Statistical Account of Bengal*, Vol. VII, p. 299.

105. *Ibid.*

106. J. A. Vas, *op. cit.*, p. 71.

107. A. P. MacDonnell, *op. cit.*, p. 241.

108. Minute by the Hon'ble Sir Richard Temple, K. C. S. I., Lieutenant Governor of Bengal, dated the 31st October 1874, MSS EUR F486/21.

109. A. P. MacDonnell, *op. cit.*, p. 243.

110. Richard Temple, *op. cit.*, p. 402.

111. Document 11. Annual Report 1874-75: weather crops and prices in Bengal, meeting of food deficiency, effect of the rain on crops, floods in the northern districts in Amiya Kumar Bagchi, and Arun Bandopadhyay (eds.)., *op. cit.*, p. 173.

112. Fifth Special Narrative of the Drought from the 6th to the 12th December 1873. Mss Eur F86/127: 1874.

113. *Ibid.*

114. *Ibid.*

115. *Ibid.*

116. Sixth Special Narrative of the Drought from the 13th to the 18th December 1873, MSS EUR F86/127: 1874.

117. Minute by the Hon'ble Sir Richard Temple, K. C. S. I., Lieutenant Governor of Bengal, dated the 31st October 1874, MSS EUR F486/21.

118. Sixth Special Narrative of the Drought from the 13th to the 18th December 1873.

119. Tenth Special Narrative of the Drought from the 23rd January to the 4th February 1874, MSS EUR F86/127: 1874.

120. *Ibid.*

121. *Ibid.*

122. *Ibid.*

123. The average rainfall of the four years 1871-74 had been 73.89 inches, the rainfall of 1865 was 80.2, and that of 1873, 37. 13 or 47 inches less than the normal fall. J. N. Gupta, *District Gazetteers of Eastern Bengal and Assam: Bogra*, Pioneer Press, Allahabad, 1910, p. 75.

124. *Ibid.*

125. *Ibid.*, p. 76.

126. *Ibid.*

127. W. W. Hunter, *A Statistical Account of Bengal, Vol. VIII: Districts of Rajshahi and Bogra*, Trubner & Co., London, 1876, p. 253.

128. *Ibid.*

129. *Ibid.*, p. 254.

130. *Ibid.*

131. *Ibid.*

132. J. N. Gupta, *District Gazetteers of Eastern Bengal and Assam: Bogra*, p. 77 and 75.

133. Hunter, *A Statistical Account of Bengal, Vol. VIII: Districts of Rajshahi and Bogra*, p. 256.

134. Situation became somewhat better in July due to the favourable rainfall of a total of about 4 ½ inches.

135. Seventh Special Narrative of the Drought from the 19th to the 31st December, 1873, MSS EUR F86/127: 1874.

136. A very small amount of rice was exported to Bihar by this route and the figures of this upward trade past Sahebganj were, for the period between the 1st November and the 23rd December, pulses 1,05,000 maunds, and rice 88,000 maunds. *Ibid*.

137. *Ibid*.

138. *Ibid*.

139. *Ibid*.

140. *Ibid*.

141. Minute by the Hon'ble Sir Richard Temple, K. C. S. I., Lieutenant Governor of Bengal, dated the 31st October 1874, MSS EUR F486/21.

142. Though the Maharani could not physically appear in the public due to 'her sex and caste', but this work is more efficiently and liberally performed by her agent, Baboo Rajib Lochun Roy Rai Bahadur. *Ibid*.

143. 'From the Officiating Secretary to the Government of Bengal in the Statistical Department, to Major Lindsay, R. E., Superintending Engineer, Northern Bengal (State) Railway, No. 3412,Calcutta, the 13th November 1873,' in Correspondence between the Government of India and the Secretary of State in Council, Part I.

144. Seventh Special Narrative of the Drought from the 19th to the 31st December, 1873, MSS EUR F86/127: 1874.

145. *Ibid*.

146. *Ibid*.

147. W. W. Hunter, *A Statistical Account of Bengal, Vol. VIII: Districts of Rajshahi and Bogra*, p. 78.

148. L. S. S. O'Malley, *Bengal District Gazetteers: Rajshahi*, Bengal Secretariat Book Depot, Calcutta, 1916, pp. 89-90.

149. In general, throughout the district the *aus* or autumn crop was one-half or 8 annas, and the *aman* or winter crop was 6 annas or three eights of an average crop. *Ibid.*, p. 90.

150. *Ibid.*

151. *Ibid.*

152. *Ibid.*

153. L. S. S. O'Malley, *Bengal District Gazetteers: Pabna,* The Bengal Secretariat Book Depot, Calcutta, 1923, p. 45.

154. W. W. Hunter, *A Statistical Account of Bengal, Vol. IX: Murshidabad and Pabna,* Trubner & Co., London, p. 328.

155. L. S. S. O'Malley, *Bengal District Gazetteers: Pabna,* p. 45.

156. *Ibid.*

157. Eighth Special Narrative of the Draught from the 1st to the 15th January 1874, MSS EUR F86/127: 1874.

158. *Ibid.*

159. *Ibid.*

160. Tenth Special Narrative of the Drought from the 23rd January to the 4th February 1874, MSS EUR F86/127: 1874.

161. *Ibid.*

162. *Ibid.*

163. Eleventh Special Narrative of the Drought from the 5th to the 19th February 1874, MSS EUR F86/127: 1874.

164. *Ibid.*

165. Twelfth Special Narrative of the Drought from the 20th February to the 15th March 1874, MSS EUR F86/127: 1874.

166. *Ibid.*

167. *Ibid.*

168. Minute by the Hon'ble Sir Richard Temple, K. C. S. I., Lieutenant Governor of Bengal, dated the 31st October 1874, MSS EUR F486/21.

169. Twelfth Special Narrative of the Drought from the 20th February to the 15th March 1874.

170. W. W. Hunter, *A Statistical Account of Bengal, Vol. X: Districts of Darjiling, and Jalpaiguri and State of Kuch Behar,* p. 395.

171. Harendra Narayan Chaudhury, *op. cit.*, p. 307.

172. Resolution. Scarcity and Relief Department., Calcutta, the 20th January 1874, Papers. Bengal Famine. MSS EUR F86/125: 1873-1874.

173. *Ibid.*

174. *Ibid.*

175. Enclosure No. 6 to the Thirteenth Special Narrative, C. Bernard, Officiating Secretary to the Government of Bengal, Calcutta 14th March, 1874, Further Correspondence between the Government of India and the Secretary of State in Council, Part III.

176. Enclosure 3 to the Fifteenth Special Narrative, in Further Correspondence between the Government of India and the Secretary of State in Council, Part V.

177. Arun Mukherjee, 'Scarcity and Crime: A Study of 19th Century Bengal,' *Economic and Political Weekly,* Vol. 28, No. 6 (Feb. 6, 1993), p. 237.

178. Cited in *Ibid.*, p. 239. (Extracted)

179. Thirteenth Special Narrative of the Drought from the 6th to the 19th March 1874, MSS EUR F86/127: 1874.

180. *Ibid.*

181. *Ibid.*

182. *Ibid.*

183. *Ibid.*

184. Fourteenth Special Narrative of the Drought from the 20th March to the 2nd April 1874, MSS EUR F86/127: 1874.

185. *Ibid.*

186. *Ibid.*

187. Fifteenth Special Narrative of the Drought from the 3rd to the 16th April, 1874, MSS EUR F86/127: 1874.

188. Twentieth Special Narrative of the Drought from the 12th to the 25th June 1874, MSS EUR F86/127: 1874.

189. *Ibid.*

190. *Ibid.*

191. *Ibid.*

192. Minute by the Hon'ble Sir Richard Temple, K. C. S. I., Lieutenant Governor of Bengal, dated the 31st October 1874, MSS EUR F486/21.

193. *Ibid.*
194. *Ibid.*
195. *Ibid.*
196. From Sir W. J. Herschel, Bart., Commissioner of the Cooch Behar Division, to the Officiating Secretary to the Government of Bengal, Scarcity and Relief Department. – (No. 420 – S.R., dated Julpigoree, the 14th November 1874), progs no. 34, Proceedings of the Lieutenant-Governor of Bengal. Scarcity and Relief department, Calcutta, January 1875, West Bengal State Archives (Henceforth WBSA).
197. *Ibid.*
198. From C. Bernard, the Officiating Secretary of the Government of Bengal, Scarcity and Relief Department, to the Commissioner of Cooch Behar. – (No. 6750 – S.R. dated Calcutta, the 20th November 1874), progs. no. 35, WBSA.
199. It was argued that in dealing with the Parliamentary returns called for and since the funds were supplied by a Native State, therefore, the returns should be drawn up for the whole district as a whole, by treating the Cooch Behar expenditure as a contribution to the Government treasury. Finally, it was concluded that the work was wholly done by Government officers or under their orders. progs no. 34, Proceedings of the Lieutenant-Governor of Bengal. Scarcity and Relief department, Calcutta, January 1875.
200. *Ibid.*
201. John F. Gruning, *Eastern Bengal and Assam District Gazetteers: Jalpaiguri,* Pioneer Press, Allahabad, 1911, p. 79.
202. He further stated that 'in case, where advances have been made direct, and where the zemindars have not stood security for repayment, it may be best to realise through such zemindars as may tender their services, and may be trusted not to realise more than is due.' From the Officiating Secretary to the Government of Bengal, Scarcity and Relief Department, to the Relief Commissioner of Dinagepore. – (No. 6860 – S.R., dated Calcutta, the 30th November 1874), progs. no. 21, Proceedings of the Lieutenant-Governor of Bengal. Scarcity and Relief department, Calcutta, January 1875, WBSA.
203. *Ibid.*
204. The realization of advances was declared to be collected as soon as possible and the instalments were also to be collected during this first six months. *Ibid.*

205. From A.C. Brett, EsQ., Joint-Magistrate, in charge of the Dinagepore Magistracy, to the Officiating Secretary Government of Bengal, Scarcity and Relief Department. – (No. 2109 – S.R., dated Dinagepore, the 14th December 1874), progs. no. 116, Proceedings of the Lieutenant-Governor of Bengal. Scarcity and Relief department, Calcutta, January 1875, WBSA.

206. From R. Knight, the Assistant Secretary to the Government of Bengal to the Relief Commissioner of the Rajshahye. - (No. 7286, dated Calcutta, the 30th December 1874), progs. no. 23, WBSA.

207. From W. LeF. Robinson, EsQ., Relief Commissioner of the Rajshahye Division, to the Officiating Secretary to the Government of Bengal, Scarcity and Relief Department. – (No. 2411, dated Dinagepore, the 21st December 1874), progs. no. 22, Proceedings of the Lieutenant-Governor of Bengal. Scarcity and Relief department, Calcutta, January 1875, WBSA.

208. *Ibid.*

209. From F. Wyer, EsQ., Magistrate-Collector of Maldah, to the Officiating Secretary Government of Bengal, Scarcity and Relief Department. – (No. 694, dated Maldah, the 14th December 1874), progs. no. 117, Proceedings of the Lieutenant-Governor of Bengal. Scarcity and Relief department, Calcutta, January 1875, WBSA.

210. *Ibid.*

211. From W. LeF. Robinson, EsQ., Relief Commissioner of the Rajshahye Division, to the Officiating Secretary to the Government of Bengal, Scarcity and Relief Department. – (No. 2411, dated Dinagepore, the 21st December 1874), progs. no. 22, WBSA.

212. Moreover, he was of the opinion that though in some parts of the country there was in fact no other harvest, but in some portions where there were cold-weather crops a second instalment, be fairly asked for in April, after what was called here the *chitali* harvest, i.e., all cold-weather crops had been gathered. *Ibid.*

213. From R. Knight, the Assistant Secretary to the Government of Bengal to the Relief Commissioner of the Rajshahye. - (No. 7286, dated Calcutta, the 30th December 1874), progs. no. 23, Proceedings of the Lieutenant-Governor of Bengal. Scarcity and Relief department, Calcutta, January 1875, WBSA.

214. From the Officiating Secretary to the Government of Bengal, Scarcity and Relief Department, to the Deputy Secretary to the Govt. of India, Department of Revenue, Agriculture and Commerce. – (No. 6643 – S. R., dated Calcutta, the 14th Nov. 1874).

215. C. E. Buckland, *op. cit.*, vol. II, p. 582.

216. Malavika Chakrabarty, *Famine of 1896-97 in Bengal: The Availability or Entitlement Crisis*, Orient Blackswan, New Delhi, 2004, p. 232.

217. For example, mention can be made of Jalpaiguri, where prices of rice would never have reached to 8 or 6 seers for the rupee by May 1874, but for the exceptional rate of exports by traders coming in from Purnea, Rangpur, Dinajpur and Darjeeling. *Ibid.*, p. 234.

218. Report of the Indian Famine Commission, Calcutta, 1901, p. 2.

219. C. E. Buckland, *op. cit.*, Vol. I, p. 566.

220. Richard Temple, *op. cit.*, p. 405.

221. *Ibid.*, p. 393.

222. Romesh Dutt, *op. cit.*, p. 1.

223. 'Census of Bengal, 1881', Journal of the Statistical Society of London, vol. 46, No. 4 (Dec., 1883), p. 682.

224. Document 12. Annual Report 1875-76: Weather, crops, and Prices of Bengal in Amiya Kumar Bagchi, and Arun Bandopadhyay, *op. cit.*, p. 177 and 180.

225. *Ibid.*, p. 180.

226. *Ibid.*, p. 181.

227. *Report of the Indian Famine Commission, 1898,* Government Central Printing Office, Simla, 1898, p. 9.

228. *Ibid.*

229. *Ibid.*

230. Relief works were, as stated, provided by the district boards. *Ibid.*, p. 11.

231. F. W. Strong, *op. cit.*, p. 67.

232. *Report of the Indian Famine Commission, 1898,* p. 27.

233. *Ibid.*, pp. 27-28.

234. *Ibid.*, p. 28.

235. F. W. Strong, *op. cit.*, p. 67 and *Report of the Indian Famine Commission, 1898*, p. 28.

236. Labourers in class 'a' received the full ration wage of the code on performing a given quantity of work, and a corresponding smaller wage if they failed to complete it. They were not permitted to earn more than the full ration wage, nor was any minimum wage secured to them. Labourers in class 'b' were required to do a fair task for people of their calibre for a ¾ths wage. If they did less they were fined, but never received less than the minimum wage. Persons in class 'c' were encouraged to do what they could, but their work was not measured, and they received the minimum wage. *Report of the Indian Famine Commission, 1898*, p. 29.

4

Famine, Relief and the Colonial State in North Bengal, 1896-1909

According to the *Report of the Indian Famine Commission 1898*, the famine of 1896-97 affected an area of about 225,000 square miles in British India and a population of 62 million.[1] The meteorological conditions in India in 1895 and 1896 was on the whole unfavourable due to the failure of monsoons which was coupled with series of cyclonic storms 'that degraded land.'[2] During the winter season of 1896, famine conditions had prevailed in a vast area of northern and southern India.[3] Romesh Dutt had argued that 'deaths were prevented in Bengal and elsewhere, but in the Central Provinces the death rate rose from an average of thirty-three per mile to sixty-nine per mile during the year.[4] Bengal had become a serious victim of the 1896-97 famine. Though entire Bengal had been suffered from the famine, there was remarkable variations in regards to the nature, extent and duration of the crises in several districts of colonial Bengal. The district-wise account of famine condition that prevailed in 1896-97 deserves a special attention because ecological variations in terms of rainfall distribution was different for the different districts. The relief measures which were adopted by the colonial administration and the participation of the sufferers in the government works had largely varied in different districts. Thus, the present chapter intends to explore the dynamics of rainfall, ecology and market which were instrumental for the causation of the 1896-97 famine in the districts of north Bengal. The districts of north Bengal had also shown certain peculiarities in terms of market-economy, famine-relief, public response during the famine years. Apart from the 1896-97 famine, the chapter also includes a brief description about the local scarcities of 1908-09 which was limited to the certain districts of north Bengal.

Figure 4.1

Famine in India, 1896-97

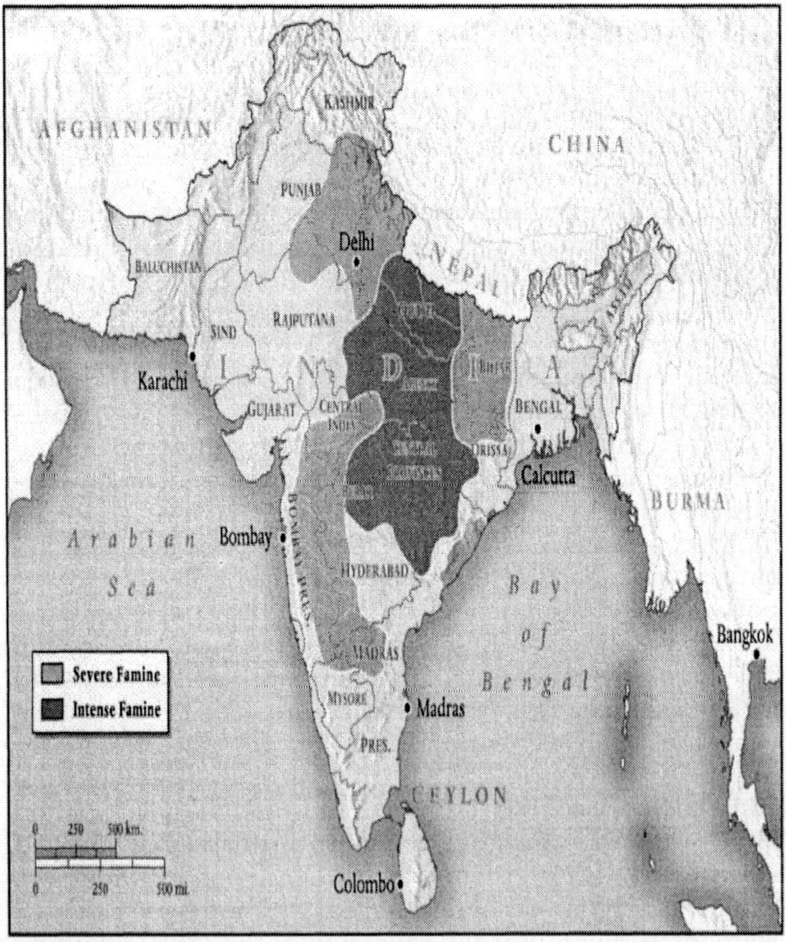

Source: Mike Davis, *Late Victorian Holocausts: El Nino Famines and the Making of the Third World*, Verso, London, 2001, p. 145.

The Census of Bengal, 1901 had mentioned about the comparative vulnerability of the Bengal districts which were liable to famine or severe scarcities. According to the Census of 1901, the only districts which were 'free from all danger of famine', were the 24 Parganas, Darjeeling and the districts of Eastern Bengal.[5] Apart from these districts, the other districts of Bengal had suffered from scarcities and famines according 'to the character of population and the nature of the neighbouring country.'[6]

Table: 4.1

Area and population of Bengal liable to famine, 1891-1901

Division	*Total area*	*Area liable to famine*	*Population of area liable to famine*	*Maximum number of persons likely to require relief in severe famine*
Burdwan	13,949	7,449	3,130,634	164,507
Presidency	12,066	4,355	2,565,241	131,437
Rajshahi	17,356	9,853	5,143,794	287,097
Patna	23,686	16,795	11,091,272	710,382
Bhagalpur	20,511	13,629	5,702,598	339,680
Orissa	9,841	4,342	1,396,149	248,985
Chota Nagpur	26,963	26,963	4,900,429	287,476
Total	124,372	83,386	33,930,117	2,169,564

Source. E. A. Gait, *Census of India, vol. VI: Part I, the Report*, (1901), p. 12.

The above table shows that the Rajshahi division, among the other divisions of Bengal proper (in comparison with the Burdwan and Presidency) had the largest area and population, which were liable to the famines. Also, the number of persons who would require relief in famine was the highest in the Rajshahi Division. Despite of this fact, the narratives of sufferings of the people of the Rajshahi Division did not receive any adequate attention by the famine-historians, so far. Hence, this chapter intends to fill up this gap in regards to the extent and severity of the 1896-97 famine in the districts of Rajshahi Division.

I. Drought, Ecology and Economy: 1896-97 Famine in North Bengal

W. H. Grimley, the Chairman of the Bengal Executive Committee of the Indian Famine Charitable Relief Fund, in his *Report* had attributed the reason for the 1896-97 famine to the 'failure of the monsoon rains, and...two successive bad seasons' like all the previous famines.[7] The situation created by the shortage of the rainfall had been many times compared with the 1873-74 famine. The failure of rains and the subsequent crop failure that occurred in the Province of Bengal had 'extended throughout India, and caused an unprecedented rice in prices.'[8] The failure of the September rice of 1896 had made the *aman* prospects doubtful which contributed to the abnormal price-rise in the market. Throughout the year of 1896, prices had been much upwards and it rose suddenly since the mid-October and persisted for a long time.[9] Although the harvesting season of 1895 was on the whole favourable to *bhadoi* crops but it was good for the production of winter rice and the rainfall of 1896 was very nearly as short as it was in 1873 and had been un-proportionately distributed.[10] The *bhadoi* crops had to suffer from short rainfall in all parts of the province except in Orissa, and the average outturn of the whole province was estimated at 10½annas. The harm caused to the winter rice crop by deficient rainfall during the sowing and transplanting season had been affected by the overall cessation of the rains at the most crucial period when no rain fell after the 19th September.[11] The acute scarcity of grains had produced grain-riots in many areas of Bihar. Though the government had provided a subsidy grant of 8 *annas* per maund on the import of rice in the affected areas, the hindrances in transporting the grains through roads and shortage of carts had caused serious inconvenience in trading food-grains.[12]

However, many regional or local factors which were closely associated with broad ecological changes had brought out the peasant-society in an acutely vulnerable position. Lance Brennan and other argue that behind the famine of 1896–1897 in Nadia District in Bengal there was a series of ecological disasters - from the drying up of some of the Ganges tributaries to the debility of the population caused by epidemics of malaria (linked to stagnant water from atrophying rivers and railway embankments).[13] On the other hand, Bihar and Lower Bengal was the worst sufferer of the failure of the winter rice which coupled with excessively low wages 'remained practically unaltered for the past 20 years or more' was turned into a zone of acute scarcity and starvation.[14] Although it was widely accepted in the contemporary official and semi-official documents that the districts of northern Bengal were 'slightly affected' by the famine, detailed investigations and objective analysis of the fact had provided sufficient evidences to situate these areas at par with the other areas which were critically affected by the famine of 1896-97.

Famine operations in the province of Bengal was commenced in the Patna division, where test works were opened in October and were followed by relief works in November 1896. The only clear direction of the provincial Code on the point of relief administration was that each affected district should be divided into relief circles and a relief inspector should be appointed to each circle to discharge prescribed duties, the chief of which were concerned with the preparation of gratuitous relief lists in villages and the superintendence of this form .of relief.[15] The overall meteorological condition in India which instigated the advent of famine in 1896, as mentioned in the 'Narratives' of the famine was as follows:

> "The cause of the famine of 1897 was the early cessation of the autumn rains of 1896. The south-west monsoon was late in establishing itself in June 1896 on the West Coast, and from its first appearance was ill-distributed and fitful in character. Throughout July the rainfall

Table: 4.2

Rainfall and price-rise in the Rajshahi Division from May to September 1896 (extracted)

District	Rainfall from 16th May to 15th Sept.			Price of common rice on 31st Aug. (seers per rupee)		Proportion borne by *bhadoi* to total rice crop of district	Estimated outturn of *bhadoi* in annas
	Actual	Average	Deficiency	seer	chatak		
Rajshahi	31.30	41.06	- 9.76	9	0	13.6	8
Dinajpur	30.97	53.76	- 22.79	9	10	8.9	8
Jalpaiguri	55.89	100.92	- 45.03	11	0	28.3	6
Darjeeling	92.33	96.32	- 3.99	11	0	32.3	6 in hills 4 in Terai
Rangpur	46.03	61.11	- 15.08	9	0	22.0	12.5
Bogra	37.26	49.56	- 12.30	9	12	33.3	12
Pabna	38.62	43.28	- 4.66	10	8	16.2	10

Source: From P. Nolan, the Commissioner of the Rajshahi Division, to the Secretary to the Government of Bengal, Revenue Department.[17]

> was more ·or less deficient in Bengal and Central and Northern India, and gave rise to apprehensions. In August the monsoon appeared to have recovered strength, and frequent cyclonic storms gave heavy rain to the Central Provinces, Central India, and Rajputana. Elsewhere in Upper India the rainfall was in defect. Early in September the hopes of an improving monsoon were disappointed."[16]

The Rajshahi Division had to go through an acute shortage of rainfall since May 1896, which caused remarkable rise in the price of rice.

It is evident from the Table 4.2 that the district of Jalpaiguri and Dinajpur were suffered from deficient rainfall. For Jalpaiguri, the deficiency was almost half the average. It is to be noted that the *bhadoi* crops which formed a chief share of the total rice crop of the districts had been considerably affected, and in Jalpaiguri, Darjeeling, Rangpur and Pabna the distress was more serious. The Collector of Pabna had sought for financial assistance of Rs. 5,000 as agricultural loans, which was to be distributed among the agricultural populations.[18] At the middle of November 1896, it became already clear that due to the unprecedented low level of the floods and the almost total absence of rain since the last week of September the winter rice crop would yield a poor outturn.[19] The Collector of Pabna revealed that rice was always imported for Pabna during this time of the year from Dinajpur, Bogra, and Rangpur districts; and for this year, especially, only two or three per cent of the cultivators had stocks of rice or paddy by which they could only sustain till July 1897.[20] Influenced by the price-rise the dealers had also sold of their stocks which caused a serious shortage of rice in the district of Pabna.[21] The Collector of Rajshahi was afraid about the condition in his district which would probably face a severe 'water famine' due to the total failure of rains in the district.[22] Therefore, excavation of 'as many

Table: 4.3

Comparative Rainfall in the subdivisions of Rajshahi district between Jul. and Oct. 1873-74 and 1896-97

Subdivision	*July*			*August*			*September*			*October*		
	Normal	*1873-74*	*1896-97*	*Normal*	*1873-74*	*1896-97*	*Normal*	*1873-74*	*1896-97*	*Normal*	*1873-74*	*1896-97*
Sadar	11.67	6.73	8.87	12.05	11.27	4.70	11.27	3.12	6.55	4.44	0.32	No rain
Nator	11.86	9.05	14.98	12.16	13.60	4.75	11.64	6.08	4.12	4.46	0.14	No rain
Naogaon	11.25	No rain	7.88	8.75	No rain	3.88	12.68	No rain	8.14	2.29	No rain	No rain
District Average	11.72	7.89	11.97	10.15	12.43	4.01	10.21	4.60	6.27	3.73	0.23	0.16

Source: From P. Nolan, the Commissioner of the Rajshahi Division, to the Secretary to the Government of Bengal, Revenue Department.[27]

tanks' were ordered by him to meet the water scarcity of the district. In fact, within March 1897, want of drinking water was severely felt and it became necessary to 'excavate or re-excavate the tanks before the rains sets in.'[23] Due to a severe shortage of rains which was almost half the average, the District of Jalpaiguri had suffered the worst. While on the hand, the outturn of rice crops got massively affected, on the hand the influx of tea labourers in the district had made the situation more complicated. As per the official information, Falakata and Alipur Duar were the two 'worst' tahsils which faced acute shortage of production.[24] In December 1896, the Deputy Commissioner of Jalpaiguri had reported that

> "The prospects in Alipur and Falakata being so much worse than either Mynaguri to the west or Bhalka to the east...that the land cultivated are much higher and therefore much drier than towards the Tista, and as regards Bhalka, the people there are aboriginal Meches who resort with success to artificial means of irrigation."[25]

However, in the January 1897 the situation had further deteriorated. The growing apprehensions of an impending scarcity and continuous increasing demand from the tea labourers had contributed to the rise of coarse price in the mufassil areas of Alipur and Falakata. The Inspector of Alipur subdivision had reported that people had already started eating 'boiled kachu with their meals, with a proportionately small quantity of rice.'[26]

The above rainfall statistics (in Table 4.3) has shown that there was continuous shortage of rainfall between July and October 1896 in the Rajshahi Division. The district Sadar, Nator, and Naogaon did not receive any rain in October, that made the situation worse for the crop production. Acute scarcity of water had increased the apprehension for abnormal price rise which further intensified the subsistence crisis.

Table: 4.4

Estimate of outturn of winter rice crops in Rajshahi

Tract	*Soil*	*Area in square miles*	*Population*	*Outturn in annas*
Gangetic	Grey sand	700	500,000	4
Barind	Red Clay	500	200,000	8
Swamps	Black loam	1100	600,000	12

Sources: From P. Nolan, the Commissioner of the Rajshahi Division, to the Secretary to the Government of Bengal, Revenue Department.[28]

It is pertinent to mention here that the Rajshahi district had been divided into three distinct regions for agricultural purposes, viz., the Gangetic tract (composed of grey sandy soil), the *Barind* (made of red clay with an undulated surface), and the marshes or black loam (deposited by the great Chalan Bil and surrounding pools.[29] The outturn of crops in all these three parts were considerably affected, and among these the Gangetic tract had produced the minimum outrun which was 2 to 4 annas in comparison with the *Barind* and marshes that yielded 6 to 8 annas and 8 to 12 annas respectively.[30] During the mid-June, the situation in the *Barind* tract had deteriorated and the Commissioner had asked for a 'special report' for this region.[31] The Commissioner had expressed his 'anxiety' for this area where people needed more assistance from the government.[32]

The relief operations in the district of Jalpaiguri had included large scale sanctioning of roads throughout the district which provided a great scope of employment for the labourers. The sanctioned road-works were as follows:

(a) Road from Falakata to Lachman Dabri, sanctioned by District Board, which was prepared to pay and it was estimated that 500 people would find employment for two months.

(b) Patlakhoa to Jaigaon.

(c) Mahakalguri to Hatipota Tea-graden.

(*d*) Mohakalguri to Chikliguri road which passed through many villages of the eastern part of the district had been also proposed for improvement.

(*e*) Chikliguri to Bhalka (an old road)

(*f*) Alipur to Gharghoria. This road was proposed to connect Alipur with the road passing by the south of the Kaljani from Kholta at the point where it entered into Cooch Behar.

(*g*) For the Santhals, road connecting villages within the settlement.

(*h*) For Bhutias – the road from Santrabari to Chunabhati that passed through Buxa Bazar.[33]

The Indian Famine Charitable Relief Fund was established in 14th January 1896 at a public meeting held in Calcutta and presided over by the Viceroy himself. However, further arrangements were made to form a Provincial Committee for Bengal, which included representatives of every division and district. The first Chairman of the said Executive Committee was C. C. Stevens who was later replaced by Mr. W. H. Grimley, the then senior member of the Board of Revenue.[34] Subsequently, instructions were issued to form District Relief Committees. Murshidabad was the first district to form a Relief Committee which was constituted on the 30th January 1896 under the presidency of the District Judge. Bogra, Malda and Chittagong were also prompt in forming district relief committees.

The district of Bogra had been suffered from severe crop failure during this time. There was considerable deficiency of outturn in areas east to the Karatoya river, which was extended to the thana Shariakandil, Dhunot, Shibganj, Bogra and Sherpur.[35] In Bogra, rainfall was deficient during the years of 1895-96 and 1896-97 and as a result crops had to suffer a great loss. Although there was a widespread failure of crops in the district but the 'actual scarcity [was] only in the portion of the district east of the Karatoya in *thanas* Shariakandi and Dhunot and a famine charitable relief fund had to be opened towards the close of the year.'[36] The famine in Murshidabad was called forth by the failure of crops caused by the shortage of rainfall. This time prices rose in an unprecedented manner during the later part of the famine which severely had affected parts of Sadar subdivision, which was located on the east of the river Bhagirathi and was known as the Bagri, along with a few areas on the west of the river in the Kandi subdivision.[37] Short rainfall and the lowness of the rivers in 1895 was resulted in a partial failure of the autumn and winter crops and in 1896 in many parts of the district autumn rice had completely failed to yield a full turn.[38]

Table: 4.5

Comparison of the outturns of the various crops in 1895-96 and 1896-97 and 1873-74 in Murshidabad

Crop	*1895-96*	*1896-97*	*1873-74*
	Annas	*Annas*	*Annas*
Aman paddy	8	7	6
Aus paddy	9	8	12
Wheat	8	3	12
Pulses	14	7	12
Other *rabi* crops	10	8	12

Source: L. S. S. O'Malley, *Bengal District Gazetteers: Murshidabad*, p. 112.

This time the situation was worse than what was in 1873-74. Test-works had been introduced in February and the maximum wages which the workers were allowed to earn in a day was 1½ annas for a task of 66 cubic feet. Since increasing number of people were engaged in the tasks so the administration towards the end of April found it necessary to convert the test-works into ordinary relief works under the Famine Code. The supply of gratuitous relief was started in March in Barwa and Bharatpur thanas which were the most severely affected parts of the district.[39] The suffering was predominantly experienced by the landless and labouring classes, and by those who in ordinary years were relied on the charity of the others.[40] During the month of July the situation became more severe and the price of common rice was prevailing between 6 to 7½ seers per rupee in the affected areas. The Government had to open new relief centres at Nawada at the end of April and later on at Jalangi. The whole of the Sadar subdivision was more or less affected, and where circles were not opened, relief was administered by private enterprises like zamindars, big landlords of the district. [41] Mention can be made of Maharani Swarnamayi, the Nawab Bahadur of Murshidabad, Rai Sitab Chand Nahar Bahadur, Rai Budh Singh Dudburia Bahadur of Azimganj, Babu Jogendra Narayan Rai of Lalgola, Bibi Hani Mena Kumari and Babu Narpat Singh and many others.[42] There is no doubt that these private charities were in many respect had contributed to the lessening of the severity and duration of the distress caused by the famine and had complemented the Government relief operations in the district.

In Rajshahi, crop was half the average in 1896 and as a result *boro* rice was planted on an abnormally large area of field (77,000 acres). Though there was no such great deficiency in rainfall during the early monsoon period but by the coming of August there was a serious shortage and the drought persisted even till the middle of September.[43] October went rainless. The crop production in lands which were nearer to the river beds was also below the average due to the short-lasting of the floods of this year. However, it was the 'abnormal meteorological conditions and the abnormally low inundations of the Padma [which] injured the year's winter harvest, prejudiced the prospects of the coming spring crop, and affected the condition of the people at large.'[44] There were contradictory estimates put forward by the Collector and Commissioner of the district.[45] There was complete absence of any work in the agricultural fields between mid-October and end-November and the price of agricultural labour had become drastically low viz. 1 *anna* per diem in the Boalia and Durgapur outposts.[46] Though in 1873 the worst affected part of the district was the Barind tract but in 1896-97 famine the areas which were severely affected were located in *thanas* Boalia, Puthia, Charghat, the southern half of Bagmara and that portion of the Nator *thana*. The prices of rice had eventually increased - the market price of common rice was 7½ seers per rupee at Rampur Boalia in October 1896 and at Nator in November and it rose abnormally high in July 1897 when rice was selling at 6 seers to 7 seers 12 *chittaks* and in August it was 6½ seers at Puthia and 8 seers at Mahadebpur.[47] In these circumstances, gratuitous relief was undertaken by the Government and as a result 9,000 persons were relieved from the Charitable Fund who were mostly impoverished women and children and a great portion of the relief was extended in form of gratuitous doles of rice.[48] When the test works were started it was initially found that except from the place near to the Ganges, where the people were hard hit by the decline of silk industry and there was constant want of employment, no such demand was raised for it. The test works in the primary stage was aimed to bring the Ganges water into the inland *bils* and was limited in the two canals of Narad Khal and Bairagi Khal for this purpose, the former was 5½ miles and the later was 3 miles long.[49]

P. Nolan, the Commissioner of the Rajshahi Division on his *Resolution on the Rajshahi Report* had noted the impoverished condition of the people of the Rajshahi Division and asserted that 'the general condition of the people was said to have got worse during the fortnight; a result which is unfortunately to be expected as the season advances and with reference to the insufficient fall of rain.'[51] The assertion had shown an attendance at test-works averaging 670 male units during the first week and only 626 in the second which overall demonstrated that no woman or child was employed, since as it was believed, 'the result of the test in regard to the existence of famine [was] negative.'[52] But it was noticed that there had been a marked increase of participation in test works since the close of the

Table: 4.6

Statement showing the actual expenditure incurred in Pabna and Rajshahi for 1896-97

District	Relief work and gratuitous relief					Amount advanced for village works under the modified rules under the Land Improvement Loans Act.	Total expenditure debited to general revenues
	Amount paid as wages	Amount spent in giving gratuitous relief	Cash of establishment tools and plant, &c.,	Total cost of relief works and gratuitous relief	Portion of cost defrayed from District Funds.		
1	2	3	4	5	6		
	Rs. A. P.	Rs. A. P.	Rs. A. P.	Rs. A. P.	Rs. A. P.	Rs. A. P.	Rs. A. P.
Rajshahi	3,748 13 3	136 3 0	1,336 8 6	5,221 8 9	5,221 8 9	1,400 0 0	1400 0 0
Pabna	51 9 4 0	------------	78 15 3	598 3 3	598 3 3	1000 0 0	1000 0 0

Source: Extracted from letter from P. Nolan, EsQ., Commissioner of the Rajshahi Division, to the Secretary to the Government of Bengal, Revenue Department.[50]

fortnight probably due to the opening of new works. The gratuitous relief under the Famine Code, which was also an indication of the degree to which scarcity prevails, had been reported as nominal, the cost being Rs. 3-10. Public health is reported fair, although cholera has appeared, as is usual in this season. As a method of test works coolies were sought by the administration. Nolan stated that:

> "I called the Collector's attention to the demand for 5,000 coolies on the Bogra Railway adjoining his district, and would glad if he can state in his next report under the head of emigration, whether the labourers of Rajshahi have availed themselves of this opportunity. The opening of new test-works is in accordance with my instructions. ...... It is to be recommended that a work not conducted in strict accordance with the Code is no "test" so far as Government is concerned."[53]

In his letter on 19th April 1897 N. K. Bose, The Collector of Rajshahi wrote to the Commissioner of the Rajshahi Division that 'The general condition of the affected tracts [was] gradually becoming worse and worse, particularly portions of Boalia, Nowhatta, Charghat and Rajapur Circles.'[54] There was 6.30 inch of rainfall in Naugaon till the third week of April, but practically there was no rain elsewhere. Although it was reported that the condition of *boro dhan* in Tanor was good, and *boro dhan*, onions and jute in Bagmara were also good, but in parts of Godagari, *boro* and *jail dhan* was said to be drying for want of rain. Only a quarter crop of *til* and sugarcane were expected in Charghat and elsewhere in the Sadar Subdivision the prospects were not positive and in Rajapur the condition was noticeably worst.[55] Importation from Panchupur and Singra *thanas* into Boalia and from Dinajpur had been going on, but not in sufficiently large quantities to meet the demand. In ordinary years the price of rise did not get much higher but in 1897 the condition was alarming due to the shortage of rainfall, as the *rabi* crops did not turn out well. In these circumstances the District Superintendent reported that 'only the well-to-do cultivators had any food-stocks; many poor persons [were] subsisting on fruits or berries, greens, kachu, &c., and [had] to do without cooked food for a day.' The scarcity of food and water had been accompanied by severe cases of cholera in Boalia, Putia and Baraigram *thanas* and there were 31 cases reported in Boalia town alone. Till the middle of April there had been three test relief works open and the price of rice at the relief works had fluctuated between 8 to 9 seers per rupee. Besides the above test works initiatives had been taken there to open several works in which the labourers were paid wages according to the Famine Code. Two tanks near Purila were being excavated under the modified piece-work system where 80 persons on an average could work daily. Eight works were being carried out with the loans granted under the modified rules under the Land Improvement Loans Act. Besides these works, opening of several tanks were being executed throughout the district by some private individuals either from their own funds or from loans granted under the ordinary rules under the Land Improvement Loans Act.[56] The Collector of the district of Rajshahi had informed about the opening of three new test- works in the district which were 'ready to be started at a moment's notice' – in Boalia the Narad Khal, Tank at Hat Godagari and Tank at Sridharpur. In the meanwhile, the work at Narad Khal had already begun, and regular estimates had been sanctioned for the tanks at Hat Godagari and Sridharpur. But despite of all these initiatives there were only 16 cases of gratuitously relieved people informed by the police under section 12 of the Famine Code. Till the end of 15th April, nearly 8,000 people were gratuitously relieved from the Charitable Relief Fund.

From the Table 4.7 it is evident that among the recipients of gratuitous relief of the district of Rajshahi women formed the overwhelming portion viz. almost 69%. This shows the relatively increased crisis prevailed among them and their

Table: 4.7

Statement of gratuitous relief by Police for the two weeks ending 15th April 1897 in

Name of circle and Heads of gratuitous relief.	Number of persons receiving gratuitous relief				Money expended		
	Men	Women	Children.	Total	Rs.	A.	P
Relief by Police under section 12							
Godagari	....	3	....	3	0	3	6
Tanor	1	2	3	6	0	8	6
Rajapur	1	6	......	7	0	13	6
Lalpur	Particulars of men, women, &c., not given. Gratuitous relief administered by the Charitable Relief Committees were not shown here.				2	0	6
Total	2	11	3	16	3	10	0

Source: From N. K. Bose., EsQ., Collector of Rajshahi, to the Commissioner of the Rajshahi Division. – (No. 228G., dated Rampur Boalia, the 19th April 1897), WBSA.

sheer dependency on the government relief. This has also reflected that the drought had peeped into the domestic order which was shaken vigorously by the scarcity and wanting of food. Gendered social hierarchies became more intense during the crisis time viz. famine and scarcities when women did not get even for their bare subsistence and their male counterpart captured the whole subsistence. In November 1896, it had been informed that in Hatia and other affected areas of Noakhali-Chittagong rice obtained from the relief actions were consumed by the 'pater familias, at the cost of the female, minor, old and infirm members of the family.'[57] As 'for many of the poorer households survival was a balancing act requiring the strategic operation of all economic and cultural resources',[58] thus the household itself became a site of competition and contestation instead of showing cooperation in a time of crisis. Bina Agarwal argues that 'there is a systematic anti-female bias in the allocation within rural households of subsistence resources controlled by men, including resources used for food, health care' etc.[59]Moreover, since the women had mostly relied on the 'specialized' job, they had to go through within a severe crisis of employment during the time of drought or scarcities when the occupational opportunities gradually contracted and ultimately stopped.

Table: 4.8

Statement of gratuitous relief by Police for the two weeks ending 15th May 1897

Name of circle and heads of gratuitous relief	*Number of persons receiving gratuitous relief*			
	Men	*Women*	*Children*	*Total*
Tanor	11	17	35	63
Rajapur	1	5	1	7
Total	12	22	36	70

Source: Selection of papers relating to the famine of 1896-97 in Bengal. Revenue Department, Bengal, vol. VIII (May - June 1897), IOR/V/27/830/44.

In May, 1897 the number of people who had received gratuitous relief had increased, among them women and children were the majority. This revealed the intensification of the famine which had critically affected the household also. While men were involved in the task works, women and children were treated with gratuitous relief. The police report of 15th June 1897 had also reflected the increasing number of women and children in comparison with the men who had received gratuitous relief during that period.[60] However, a comparatively greater participation of women at the works of 'bailing and turfing' in the district of Pabna had revealed a 'greater' distress 'in this district than in Rajshahi.'[61] Arup Maharatna argues that 'the age-sex composition of mortality effects of famine is usually an outcome of two factors, namely, physiological vulnerability and social protection.'[62] In Rajshahi and Pabna, paddy-husking was provided on a large scale, and for Pabna, especially, advances of cotton-thread for weaving and jute for twisting were also made.[63] The total amount expended for paddy-husking and jute-twisting was Rs. 77,100 by which 3,098 persons were relieved.[64] In May 1897, Mr. Finucane, the Secretary to the Government of Bengal had asserted that the prices were very high and 'for the week ending 3rd May show[ed] that the numbers on the test works were 781 in Rajshahi and 492 in Pabna.'[65]

There were also certain peculiar characteristics which prevailed in the district of Pabna. The Commissioner of Pabna had remarked that the lower class of Muslim women in Pabna did care very little for the *purda*, which was used for hiding themselves behind a curtain, but it did not follow that they had no objection to earthwork – on the contrary it was observed in Rajshahi by their abstention from doing the work despite of prevailing the same condition in that district.[66] The Collector pointed out that the women had no prejudice against husking rice – a task assigned to them in the ordinary course of village industry. Employment of this class, however, was afforded from charitable funds – not by the Government. C. A. Radice, the Officiating Collector of Pabna in a letter to the Commissioner of the Rajshahi Division (18th July 1897) had remarked that he was informed by native gentlemen of Pabna that Muslim women did not care much for the *purda* in this district, this idea, as argued by him, had been attested fully by his personal observation.[67] It was found that at the relief circles the paddy huskers were almost all Muslims, mostly widows, many with several children and when they came for their paddy from villages even 5 or 6 miles distant many appeared to be endowed with very little modesty. The incident had shaped the Governmental apathy of the fact that the number of women recipients were gradually increasing and also guided them to be 'greatly disinclined to attach importance to the fact that women still [came] to the test-works and they [had] taken to carrying earth as well as turf on the Rajapur-Dasuria road work.[68] It was further noted that despite of the considerable presence of women workers it was reported that 'their number [had] moreover, remained on the whole comparatively constant,' and the numbers of males was increased by the junior males of less indigent families who were attracted by the lightness of the tasks set.[69] The was a 'rumour', according to the administration, of several deaths in Sara jurisdiction and the 'rumour' of these several deaths from famine had resolved itself on enquiry into one death only, that of a child about 7 years old, the son of a chaukidar who was of the opinion that the death was due to fever. But further enquiries which were conducted amongst some women of the same village showed that the boy had had nothing to eat for two days and had taken a long drink of water for which he began to vomit and died.[70] In the tribal societies where social restrictions were not powerful to restrict them, the tribal women had shared their duty in the initial years of famine – women were engaged in collecting jungle products and men went to the relief works, whereas during the critical famine years men were first to respond to the outward migration leaving their families behind in the famine areas but ultimately the women too had to migrate for the tea gardens of Duars and Assam and for the coal mines of Bihar and Bengal.[71] There existed forms of social prejudices and bindings which were predominant among the poor people even in the days of acquiring famine relief and test-works. Though women were not much familiar with the works that they had to perform for obtaining the reliefs but sometime they still went out from their houses to do such works. This propensity became so widespread that even the Muslim women did join and perform the test-woks for which they had to go beyond their *purda* restrictions. Apart from the central and eastern Bengal, these kinds of practises were prevailed in north Bengal. The higher and lower class women of Hindu and Muslim families came to join the test-works during the relief periods when they had to do rice-husking, jute twisting etc. and other women were engaged in cleaning Burma rice.[72] The women's participation in the test-works had disclosed the severity of famine-condition which had critically impoverished the household of the poor and dragged the women from their *antapur*. The acute scarcity in the district of Pabna had brought the Muslim women into the test-woks where they could care very little for their *purda*.[73]

In the district of Pabna there were no crops of importance on the fields except the *boro dhan*. The sowing of the *aus* had been delayed by the want of rain. There was no rain during the middle of April in Pabna and this had prevented *aus* sowing and kept the price of rice even higher than it would probably otherwise had been. The normal for the Sadar Subdivision for the whole month of April was 3.12 inches.[74] The retail prices of common rice and paddy was returned as follows from the different police stations. The figures were standard seers of 80 *tolahs*. (80 *tolahs* = 1 *seers*)

Table: 4.9

Retail prices of common rice and paddy of different police stations in Pabna

Thanas	*Rice*	*Paddy*
Pabna	9	13
Sara	8¼	13
Chatmohar	10½	25
Faridpur	10	Not returned
Dulai	8	Ditto
Mothura	8	15
Ullapara	9	14
Khamarkhand	8	13
Shazadpur	8¼	13Q!
Sirajganj	8	13½
Subgacha	8¼	13
Raiganj	9	14
Taras	10	20
Chohali	9¼	13

Source: From W. Maude, EsQ., the Collector of Pabna to the Commissioner of the Rajshahi Division, dated Pabna, the 19th April 1897), WBSA.

The above table has shown the great variations in the prices of rice and paddy at different places due to the state of local supplies and the peculiar fact that, although owing to rain holding off the price of paddy had been steadily increasing up whereas the price of rice has remained stationary. The rise in the price of paddy and the great increase in the numbers attending the one test work which was open during by that time indicated that the position was one of considerable deterioration which had been attributed chiefly to the rain having kept off altogether. On the other hand, the Subdivisional Officer of Sirajganj had further reported that distress in his subdivision was confined to the very poorest people.[75] The imports and exports of food grains registered during that time was as follows: -

	Standard maunds
Imports	28,682
Exports	2,123

The remarkable feature of the relief works during the 1896-97 famine was that this time Government had acknowledged the necessity of both import and export from the districts affected by the famine whereas in the previous famines import and export had both become a matter of dissension among the Government officials. The policy of restrictions on export and increasing quantity of import became widespread in many affected districts of the Presidency. The Collector of Darbhanga observed that

> "The local feeling, as is invariably the case on such occasions, was very strongly in favour of measures being taken to check the export of food grains from the district, and of Government taking measures to import food grains; Measures to check exports have never been adopted by Government as a part of their famine policy, but in 1897 Government was obliged to import largely."[76]

The total numbers of task-works, persons who had been relieved by the gratuitous relief and the cost of the same at the circles of Pabna and Dasuria were as follows:

Table: 4.10

Total numbers of task-work, relieved persons and their cost in Pabna and Dasuria

Circle	*Task Work*	*Gratuitous*	*Cost (Rs.)*
Dasuria Pabna	1,172343	Nil223	1,997269

Source: From W. Maude, EsQ., the Collector of Pabna to the Commissioner of the Rajshahi Division, dated Pabna, the 19th April 1897), progs. no. 393-94, WBSA.

The condition of the tracts threatened with distress in the districts of Rajshahi and Pabna, during the first half of the April had been demonstrated from the Secretary of the Government in the following manner:

> "It appears to the Lieutenant Governor that the Collector of Rajshahi [was] inclined to take an unduly gloomy view of the state of things in his district and I am to request that you [would] take steps to check this tendency on the part of Mr. Bose. His Honor [did] not think that there can be any severe pressure at present in this or any other district in the Rajshahi Division."[77]

N. K. Bose was of the opinion that the price of rice at the relief works varied between 8 and 9 seers, and as a result of this he had therefore raised the maximum wage from 8 pice to 9 pice.[78] As the operations in the district of Rajshahi were still at the test-work stage, the Lieutenant Governor was of opinion that two *annas* a day should be sufficient as a maximum wage on test works, and that the tasks were to be strictly enforced with an objective to ascertain whether the people were under the necessity of working on a mere subsistence wage.[79] But on a sharp contrast with the Government, A. M. Bose., President of the Indian Association wrote in a telegram about the severe famine condition of the Rajshahi district in following terms:

> "Funds for charitable relief in Rajshahi completely exhausted. Rice selling 8 seers, even less, and at places no adequate quantity procurable for money. Scarcity and starvation prevailing. Advance of seed grains to cultivators necessary. Unless Government or Central Relief Committee comes to rescue immediately, many will die."[80]

The telegram had disclosed an extent of distress which required the immediate attention of the Government. Rai

Raj Kumar Sarvadhikary, Bahadur, Secretary, British Indian Association had also acknowledge the 'prevalence of severe distress in the Rajshahi district' to the Secretary of the Government of Bengal.[81] For the time being, there was a situation 'of stoppage of work' in the Sirajganj Jute Mill which was seriously affected by the 1897 earthquake.[82] This caused a cessation of work for the labourers who were working there as a part of famine-work.

The Collector of the district of Pabna had anticipated a good *aus* crop by the middle of May which was generally coming up well and was already six inches high in many parts. The crop had been 'benefited by the break without rain for the last week' for which 'good occasional showers were needed to bring it along well.' Therefore, it was expected that there was 'a good deal to make up during the next fortnight, but constant heavy showers may now be confidently expected.'[83] But there had been a steady rise in price all over the district. This had been attributed to the uncertainty of the probable fate of the *aus* crop owing to the long drought that had prevailed up to the middle of April. There had been a large import of Burma rice, both in Pabna and Sirajganj. The Sub-divisional Officer of Sirajganj wrote most miserably in his reports about 'the very high prices and on general rumours' –

> "... in the Sadar, at any rate, things are much in the same condition as before, and, if anything, slightly ameliorated by the recent rains and the promising condition of the aus paddy crop. I am satisfied that the distress is much exaggerated."[84]

The Naib of Shazadpur reported on the first week of May that there was great distress in some of his villages which required serious attention on the part of the Government. Although Government wanted to tackle the problem through the introduction of test-works for the victims but the Naib 'replied with equal promptness that they would not.' On the other hand the Naib had insisted the Collector to compel the mahajans to lend money at a small rate of interest. The proposal did not get any approval from the Government which instead of extension of any further loans to the peasants had suggested that the estate (the Tagore's) should lend money to their tenants at a reasonable rate and as a result the 'old idea that Government [would] give innumerable loans [was] still hanging on.'[85] There had been importation of 18,141 maunds of food grains whereas 1,207 maunds were exported from the district. Though cholera had again overwhelming presence in the district of Pabna too but gradually cholera was receding from there. The amount which had been allotted for the districts of north Bengal for relief works was as follows:

Table: 4.11

Amount of distribution of relief funds among the districts of North Bengal

District	*Amount (Rs.)*
Rajshahi	3000
Dinajpur	1000
Jalpaiguri	1000
Darjeeling	Nil.
Rangpur	1000
Bogra	2000
Pabna	2000
Reserve	8000

Source: Memorandum by P. Nolan, EsQ., Commissioner of the Rajshahi Division – Circular No. 21M., dated Jalpaiguri, the 5th April, 1897, progs no. 401-402, WBSA.

It was decided in a meeting of the Bengal Provincial Executive Committee that a sum of Rs. 25,000 (inclusive of sums already remitted to Rajshahi and Pabna) would have been disposed to the Commissioner of the Rajshahi Division for the expenditure in charitable relief in the Division. The

Executive Committee had instructed that the money would be distributed from time to time in accordance with circumstances, among the Local Committees which had been formed in all the districts of the Rajshahi Division at the Commissioner's discretion, in response to their respective needs. It seemed to be axiomatic to the Committee that no districts other than Rajshahi and Pabna were likely to require money for charitable relief. The above table (4.11) has shown the amount of distribution of this money which was in total 18,000 and the rest of 7000 had already been remitted to the Rajshahi Division.[86] The table below shows the number of persons on the relief list on the 31st March: -

Table: 4.12

Number of persons on the relief list on the 31st March, Rajshahi Division

Category of people	*Number of people*
Number of paupers gratuitously relieved	5,103
Number of huskers, spinners, &c.	1,649
Number of persons to whom rice is sold at a cheaper rate than the market rate	597
Total	7,349

From E. N. Baker, EsQ., C.S., Honorary Secretary, Bengal Branch, Indian Famine Charitable Relief Fund, to the Commissioner of the Rajshahi Division. – (No. 314, dated Calcutta, the 31st March 1897), WBSA.

In the Sadar Subdivision relief centres were opened in Boalia, Nowhatta, Bagmara, Muchmal, Tanore, Charghat, Rajapur, Putia, Durgapur and in the Nator Subdivision relief centres were opened at Nator, Lalpur and Bagatipara. These centres which were opened upto 31st March in the district of Rajshahi.

In addition to the miseries of the people caused by the shortage of rainfall and failure of crops, there had been two disastrous fires, one at Boalia, and the other at Putia, besides small fires here and there.[87] The fire at Boalia occurred on Good Friday at the poorest part of the town. Although the wind was very high but the open space afforded by the Rajshahi College compound and for the untiring exertions of some people to cut off connections by breaking down huts, the conflagration had been tamed at last but otherwise it would have been much more disastrous than it actually was.[88] A tiled hut belonged to the college and another, in the Boalia Hospital were burnt down. In Boalia, it had been roughly ascertained that 50 poor families turned out homeless and in Putia more than 40 families.[89] These poor persons deserved to get some assistance to build up some sort of shelter along with the arrangements for famine-relief. The fires had triggered the sale of food-grain by the mahajans of Murshidabad and other places. In April 1897, the Rani Mena Kumari of Jeagunj and Babu Narpat Singh of Azimganj had sold rice for 10 seers a rupee which was excessively high during the famine periods.[90] In areas of Rajshahi where there was no such systematic grain trade, rich peasants had acted as the mahajans like former and had 'controlled a large part of the surplus engaged in petty retail trade.'[91]

The Rules for the Charitable Relief in Rajshahi were as follows:

> "To advance half a maund of paddy (*kachi*) to each indigent female who can husk it, but cannot procure it for want of capital, on her undertaking to return 12 seers (*kachi*) of clean rice. By this arrangement a margin of above one seer of rice with bran and husk is left to the husker as her remuneration. To *pardanishin* ladies, unaccustomed to husking, may be insisted on a return of 10 seers of rice for half a maund of paddy.
>
> To register all lame, blind, decrepit, and infirm persons, and give them a dole of rice at two seers (*kachi*) a week (say on Sunday) and their dependent children below 10 at 1 seer each.

To make house to house search and pick out cases of starvation with a view to supply each one with so much of rice *gratis* as the committee consider necessary. The doles should be given weekly on a fixed day.

If no paddy is available, *khesari* or *musari* pulses may also be issued. Half a maund (*kachi*) may be issued to each female, who is required to return 13¼ seers (*kachi*) of clean dal.

It has been decided to give relief to indigent weavers. The police has been instructed to prepare a list of those indigent weavers who are ready to supply us with clothes and *gamchas*, with advances made from the fund. These lists will be forwarded to the Branch Committees, and they may, after due enquiry, make advances. The Committees may also on their own knowledge make advances. Not more than Rs. 10 should be advanced at one time to any person.

Each weaver taking advance shall have to execute an agreement on a stamped paper (of 8 annas value) in the form enclosed. It should be executed in favour of the Magistrate and President of the Relief Committee. The cost of the stamp should be paid from the fund.

Two or more weavers may execute a joint agreement, but the total advance made on subjoint agreement should not exceed Rs. 50.

When the weaver brings in the clothes, their market price should be appraised and paid in cash. The cloths received from the weavers should be distributed *gratis* to the poor and needy."[92]

Regarding the offering of the advances to weavers there were, however, certain pre-conditions which were set by the Government. In the matter of giving advances to the weavers, no steps were taken until the Committee were satisfied that necessity had arisen to aid them in their industry. While reports were received from the Police, as well as from the Branch Committees, that several indigent weavers were in great distress at the same time objection had been taken to the police preparing a list of indigent weavers.[93] As a matter of fact, the lists were in the first instance submitted by the panchayats, which were as far as possible checked by the police, and then they were sent to the Branch Committee. The members of the Committees were required to make due enquiries personally before any advances were made. The Committee was always in a state of receiving any better plan for preparing the list. Despite of all the above evidences and instances, famine had not been officially declared in the district of Rajshahi till the mid-April of 1987, and the rules laid down were strictly applicable to tracts in which famine prevailed. Therefore, considerable confusion prevailed centering on the question that although the affected persons were entitled to State relief; but as famine had not been officially declared in this district; then they either might be left to die of starvation or be given some relief from the Charitable Fund. In these circumstances, it was decided that supports would be given to the distress people through the weekly distribution of dole of two *seers kachi*, or 1½ seers *paki*, which implied that they were to be provided with 'only two days' subsistence allowance, leaving them to pick the other five days' diet from private charity.'[94] It was resolved finally that this form of relief would be discontinued as soon as famine would be declared to prevail in this district. P Nolan was of the opinion that in the adjoining districts of Pabna and Rajshahi there were almost identical conditions in regard to the degree of deficiency in rainfall and of failure in crops. In Pabna, the number employed on the 30th April was 407 and the only difference between them was that charitable relief had been much more freely distributed in Rajshahi.[95] From 16th April to 30th April 1897 the total rainfall in Pabna was 1.99 inches and in Sirajganj was 2.37 inches.[96] W. Maude, the Collector of Pabna wrote to the Commissioner of the Rajshahi Division that the only standing crops in Pabna were *boro dhan, jali dhan* and sugarcane. *Jali* paddy was a later kind of *boro dhan* coming between that variety and the aus crop. It was more extensively cultivated in the Sadar subdivision than the regular *boro dhan* which was rare, except in some low *bil* lands whereas *jali* paddy was cultivated on char lands. There had been a good deal of cholera prevalent, especially in Pabna town and the Pabna, Dulai and Mathura *thanas*. There was also an unusual prevalence of fever and dysentery, and general sickness around Dasuria for which a compounder was sent out with medicines.[97] The Collector of the Rajshahi Division had asked for 5000 coolies in the Bogra railway which would be subsequently placed under the head of emigration.[98]

The Collector of Rajshahi argued that till the half-month of the May there had been good rainfall throughout the district and the table below shows the rainfall recorded in the several rain-registering stations in the district:

Table: 4.13

Rainfall at different places in Rajshahi till the month May, 1897

Stations	*Rainfall (inches)*
Boalia	2.35
Naugaon	2.69
Nator	1.77
Manda	2.02
Lalpur	1.16
Mahadebpur	1.32

Source: From N. K. Bose, EsQ., Collector of Rajshahi, to the Commissioner of the Rajshahi Division. – (No. 400G., dated Rampur Boalia, the 3rd May 1897), progs. no. 405-406, WBSA.

The Collector continued to state that on the 1st May there was a very smart shower at Boalia which had contributed to the improvement of the agricultural prospects considerably. *Boro* paddy for which some anxiety was being felt had been reported to be safe and the sowing of *aus* and *aman* paddy and jute was about to start.[99] Despite of these changing conditions the prevailing high price of rice had become however, a source of great anxiety. In several hats the prices had varied from 7½ to 8 seers per rupee and paddy was still being imported in the affected tracts from Panchupur side though in very small quantities.[100] The stocks had fallen low, and the import trade was turning gradually dull which inspired the grain dealers to begin importing Burma rice from Calcutta. This was equally known to the Government who believed that 'no doubt that they [grain dealers] [would] do so if the present high prices continue.'[101] The prices of labour had largely fluctuated in several places– prices were high in Naugaon and Nator, but low in all other parts of the districts. A large number of landless labourers were searching for work in the fields, as well as in the excavation of tanks; but owing to the high price of food grains, their earnings were insufficient to maintain them and their family. Though the condition of 'public health fortunately continues fairly good' but still 'incomplete' mortuary returns had been received for the month of April from certain *thanas*, which showed that the rate of mortality was higher than in the previous month. Cholera broke out in the Boalia town, and 50 deaths were reported.[102] Although as a result of the vigorous measures taken by the Municipality at the instance of the Civil Surgeon and the Magistrate, the disease had been stamped out but in the Baraigram *thana* cholera was said to be rather bad, and a necessity for Civil Hospital Assistant for this *thana* was strongly felt by the administration. It was reported that there was no immigration of famished people, but on the other hand the District Superintendent of Police reported that some people left Bagmara, Charghat and Puthia to obtain employment elsewhere beyond the district. The demand for coolies on the Bogra-Sultanpur Railway was widely circulated throughout the district, but it was not known that to what extent it helped the labourers since it was not informed that how many of the labourers had availed themselves of the opportunity.

The last return of May had showed 881 male units on the test-works and the number for the three weeks were 646, 503, and 566 respectively. Though there was no objection in allowing the full famine wage from the Collector but the fact was that the charitable relief at the cost of Government was almost nothing.[103] The death-rate was 3.47, against an average of 4.11 for the month of April. The *boro* crop estimate had been raised from 7 *annas* to 13 by the Collector, which was to be rose to 16 *annas* but the specific estimate after the personal enquiry conducted by the Deputy Collector, as it was anticipated would be 20 *annas*. The area sown this year was 116,600 acres among which more *aus* had been sown in 1897 than usual. Since the prospect of this crop was excellent, therefore the Commissioner 's view was that 'under the favourable circumstances of the season, not a seer of seed-grain or an acre of land would be left unutilized for want of advances.'[104] Bengal Government had tried to generalise the sufferings of the people of Bengal in relation with the other parts of India regarding the long prevalence of high prices. However, the government had surprisingly commented that Rajshahi was 'in the position of those districts which shared the common misfortune of the country at large, but where the prescribed test show[ed] that there [was] at present no famine.'[105] Raiyats had been left upon the mercy of the mahajans for lending money during the famine-time which frequently turned out as perilous problem for the raiyats. Although the raiyats of Bogra and Jalpaiguri had tried to obtain loans from the mahajan for the *aus dhan* and jute, but the mahajan had declined to lend money to the raiyats till the prospects of the crops could be settled.[106]

Report of the middle of the May had disappointedly demonstrated no material change in the generally bad condition of the affected tracts, excepting that rain had fallen and had slightly improved agricultural prospects. The recent rainfall had saved the *boro* paddy. Aus paddy had been very extensively sown, and everywhere it had germinated well. At the end of the last April and in the beginning of this half-month of May crowds of raiyats came into Boalia and informed that they had no seed-grain and no money, and they would not be able to get through the next two months unless grain was advanced to them.[107] It was noticed by the Collector that 'most of these applicants appeared to be well-to-do, wearing good cloths, carrying umbrellas, and presenting none of the appearances of want or privation [whose] object was apparently to make a profit for themselves.'[108] Prices have remained high throughout the month of May, in some places as high as 7 seers 4 *chitaks* per rupee. Babu Sasi Bhusan Dutt, Deputy Collector, reported some importations from the eastern *thanas* of this district and Dinajpur, and the Subdivisional Officer of Nator stated that Messrs. Watson and Company had imported about 6,000 maunds of paddy, yet there had been no importation of Burma rice in the district.[109] There was little doubt that the high price of rice was caused by the almost total cessation of importation. Although the Collector had observed improved agricultural prospects caused by the recent rainfall but there was undeniably a good deal of distress. The majority of the people were now living on only one full meal a day, and as far as the poor and destitute, this even was not always procurable by them. Though death-rate was reduced to some extent but it did not stop. The death rate per mile during the month of the April was 3.47 against 4.11 which was the average death-rate in April for five years (1892-96). The average daily numbers of labourers at work at different relief works were 385 at the Narad Khal, and 239 at the Bagha tank. The average daily number of labourers in the Mohunpur tank and Rahimpur tank was about 30.

Government seemed to be anxious not about the deaths caused by famine but about the reports which were sent by its servants. It was argued that 'the readiness with which the false report of three deaths from starvation was at first accepted is instructive.'[110] Being confident and assured by the enquiries of Mr. Bose who had 'properly caused a full enquiry' it was stated that:

> "Rajshahi may now be classed with the rest of this Division as distinctly outside the famine line (it was never within it, but doubts existed), although the people do and must suffer greatly from the prevalence of famine prices at a time when their means have been diminished by a partial failure of crops. This causes general and searching distress which in many cases reaches the point at which charitable relief is requested."[111]

For the district of Pabna P. Nolan, had remarked that the agricultural prospect seemed to be excellent, but there prevailed the marked rise in prices in some places to six seers a rupee, the appearances of women on the test works and the increased imports indicated that there was a great pressure. On the other hand the works attracted but a limited number of labourers, the highest figure was the attendance of 414 on the first day of the month of May and the lowest 172, on the 26th, after which it again rose to 262 on the last day of the month.[112] In the middle of April 1897, W. Maude, the Collector of Pabna had reported that there had been 'no rain during the fortnight' and there were no crops of importance 'except the *boro dhan*.'[113] The remarkable price-differences between rice and paddy in the district of Pabna had been attributed to the 'great variations due to the state of local supplies…'[114] In July, the number of affected people had increased due to the high prices of food-grain. The Collector of the Rajshahi district had stated that 'the number of paupers, especially of women and children, [had] very greatly increased, they [were] wandering about in search of food.'[115] There was also a 'steady stream of famished women and children into the town from the villages of the district.[116] Nolan was of the opinion that the adjoining districts of Pabna and Rajshahi had represented almost 'identical conditions' regarding the degree of deficiency of rainfall in crops.[117] For the districts of Rajshahi and Pabna the grants allotted from Government fund for the month of April were Rs. 10,000 and Rs. 1,000 respectively, for Pubna which had been paid as advances for village works under the modified rules of the Agriculturists' Land Improvement Loan Act.[118] The estimate for the district of Rajshahi under the head of relief works and gratuitous relief for the month of May 1897 was as follows:

Table: 4.14

Estimate of relief-works and cost in the district of Rajshahi

	Estimated daily number	*Estimated cost (Rs.)*
Relief works	2000	8125
Gratuitous Relief	500	1440
Establishment, tools and plant & etc.		1000
Total		10,565

Source: From M. Finucane, EsQ., the Secretary to the Government of Bengal, to the Commissioner of the Rajshahi Division. – (Agriculture. – No. 138 T.R/(Fam), dated Darjeeling, the 4th May 1897) [File No. 3-B/6.3.], progs. no. 29, *Proceedings of the Hon'ble the Lieutenant Governor of Bengal during August 1897* – Revenue Department. (Part I), WBSA.

The estimates under (1) and (2) demonstrated a grant of 'over Rs. 4 per head for the month for relief works, and nearly Rs. 3 per head for gratuitous relief' which the Lieutenant Governor regarded as 'very high' rates for men, women and children.[119] Mr. M. Finucane, the Secretary to the Government of Bengal had ordered an investigation to find 'an explanation showing why the estimate [was] so high, and why no part of the estimated expenditure [was] to be borne by the District Board.'[120]

In such a situation, the report of the Collector of Rajshahi on 2nd June had informed that there had been good showers of rain throughout the district. But he was equally aware of the fact that the general condition of the district, however, was still bad owing to the continued high prices of food-grain. The head-constable of Godagari police-station reported three cases of deaths from starvation.[121] Babu Upendra Chandra Mukerjee, Sub-Deputy Collector, was directed by the Collector to make a full enquiry which subsequently confirmed the police report as true incident. But still it was believed that the 'report was very meagre, and the enquiry was most perfunctory.' Babu Atul Chandra Ker, Deputy Collector was therefore deputed to make a searching enquiry on the spot and his report demonstrated that 'one of the deaths was due to chronic fever, the second case reported was the result of a boy aged about 7 years, the son of the man who was 30 *bighas* of land, 2 ploughs, 4 plough bullocks, 3 cows, 4 calves, 3 fowls, 12 or 14 brass bell-metal utensils.'[122] Thus it was conceived by the Deputy Collector that it was 'absurd to think such a man will allow his son to die of starvation.' According to Babu Atul Chandra Ker, the boy probably died of cholera after eating some raw mangoes with chillies. The third case was that of a baby of 18 months old. The family consists of father and mother and three other children who all looked healthy and well fed. The report, however, did not unfolded the 'truth' behind the deaths and there still prevailed a doubt that despite of their well-to-do conditions why these people had died. It was reported that there were no immigration and emigration of famished people worth noticing, but it was, however, stated that many persons in Charghat *thana* have left their homes to seek employment elsewhere.

The Collector of Pabna had stated that from 16th May to 31st May in Pabna total rainfall was 2.56 and in Sirajganj was 6.60 inches and for the whole month of May the rainfall in Pabna was 7.08 inches and in Sirajganj 10.59 inches, against a normal fall of 6.95 and 7.27 respectively.[123] Though this statistics have shown an increase rainfall than the normal rate, but this did not contribute to the lessening of the prices of rice in the district. The price of common rice was reported as follows:

Table: 4.15

Price of common rice in Pabna in May, 1897

Places	Prices(*pucka Seers*)
Pabna	8½
Dulai	7
Chatmohar	8
Mathura	7½
Sara	7
Faridpur	8
Ullapara	8
Kamarkhand	6½
Shahzadpur	6
Subgacha	6
Chohali	6¾
Taras	7½
Raiganj	9
Sirajganj	6½

Source: From W. Maude, EsQ., Collector of Pabna, to the Commissioner of the Rajshahi Division. –(No. 424G., dated Pabna, the 3rd June 1897), WBSA.

Therefore, it can be seen from the above table that prices were very high in all parts of the district of Pabna and only few seers of rice could be obtained for a rupee which dragged the poor people in the crisis of their livelihood. Instead of acknowledging the high prices, the Government was of the opinion that there had been 'a slight but general rise in the Sirajganj subdivision, while in the Sadar subdivision prices of common rice [were] stationary.'[124] The total amount of import in the district was 31,009 maunds and on the other hand the quantity of export from the district was 1,822 maunds. The death-rate returns from February to April 1897 for Pabna were as follows as compared with the average:

Table: 4.16

The death-rate returns from February to April 1897 for Pabna

Month	*1897*	*Average*
February	3.37	1.87
March	4.00	2.05
April	4.69	3.07

Source: From W. Maude, EsQ., Collector of Pabna, to the Commissioner of the Rajshahi Division. –(No. 424G., dated Pabna, the 3rd June 1897), WBSA.

The above table has shown a considerable increase in the death-rates during the months mentioned above from the average rates. Despite of that it was stated that the state of public health showed 'a marked improvement if one may judge by the police reports.' In addition to this there had been many returns of cholera and small-pox which shows a severe deterioration of public health conditions triggered by the drought and governmental callousness.

Test-works were, however, still continuing on at the Manikair tank, the Dasuria tank, and the Pokuria tank. A test-work was tried at Gunaigacha, but did not draw due to unkbnown reasons. The chief feature of the test-work of this time was the appearance from the commencement of it of women workers on the Manikair tank. These women generally carried out baling work which was very muddy and nasty work. Their appearance showed that how deep the distress was in this particular quarter. The Collector was 'confidently assured by many babus some months since that no pinch would ever induce the women of this district to come to a Government relief work.'[125] But the acute crisis had driven the women from their home and compelled them to do such works with which they were not accustomed neither they were suitable. On the other hand, this also demonstrated that how meagre was the knowledge of babus that they could not even sense the gravity of the condition prevailing in their areas and who lived in a state of oblivion about their surrounding world. On the other hand, it was revealed that the Collector ad sent an incorrect report regarding the average death-rate which was subsequently corrected by P. Nolan, Commissioner of the Rajshahi Division. Showing the 'correct' information Nolan started that 'The statement in Mr. Maude's fortnightly report was incorrect, and the mortality in Pabna, during the months referred to, really indicated the necessity for watchfulness.'[126]

The Lieutenant Governor had sanctioned a grant of Rs. 5,000 to meet the expenditure under the above mentioned three heads and in addition to that he also approved a grant of Rs. 9,000 for advances for village works in the districts of Rajshahi and Pabna during the month of May. For the district of Rajshahi an expenditure of 3,139 Rs. 9 annas 6 paisa had been incurred for relief works and gratuitous relief, including Rs. 382 -12-3, the cost of establishment, and that the entire cost had been met from the grants of Rs. 14,000 made by the District Board. At the end of May it was found that there was still a balance of Rs. 10,860 available from this grant for expenditure in May, the estimate for which is Rs. 10,565, and the Lieutenant Governor anticipated that the grant of Rs. 5,000 sanctioned from provincial revenues (in paragraph 2 of Government order No. 138 T.R./ Fam., dated the 4th May 1897) would not be required.[127] It was also reported that from the amount placed under the Agriculturists' Land Improvement Loan Act for the district of Rajshahi and Pabna only Rs. 1,850 had been advanced in the former district and nothing in the latter.[128] The estimates for June 1897 for the Rajshahi District were as follows:

	Rs.
Relief works	4,062
Gratuitous Relief	719

Establishment, tools, plant, &c. ——	500
Total ——————————————	5,281

It was directed that out of this amount Rs. 281 only would be provided from District Funds, and that the balance of Rs. 5,000 should be paid from Provincial revenues. Along with a grant of Rs. 3,000 for Rashahi for June under the head of advances for villages, the Lieutenant Governor had sanctioned a grant of Rs. 5,000 from the Government Funds on the pre-condition that the amount could not be met by contributions from the District Fund. On the other hand, the local banias were still continuing to hoard rice in their private stores which had led to the abnormal rise in prices in Rajshahi and paved the way for grain riots in Rampur-Boalia in June-July.[129]

For Pabna the estimates for June was as follows:

	Rs.
Relief works ——————————	4,500
Gratuitous Relief ————————	Nil.
Establishment, tools, plant, &c. ——	200
Total ——————————————	4,700

The above amount which had been sanctioned by the Lieutenant Governor was to be made from the District Funds.[130] However, the estimates which had been forwarded by Mr. E.M. Konstam, Under-Secretary to the Government of Bengal, Revenue Department to the Commissioner of the Rajshahi Division had included the expenditure on famine relief during August 1897 along with the statements of actual for the month of June where it was shown that the cost of giving doles to 500 persons daily was amounted to Rs. 1,500 and the cost for establishment, tools, and plant was Rs. 500.[131] The grant applied for from Government was Rs. 2,000 for the district of Rajshashi under the heads of gratuitous relief and establishments. tools, and plant etc. The weekly telegraphic reports for the first three weeks of the month of July regarding the test-works and gratuitous relief for Rajshahi were as follows:

Table: 4.17

Weekly report for the Rajshahi district for July, 1897

Weeks	*Test-workers*	*Gratuitous relief*
3rd July	405	——
10th July	Works closed	6,901 from the charitable fund
17th July	——	6,674 from the charitable fund

Source: From E.M. Konstam, EsQ., Under-Secretary to the Government of Bengal, Revenue Department, to the Commissioner of the Rajshahi Division. – (No. 1452 (Fam.), dated Calcutta, the 24th July 1897), WBSA.

It is to be noted here that the Government wanted to initiate an enquiry against the estimate for establishment and other expenditure for the district of Rajshahi which was Rs. 500 whereas 'the estimate under this head for the district of Pabna [was] only Rs. 250, against Rs. 4,700, the estimated cost of test-workers and gratuitous relief.'[132] But the fact was that the circumstances in terms of intensity of scarcity and number of populations were not identical for the two districts. The rainfall had been insufficient in the Pabna subdivision to allow transplantation of the *aman* to begin which had added a new difficulty in the existing state of crisis.[133] It was said to believe that since the residents of the Gangetic tract of Rajshahi were well-off than the average of Bengal in terms of wealth, therefore, the local workers of this tract and also the workers of Bogra and Pabna did not incline to work at the famine rate on 2 *annas* a day.[134] This tendency of 'sacrifice' was much prominent in Pabna, and at Sirajganj in Pabna, the workers and coolies were demanding for more wages despite of the fact that they had been paid at the 'high rate of four to five rupees per thousand cubic feet.'[135]

To meet the famine situation and to prevent such condition in coming days the Government of Bengal had placed a scheme of advances to the Land Revenue Department. It was stated that 'the proposed advances should be given freely in tracts declared by the District

Officer, with the sanction of the Commissioner, to be affected by scarcity or famine, care being taken to see that the works for which the advances [were] given [we]re really executed, and that the money advanced [was] not spent on purposes other than those for which it is advanced.'[136] For the maintenance and proper functioning of the scheme it was decided that the advances should be made in instalments, no further instalments would be made till the Government officers were satisfied that the sums already advanced had been properly spent. The works on which these advances were to spent should be directed towards relieving distress through the relief works, and for the increase supply of water for drinking and irrigation purposes for the needy people which would consist of tanks, wells, village reservoirs for the storage of water, and irrigation channels (pynes); and this work would have to be 'approved by local officers of Government.'[137] Another provision which was inflicted was that the labourers who were to be employed upon these works should not receive more than the maximum and never less than the minimum wage calculated according to the provisions of the Bengal Famine Code under the supervision of Circle Officer who would be 'able to regulate the wages paid on it and to see by periodical inspections that the condition as regards giving the minimum wage [was] fulfilled.[138] The Government of India had sanctioned not only the grant of these advances free of interest, but also the remission of a portion of the advance, representing the difference between the cost of executing the work in ordinary years and the increased cost entailed by the employment of famine labour. Since it was difficult to estimate the exact amount of this difference in each case, the Lieutenant Governor was of the opinion that 'if the work [was] completed to the satisfaction of the collector, one-third of the total amount advanced [would] be remitted.'[139] Citing the instance of a notification of 1873-74 Famine dated the 20th November 1873 which was published for relaxing temporarily some of the rules under the Land Improvement Act then in force (XXVI of 1871), the Lieutenant Governor had suggested that a similar notification should now be issued in order to modify the existing rules under the Land Improvement Loans Act. In addition to the above mentioned clauses the chief modifications of the Act were as follows:

> ".... (Rule 4.) – The Lieutenant Governor thinks that the limits upto which Collectors and Commissioners may sanction individual loans may, under the special circumstances of the case, be raised from Rs. 1,000 and Rs. 5,000 to Rs. 5,000 and Rs. 10,000, respectively....
>
> (Rules 9 and 10). - The Lieutenant Governor does not think it desirable that in the present case the maximum period for repayment of the advance should be ten years. It is sufficient to provide that the first instalment shall be paid by the end of February 1898, subsequent payments being made in equal half yearly instalments till the debt is discharged in five years from January 1898."[140]

The modified rules of the Land Improvement Loans Act, XIX of 1883, had issued the following provisions regarding the relief works for tracts affected by scarcity or famine which had come into existence from the 5th January 1897.–

> "....It will be in the power of the Commissioners to divide the sum so allotted among the Districts of their Divisions at their jurisdiction, and to transfer assignments from one district tom another, but expenditure in the Division must be kept within the amount assigned.
>
> ...subject to the provisions of these rules, the Collector may sanction loans not exceeding Rs. 5,000, provided the district allotment is not exceeded without the sanction of the Commissioner of the Division. Loans

exceeding Rs. 5,000 require the sanction of the commissioner, and exceeding Rs. 10,000, the sanction of the Board."[141]

Table: 4.18

Statement showing the net imports and exports (tons) of food-grains from January to September 1897 in Rajshahi Division [Net Import +] [Net Export -]

Districts	*January to March*	*April to June*	*July to September*	*Total*
Rajshahi	+ 5, 573	+5,084	+1,260	+11,917
Dinajpur	-7,920	-4,930	+23	-12,827
Jalpaiguri	+ 3,018	+5,148	+4,523	+12,699
Darjeeling	+1,793	+2,171	+1,965	+5,929
Rangpur	-408	+433	-889	-864
Bogra	-5,631	-4,632	+1,712	-8,551
Pabna	+3,894	+4,864	+702	+9,460

Source: T.W. Holderness, *Narrative of the Famine in India in 1896-97, Appdx VII.*

The figures for the districts have included the quantity of import and export done by only the rail borne traffic. The figures mentioned above have indicated the net figures, i.e., the imports have been deducted from the exports, or vice-versa. Since the imports of one district were the exports of another, therefore, no inference as to the gross volume of trade could be made by taking the aggregate totals. As the above table have included the figures of the districts which were engaged in the rail-born traffic of grains, so it can be said that by the end of the nineteenth century the districts of northern Bengal had already been connected with the railway networks that helped to import to and export from the districts of this part of Bengal. So far the import was concerned, the districts of Rajshahi, Jalpaiguri and Pabna had the largest amount of import, and on the hand the districts of Dinajpur and Bogra had witnessed largest export from the districts. This revealed that the famine condition was more intense and critical in the former districts and relief operations were largely carried out through the export of grains from the later districts to meet the necessity of former districts. In regards to the famine-condition of the district of Dinajpur, the Commissioner of the Rajshahi Division had asserted that '...Dinajpur itself and to the west there are dry tracts where the crop is only 4 annas to 6 annas, which will eventually feel the pinch.'[142]

It is to be noted here that despite of having a greater degree of import the district of Jalpaiguri did not receive much attention in the relief administration or official correspondence. In some of the codes viz. Bengal and others District Boards were deemed to form an integral part of the administration and to be the primary agency for coping with famine, to which object they might subordinate the ordinary objects and methods of their expenditure.[143] The position assigned to the chief revenue authority in .regard to famine relief administration did vary greatly in the different provinces. In Bengal and the North- Western Provinces the Board of Revenue finds no place. Regarding the detailed management of relief works, the prescriptions of the Bengal famine code were found as imperfect as those of the code of the North-Western Provinces. The code in recommending the grouping of the relief workers into gangs did not specify the size or composition of the gang, and its schedule of tasks proved to be unworkable.[144] But in a later development, the Indian Famine Commission of 1901 agreed with the 1898 Commission that 'a considerably low wage should be given on village works, because 'experience [showed] that people [could] live on less at home than elsewhere.'[145]

The famine of 1896-97 had been also attended by numerous cases of cholera in different parts of northern Bengal. Cholera usually became frequent when there was a scarcity of water. During the time of drought as a result of the absence ample source of water people were compelled to consume dirty and polluted water which caused severe cholera. Many parts of the districts of Rajshahi and Pabna were affected by serious cases of cholera which aggravated the overall condition of public health. Despite of prevalence of many cases of cholera, most surprisingly the year of 1897 had been declared as one of the comparatively 'healthy' year 'owing perhaps to short rainfall, which caused many of the shallower *bils* to dry up.'[146] The people of the district was generally depended on *bils*, ponds etc. for their regular water supply. Due to the shortage of rainfall when the regular source of water had been dried up then the people had to take any other source of water which was not properly maintained or got polluted. Moreover, during the hot weather tanks were either dried up or became very low and the water was polluted by the indiscriminate washing of cloths, house linen, and kitchen utensils and by the bathing of cattle as human being who frequently had to drink the same water. This tendency turned into practices during the prolonged season of drought which triggered the appearances of severe cases of cholera. The district of Pabna as a whole became unhealthy due to the long absence of inundation since 1871 when in a report 'the beneficial results of flushing by the rivers and the deterioration caused by their failure [had] long being recognized in this district.' Mr. W. V. G. Tyler, the Collector of Pabna in a report had argued that:

> "Within the districts [were] tracts, at places miles in extent, almost without a ryot, and there [had] been a time when they were as highly cultivated as the best tracts are now. These results were generally due to the simple cause that the rivers' inundations [had] ceased to extend so far.... When the river ceased to keep open the jolas and water courses, they became gradually choked up and all the hollows of the plain became an unhealthy plain. This breeds fever. The prosperity and energy of the ryots die[d] away, they allowed their own drinking water to become

> foul...sickness increase[d], cultivation decrease[d], and the small remnant [were] driven away by the wild beasts. This was happening...within a few miles of the Sadar station, as it had happened over and over again in the interior."[147]

The environmental transformations in terms of dying of river channels of the district had contributed in intensifying ecological vulnerability which was also responsible for the heightening of tensions of famine. The official discourse regarding the famine and relief had hardly looked into this sort of problem. Supplying of clean water in the drought-affected areas was not a part of governmental concern which only blamed the habits of the people of having polluted water. What appears more interesting in this situation was the Governmental refusal of acknowledging the actual conditions caused by cholera in the affected parts. For several occasions the Government had declared the public health condition as 'fairly good', without taking into consideration the prevalence of cholera in the district or it was observed that in a widespread attack of cholera only minimum initiatives had been under taken by the administration. Government was indifferent towards securing the supply of clean and hygienic source of drinking water, and as a result cholera made its repeated visits in a single famine year which proved disastrous for the health of the poor and distressed who were already suffering from starvation, malnutrition and absence of any proper medical care or treatment. The death-rate in the 1896-97 famine was quite high in comparison with the previous 1873-74 famine. Deaths were caused by starvation and disease viz. cholera, influenza etc. But Government in no occasion had admitted the fact that death were caused by the starvation or failure of obtaining food either from the market or through the relief operations. It was projected either as health problem or any other causes. This showed that relief administration was not successful in rescuing the people from starvation and death. Till the end of the nineteenth century communication and transport remained a major problem which acted as serious impediment in the organization and circulation of relief operations. The interior areas were still going on without any relief or assistance that could resist the poor people from deaths. Moreover, the reports collected and sent by the district officials were in many cases not only incomplete or contradictory but even generated much confusion in the official circles which misguided the relief operations in the affected areas. In several occasions, the estimates and account of food-movement, crop failure, and death-rates sent by the Collector or Deputy Collector proved to be unreliable by the Commissioners or Secretaries who had to but rely on the reports of the formers. Police reports could not even provide the actual truth regarding the famine conditions prevailed in different *thanas* or police stations. Thus the whole set of ground level administrative machinery sometime became a source of misconception which ultimately misguided the famine administration.

The government, in the middle of May 1897, had ordered not to issue any new loans under the Land Improvement Loans Act, as 'some of the instalments in several cases' had fallen due.[148]

The zamindars and local landlords had contributed in the famine charitable relief fund. The members of the Rajshahi District Committee, both Indians and Europeans had provided subscriptions. However, the local zaminards and landlords, the Ranis had contributed the highest amount of subscription in the district charitable relief.

Table: 4.19

Subscriptions by the Rajshahi District Committee of the Indian Famine Charitable Relief Fund (Bengal Branch), 1900

Name	*Amount of subscriptions*
Raja Pramada Nath Roy of Dighapatia	3,000
Rani Hemanta Kumari Devi	1,000
Maharaja Jagadindra Nath Roy	1,000

Rani Syama Sundari & Uma Sundari Chaudhurani	600
Raja Shashi Sekhareswar Rai Bahadur	500
Rani Mon Mohini Devi	500
Kumar Saradindu Roy	500
J. Fraser Forbes	250
R. S. Greenshields	200
A.F. Steinberg	200
Rai Kedar Prasanna Lahiri Bahadur	200
Kumar Bahadur of Dubalhati	160

Source: Annexure E., Indian Famine Charitable Relief Fund. Bengal Fund. Bengal Branch, Report of the operations of the Bengal Branch of the Indian Famine Charitable Relief Fund, 1900.Calcutta, 1901. IOR/V/27/830/53: 1901.

In the Dinajpur District Committee, Maharaja Bahadur of Dinajpur and Rai Radha Govinda Rai Saheb had contributed subscription of Rs. 500 each, and Srimati Hari Mani Debya had contributed Rs. 200.[149] Raja Pramada Nath Roy of Dighapatia of Rajshahi had alone contributed Rs. 3000; Rani Hemanta Kumari Devi, Maharaja Jagadindra Nath Roy, both from Rajshahi, had provided subscriptions of Rs. 1000 each; and other local landlords and rich people of the District had also donated cash to the District Relief Committee.[150]

Table: 4.20

Subscriptions received by the District Relief Committees of Rajshahi Division (extracted)

District Relief Committees	*Amount of subscriptions received (in Rs.)*
Rajshahi District Committee	9,014
Dinajpur District Committee	4,732
Jalpaiguri District Committee	3,830
Darjeeling District Committee	11,580
Rangpur District Committee	14,286
Bogra District Committee	4,688
Pabna District Committee	3,639

Source: Annexure E., Indian Famine Charitable Relief Fund. Bengal Fund. Bengal Branch, Report of the operations of the Bengal Branch of the Indian Famine Charitable Relief Fund, 1900.Calcutta, 1901. IOR/V/27/830/53: 1901.

According to another estimate, Raja Pramada Nath Rai of Dighputhia had contributed a subscription of Rs. 5000 to the district relief committee.[151] However, the district relief committees of the districts of Darjeeling, Rangpur, Jalpaiguri, Pabna and Bogra had received considerable amount of subscription from the local zamindars, landlords and wealthy people. It is evident from the above table that the District Relief Committee of Rangpur had received highest amount of subscriptions than the other committees, which reflected the severe prevalence of 1896-97 in the district.

So far the public works in southern India as a means of relief measures for the victims were concerned, Roy argues that in 1896-97, the government, introduced an 'elaborate classification of suitable tasks' that ranges from Class A (stone-breakers) to E (child helpers).[152]

II. Crops and Scarcities in North Bengal (1908—09)

The district of Dinajpur was again visited by a scarcity during the autumn of 1908-09. Although the rainfall in 1908-09 was normal in May, and both the jute and *bhadoi* crops were good, but it did not continue for long because a prolonged draught persisted in June, July and August.[153] As a result the *bhadoi* was spoiled and jute did not turn well due to the lack of steeping water. The continuous drought severely affected the main crop of Dinajpur – winter rice. The almost total absent of rain made it impossible for transplanting of paddy seeds for most parts of the district. The rain in September was too late to save the crop and the result was a total loss of winter rice in the *thanas* of Pirganj, Hemtabad, Raiganj, Itahar, and Ghoraghat, and there was widespread loss in all over the Balurghat subdivision and also in parts of Thakurgaon and Birganj.[154] The rabi crops which were to be followed later was also in a state of total failure except in Kaliyaganj and Gangarampur, where a small crop of chillies was obtained. In the district of Rangpur, the scarcity of 1908-09 was like what was in 1873-74. The scarcity of 1908-09 was felt in the *khiyar* tract of the district of Rangpur and its adjacent parts. This was caused by the partial failure of rain in 1907 and 1908. The hard *khiyar* soil which was found chiefly in the *thanas* of Govindganj, Pirganj, and Mithapukur, was capable of producing only one good crop namely, the winter rice but as there were no system of irrigation in these tracts so people had to solely rely on the rainfall.[155] Although there was a dire necessity of heavy rain in July and August for the betterment of rice crop but this was in total absence in both 1907 and 1908. The outturn of the winter *aman* rice was much below the normal in the rest of Rangpur and in other parts of the province the price of rice rose in February 1908 to 7¼ seers per rupee which remained same till the July when, at cost of the failure of the monsoon rain, it started to rise again and in September the price reached its maximum limit - 5¾ seers.[156] This situation had continued till December 1908, when the price fell to 7 seers per rupee and remained stagnant at that figure throughout 1909, till a good crop of *aman* had contributed to the lessening of prices to 11 seers in January 1910. The *barind* tract of the district of Rajshahi had been also suffered by scarcity in 1908-09 caused by the deficient rainfall which led to a partial failure of the *aman* crop.[157]

In the district of Dinajpur, the real distress was not due to so much of a shortage of stocks in the market, which were 'ample', nor to high prices, but rather to the inability of the people to buy food owing to lack of money and the contraction of credit. Because, as it was reported by the Collector of the District, the total loss of one season's crop could not ordinarily cause a famine or even a serious distress in the district for the fact that people had 'become thriftless and extravagant.'[158] The shortage of money was caused by the fact that in the previous year when the price of paddy suddenly rose up with remarkable rapidity to the unprecedented figure of Rs. 3-12-0 per maund, the cultivators had hurriedly sold their entire stocks and in some cases, even seed grain. The shortage was remarkably present in the *pali* areas which was nearer to the railway exposition and where recurrent crops being possible the raiyats had larger stocks.[159] It was not, however, stated that since the raiyats had received extra money for selling their crops then why in the next year they did not have any money to spend for buying food. When the scarcity was apprehended in the *khiyar* tracts a famine programme had been commenced there, but the greatest distress was prominent in the *pali* area. Although in comparison with the 1873-74 famine, the scarcity of 1908-09 had been regarded as less severe but it should be noted here that the smallness of the affect was due to the shortness of the duration of the scarcity. It was argued that the scarcity was met by the governmental relief and by the 'general increase in prosperity among the agricultural classes resulting from the high prices for produce obtained in recent years,' and by the 'improved communications and better organization of trade which enabled rice to be exported from Burdwan, Buckergunj, and Burma into the district.'[160] The famine of 1908-09 in the district of Dinajpur had been declared by the administration as 'a money famine.'[161]

In Rangpur, in order to meet the distress, large quantities were imported by merchants through the nearest railway stations, viz. Mohimganj and Panchbibi and a great part of the imported rice was imported from Burma.[162] People were, however, did not show much inclination in accepting this imported rice due to its coarse quality. Although the distress had extended to many places but relief measures were confined to an area of about 40 square miles around the village of Kamdia and Govindganj *thana*. Rangpur District Board had spent Rs. 12,000 on repairing the roads in this area and Rs. 15,000on the excavation 15 tanks which eventually provided works to the able-bodied men and women.[163] A considerable amount of money had been collected through public subscription for the distribution of gratuitous relief to the old and infirm, and to women and children with a definite belief that starvation did not cause any loss of life, yet it triggered the process of migration of people into the other parts of the district.[164] Apart from this, loans of about Rs. 1,20,000 were distributed under the

Agriculturists Loan's Act of 1884 which coupled with the 'improved state of district, inter-district and railway-communications' had contributed in the rapid recovery of the district from the scarcity.[165] In the districts of Rajshahi, test works were opened and agricultural loans were also distributed. But no other relief measures were carried out in the affected tracts of the district.[166]

From the above discussion it can be said that the 1896-97 famine in North Bengal had sought for a greater and serious intervention on the part of the colonial administration in conducting relief in this region. However, the nature of public response towards governmental measures were not always uniform in all parts of North Bengal. The chief feature of the relief operations in 1896-97 was the participation and involvement of the district relief committees. Though the district committees had played a crucial role towards the official functioning of the governmental relief, the performances of these committees were not always adequate and timely. Several native landlords and zamindars had contributed cash as donations to these relief committees. Public health conditions were also declining during the famine years due to the prevalence of disease and epidemics. The famine condition which was caused by the shortage of rainfall and colonial administrative policies were further aggravated due to the absence of any artificial system of irrigation in the large agricultural tracts of North Bengal.

REFERENCES

1. Report of the Indian Famine Commission 1898, Simla: Government Central Printing Office, 1898, p. 196.
2. Tirthankar Roy, *Natural Disasters and Indian History,* New Delhi: Oxford University Press, 2014, p. 53.
3. Ibid.
4. Romesh Dutt, *Indian Famines: Their Causes and Prevention,* Westminster: P. S. King & Son, p. 2.
5. E. A. Gait, *Census of India, vol. VI: Part I, the Report,* Calcutta: Bengal Secretariat Press, 1902, p. 12.

6. *Ibid.*
7. *Report on the Administration of the Indian Famine Charitable Relief Fund in Bengal, 1898*, p. 7.
8. *Ibid.*
9. Malavika Chakrabarty, *Famine of 1896-97 in Bengal: The Availability or Entitlement Crisis*, Orient Blackswan, New Delhi, 2004, p. 296.
10. C. E. Buckland, *Bengal under the Lieutenant Governors: A Narrative of the Principal Events and Public Measures during Their Periods of Office from 1854 to 1898*, Vol. II, S. K. Lahiri & Co., Calcutta, 1901, p. 988.
11. *Ibid.*
12. Malavika Chakrabarty, *op. cit.*, p. 304 and 305.
13. For details see Lance Brennan, Les Heathcote, and Anton Lucas, 'The Causation of Famine: A Comparative Analyses of Lombok and Bengal, 1891–1974,' South Asia, Vol. 7, no. 1 (1984): 1–26.
14. C. E. Buckland, *op. cit.*, vol. II, p. 990.
15. Report of the Indian Famine Commission, 1898, p. 65.
16. T. W. Holderness, *Narrative of the Famine in India in 1896-97*, Government Central Printing Office, Simla, 1897, p. 1.
17. No. 618 Met., dated Darjeeling, the 18th September 1896, in Selection of Papers Relating to the Famine of 1896-97 in Bengal, vol.1, W 835. IOL, British Library.
18. From P. Nolan, the Commissioner of the Rajshahi Division, to the Secretary to the Government of Bengal, Revenue Department, No. 442 M., dated Jalpaiguri, the 1st December 1896, in in *Selection of Papers Relating to the Famine of 1896-97 in Bengal,* vol.2, W 835. IOL, British Library.
19. From J. H. Lea, the Collector of Pabna, to the Commissioner of the Rajshahi Division, No. 1430G., dated Pabna, the 16th November 1896, in *Ibid.*
20. *Ibid.*
21. The Collector informed that in all the major marts of the Sirajganj subdivision, including Sirajganj bazar, there were not more than 10,000 to 12,000 maunds of rice or paddy, against the usual stock of 40,000 to 50,000 maunds. *Selection of papers relating to the famine of 1896-97 in Bengal.* Revenue Department, Bengal, vol. II (Nov – Dec 1896), IOR/V/27/830/38.

22. N. K. Bose, the Collector of Rajshahi to the Commissioner of the Rajshahi Division, No. 1606G., dated Rampur Boalia, the 17th November 1896, in Selection of Papers Relating to the Famine of 1896-97 in Bengal, vol.2, W 835. IOL, British Library.
23. N. K. Bose, the Collector of Rajshahi to the Commissioner of the Rajshahi Division, No. 3052G., dated Boalia, the 8th Mach 1897, in Selection of papers relating to the famine of 1896-97 in Bengal. Revenue Department, Bengal, vol. VI (March– April 1897), IOR/V/27/830/42.
24. P. Nolan, the Commissioner of the Rajshahi Division, to the Secretary to the Government of Bengal, Revenue Department, No. 794 Met., dated Camp Rampur Boalia, the 14th December 1896, in Ibid.
25. From Lieut-Colonel, A. Evans-Gordon, Deputy Commissioner of Jalpaiguri, to the Commissioner of the Rajshahi Division, No. 2197G., dated Camp Barodighi, the 9th December 1896, in Selection of papers relating to the famine of 1896-97 in Bengal. Revenue Department, Bengal, vol. II (Nov – Dec 1896), IOR/V/27/830/38.
26. From Lieut-Colonel, A. Evans-Gordon, Deputy Commissioner of Jalpaiguri, to the Commissioner of the Rajshahi Division, No. 2428G., dated Camp Alipur Duars, the 11th/13th January 1897, in Selection of papers relating to the famine of 1896-97 in Bengal. Revenue Department, Bengal, vol. III (Dec. 1896– Jan. 1897), IOR/V/27/830/39.
27. No. 8 M/R C.T., dated Camp Bilmaria, the 22nd December 1896, in *Ibid.*
28. No. 8 M/R C.T., dated Camp Bilmaria, the 22nd December 1896, in *Ibid.*
29. *Ibid.*
30. *Ibid.*
31. Commissioner's remark on the Rajshahi Report, under section 13 of the Famine Code, for the half month ending 15th June 1897, in Selection of papers relating to the famine of 1896-97 in Bengal. Revenue Department, Bengal, vol. IX (June – July 1897), IOR/V/27/830/45.
32. *Ibid.*
33. From Lieut-Colonel, A. Evans-Gordon, Deputy Commissioner of Jalpaiguri, to the Commissioner of the Rajshahi Division, No. 2197G., dated Camp Barodighi, the 9th December 1896,

in Selection of Papers Relating to the Famine of 1896-97 in Bengal, vol.2, W 835. IOL, British Library.

34. Report on the Administration of the Indian Famine Charitable Relief Fund in Bengal, 1898, p. 9.

35. From U. C. Batabyal, the Collector of Bogra to the Commissioner of the Rajshahi Division, No. 1092G., dated Camp Dhunot, 13th/14th January 1897, in Selection of Papers Relating to the Famine of 1896-97 in Bengal, vol.3, W 835. IOL, British Library.

36. 'One hundred and forty-two applications for loans under the Agriculturists' Loans Act were received, and Rs. 1,991 were lent to the applicants in 27 cases.' J. N. Gupta, *District Gazetteers of Eastern Bengal and Assam: Bogra,* p. 78.

37. L. S. S. O'Malley, *Bengal District Gazetteers: Murshidabad,* Bengal Secretariat Book Depot, Calcutta, 1914, p. 112.

38. In 1896 there was an early cessation of the rains, and due to prevalence of low rivers a small portion of the Kalantar was flooded which was resulted in an almost complete failure of the rice crop over a portion of the Kalantar and a partial failure in the Barh. Due to this rain, the outturn of winter rice in the Karh was about 9 annas, but the average outturn for the district did not exceed 7 annas. *Ibid.*

39. *Ibid.*, p. 113.

40. The closing of several of the silk filatures in the Barwa and Bharatpur thanas also deprived numbers of labourers of employment at a time when it was most needed. *Ibid.*

41. During the end of July when the prospects of the *aus* crop seemed good the relief operations were gradually relaxed and by the end of August when the new *aus* came into the market, prices began to fall, and the Government found it necessary to discontinue the relief works. Ibid.

42. *Ibid.*, p. 114.

43. The average rainfall for the district was only 4 annas. L. S. S. O'Malley, *Bengal District Gazetteers: Rajshahi,* p. 91.

44. *Ibid.*

45. The Collector of the district had estimated the outturn of the aus paddy as 8 annas and for aman paddy as $6^2/_3$ annas – viz., 2 to 4 annas in the Gangetic tract, 6 to 8 annas in the Barind, and 8 to 12 annas in the Barind area. The Commissioner

had provided a different account of the outturn – 4 annas for the Gangetic tract, 8 annas for the Barind, and 12 annas for the Bils. *Ibid.*

46. Malabika Chakrabarti, *op. cit.*, p. 387.

47. L. S. S. O'Malley, *Bengal District Gazetteers: Rajshahi,* p. 91.

48. *Ibid.*, p. 92.

49. *Ibid.*

50. (No. 125Met., dated Darjeeling, the 16th April 1897), progs. no. 26-27, Proceedings of the Hon'ble the Lieutenant Governor of Bengal during August 1897– Revenue Department. (Part I), WBSA.

51. Resolution on the Rajshahi Report, under the section 13 of the Famine Code, for the half-month ending on the 17th April 1897. Memorandum by P. Nolan, EsQ., Commissioner of the Rajshahi Division. – (No. 88Met., dated Darjeeling, the 22nd April 1897), progs no. 391-392, File No. 2-S/11 – 13, Proceedings of the Hon'ble the Lieutenant Governor of Bengal during August 1897– Revenue Department. (Part II), WBSA.

52. *Ibid.*

53. *Ibid.*

54. From N. K. Bose., EsQ., Collector of Rajshahi, to the Commissioner of the Rajshahi Division. – (No. 228G., dated Rampur Boalia, the 19th April 1897), Proceedings of the Hon'ble the Lieutenant Governor of Bengal during August 1897– Revenue Department. (Part II), WBSA.

55. *Ibid.*

56. *Ibid.*

57. Malabika Chakrabarti, *op. cit.*, pp. 314-315.

58. Vinita Damodaran, 'Gender, Forests and Famine in 19th-Century Chotanagpur, India;' *Indian Journal of Gender Studies,* 9:2, 2002, p. 139.

59. Bina Agarwal, 'Gender, Environment, and Poverty Interlinks: Regional Variations and Temporal Shifts in Rural India, 1971-1991,' in Mahesh Rangarajan and K. Sivaramakrishnan (eds.), *India's Environmental History, Vol. 2: Colonialism, Modernity, and the Nation,* Permanent Black, Ranikhet, 2014, pp. 460-461.

60. Selection of papers relating to the famine of 1896-97 in Bengal. Revenue Department, Bengal, vol. IX (June – July 1897), IOR/ V/27/830/45.

61. *Ibid.*
62. Women health was also an important issue in analysing the issues on infant mortality which was chiefly relied on 'prenatal exposure' and 'postnatal exposure', when the former depends on 'maternal nutritional stress and associated material infections' whereas the later is related with the 'infants' own nutritional deficiency, poor care etc.' For details see Arup Maharatna, 'Infant and Child Mortality during Famines in Late 19th and Early 20th Century India,' *Economic and Political Weekly,* Vol. 31, No. 27 (Jul. 6, 1996), pp. 1774-1775.
63. *Report on the Administration of the Indian Famine Charitable Relief Fund in Bengal, 1898,* p. 21.
64. 3,385 persons had received grain doles for an average period of 8 months, and 700 families received relief through the cheap grain shops. *Ibid.*, p. 22.
65. From M. Finucane, the Secretary to the Government of Bengal, to the Secretary to the Government of India, Revenue and Agricultural Department, in Selection of papers relating to the famine of 1896-97 in Bengal. Revenue Department, Bengal, vol. VII (April - May 1897), IOR/V/27/830/43.
66. [Proceedings No. 431-432.] Commissioner's remark on the Pabna Famine Report under section 13 of the Code for the fortnight ending on the 15th July 1897, Proceedings of the Hon'ble the Lieutenant Governor of Bengal during August 1897– Revenue Department. (Part III), WBSA.
67. From C. A. Radice, EsQ., Officiating Collector of Pabna, to the Commissioner of the Rajshahi Division. (No. 730G., dated Pabna, the 18th July 1897), Proceedings of the Hon'ble the Lieutenant Governor of Bengal during August 1897– Revenue Department. (Part III), WBSA.
68. *Ibid.*
69. *Ibid.*
70. *Ibid.*
71. Vinita Damodaran, *Gender, Forest and Famine...,* pp. 154-155.
72. Malabika Chakrabarti, *op. cit.*, pp. 389-390.
73. *Ibid.*, p. 390.
74. From W. Maude, EsQ., the Collector of Pabna to the Commissioner of the Rajshahi Division, dated Pabna, the 19th April 1897), progs. no. 393-94, Proceedings of the Hon'ble

the Lieutenant Governor of Bengal during August 1897– Revenue Department. (Part II), WBSA.

75. *Ibid.*

76. R. W. Carlyle, 'Famine Administration in a Bengal District in 1896-7,' *The Economic Journal,* Vol. 10, No. 39 (Sep., 1900), p. 425.

77. From M. Finucane, EsQ., Secretary to the Government of Bengal, Revenue Department, to the Commissioner of the Rajshahi Division. – (No. 75T.R. – Fam., dated Darjeeling, the 29th April 1897), progs. no. 395, Proceedings of the Hon'ble the Lieutenant Governor of Bengal during August 1897– Revenue Department. (Part. II), WBSA.

78. *Ibid.*

79. *Ibid.*

80. From the Hon'ble A. M. Bose., President of the Indian Association, to the Secretary of the Government of Bengal, Revenue Department. – (No. 28., dated Calcutta, the 24th April 1897), progs. no. 396, Proceedings of the Hon'ble the Lieutenant Governor of Bengal during August 1897– Revenue Department. (Part II), WBSA.

81. From Rai Raj Kumar Sarvadhikary, Bahadur, Secretary, British Indian Association, to the Secretary of the Government of Bengal, Revenue Department. – (No. 251, dated Calcutta, the 14th May 1897), progs no. 397-98, Proceedings of the Hon'ble the Lieutenant Governor of Bengal during August 1897– Revenue Department. (Part II), WBSA.

82. C. A. Radice, the Collector of Pabna to the Commissioner of the Rajshahi Division, No. 628G., dated Pabna, the 4th July 1897, in Selection of papers relating to the famine of 1896-97 in Bengal. Revenue Department, Bengal, vol. IX (June – July 1897), IOR/V/27/830/45.

83. From W. Maude, EsQ., I.C.S., Collector of Pabna, to the Commissioner of the Rajshahi Division. – (No. 334G., dated Pabna, the 18th May 1897), progs. no. 399-400, Proceedings of the Hon'ble the Lieutenant Governor of Bengal during August 1897– Revenue Department. (Part II), WBSA.

84. *Ibid.*

85. *Ibid.*

86. From E.N. Baker, EsQ., C.S., Honorary Secretary, Bengal Branch, Indian Famine Charitable Relief Fund, to the Commissioner of the Rajshahi Division. – (No. 314, dated Calcutta, the 31st March 1897), Proceedings of the Hon'ble the Lieutenant Governor of Bengal during August 1897– Revenue Department. (Part II), WBSA.

87. Ibid.

88. Ibid.

89. Ibid.

90. In November 1896, the *mahajans* had increased prices through the exportation of large stocks in Pabna, Bogra, the Santal Parganas, Hazaribagh and Singhbhum, but on the other hand in Cuttack, Puri and north Bihar majajans had retain their stocks 'in the hope of a further price rice.' Malabika Chakrabarti, *op. cit.*, p. 359.

91. *Ibid.*

92. From E. N. Baker, EsQ., C.S., Honorary Secretary, Bengal Branch, Indian Famine Charitable Relief Fund, to the Commissioner of the Rajshahi Division. – (No. 314, dated Calcutta, the 31st March 1897).

93. From N. K. Bose, EsQ., Magistrate of Rajshahi, to the Commissioner of the Rajshahi Division. – (No. 190J., dated Boalia, the 30th April 1897), Proceedings of the Hon'ble the Lieutenant Governor of Bengal during August 1897– Revenue Department. (Part II), WBSA.

94. *Ibid.*

95. Commissioner's resolution on the Pabna report under section 13 of the Famine Code for the fortnight ending 30th April 1897, progs. no. 403-404, Proceedings of the Hon'ble the Lieutenant Governor of Bengal during August 1897– Revenue Department. (Part II), WBSA.

96. From W. Maude, EsQ., Collector of Pabna, to the Commissioner of the Rajshahi Division. (No. 245G., dated Pabna, the 3rd May 1897), Proceedings of the Hon'ble the Lieutenant Governor of Bengal during August 1897– Revenue Department. (Part II), WBSA.

97. *Ibid.*

98. Resolution on the Rajshahi Report, under section 13 of the Famine code, for the half-month ending on the 17th April

1897, in Selection of papers relating to the famine of 1896-97 in Bengal. Revenue Department, Bengal, vol. VII (April - May 1897), IOR/V/27/830/43.

99. From N. K. Bose, EsQ., Collector of Rajshahi, to the Commissioner of the Rajshahi Division. – (No. 400G., dated Rampur Boalia, the 3rd May 1897), progs. no. 405-406, Proceedings of the Hon'ble the Lieutenant Governor of Bengal during August 1897– Revenue Department. (Part II), WBSA.

100. *Ibid.*

101. *Ibid.*

102. *Ibid.*

103. Commissioner's remarks on the Rajshahi Report under section 13 of the Famine Code, for the fortnight ending the 15th May 1897, progs no. 407-408, Proceedings of the Hon'ble the Lieutenant Governor of Bengal during August 1897– Revenue Department. (Part II), WBSA.

104. Ibid.

105. Ibid.

106. Malavika Chakrabarty, *op. cit.*, p. 350.

107. From N. K. Bose, EsQ., Collector of Rajshahi, to the Commissioner of the Rajshahi Division. – (No. 586G., dated Rampur Boalia, the 17th May 1897), Proceedings of the Hon'ble the Lieutenant Governor of Bengal during August 1897– Revenue Department. (Part II), WBSA.

108. *Ibid.*

109. *Ibid.*

110. Commissioner's resolution on the Rajshahi Report under section 13 of the Famine Code, for the fortnight ending the 31st May 1897, progs no. 412-413, Proceedings of the Hon'ble the Lieutenant Governor of Bengal during August 1897– Revenue Department. (Part II), WBSA.

111. *Ibid.*

112. Commissioner's remark on the report under section 13 of the Famine Code from the Collector of Pabna District for the fortnight ending the 31st May 1897, progs. no. 414-415, Proceedings of the Hon'ble the Lieutenant Governor of Bengal during August 1897– Revenue Department. (Part II), WBSA.

113. From W. Maude, the Collector of Pabna, to the Commissioner of the Rajshahi Division, dated Pabna, 19th April 1897, in

Selection of papers relating to the famine of 1896-97 in Bengal. Revenue Department, Bengal, vol. VII (April - May 1897), IOR/V/27/830/43.

114. *Ibid*.

115. N. K. Bose, the Collector of Rajshahi to the Commissioner of the Rajshahi Division, No. 1131G., dated Rampur Boalia, the 17th July 1897, in Selection of papers relating to the famine of 1896-97 in Bengal. Revenue Department, Bengal, vol. X (July - August 1897), IOR/V/27/830/46.

116. *Ibid*.

117. Commissioner's resolution on the Pabna report under section 13 of the Famine Code for the fortnight ending 30th April 1897, in Selection of papers relating to the famine of 1896-97 in Bengal. Revenue Department, Bengal, vol. VII (April - May 1897), IOR/V/27/830/43.

118. From M. Finucane, EsQ., the Secretary to the Government of Bengal, to the Commissioner of the Rajshahi Division. – (Agriculture. – No. 138 T.R/(Fam), dated Darjeeling, the 4th May 1897) [File No. 3-B/6.3.], progs. no. 29, Proceedings of the Hon'ble the Lieutenant Governor of Bengal during August 1897– Revenue Department. (Part I), WBSA.

119. *Ibid*.

120. *Ibid*.

121. From N. K. Bose, EsQ., Collector of Rajshahi to the Commissioner of the Rajshahi Division. – (No. 754G., dated Rampur Boalia, the 2nd June 1897), Proceedings of the Hon'ble the Lieutenant Governor of Bengal during August 1897– Revenue Department. (Part II), WBSA.

122. *Ibid*.

123. From W. Maude, EsQ., Collector of Pabna, to the Commissioner of the Rajshahi Division. – (No. 424G., dated Pabna, the 3rd June 1897.), Proceedings of the Hon'ble the Lieutenant Governor of Bengal during August 1897– Revenue Department. (Part II), WBSA.

124. *Ibid*.

125. *Ibid*.

126. The 'correct' figures for column 3 of the statement regarding the average death-rate, as started by Nolan, would be February - 1.98, March – 2.35, April, 3.65, May, 2.70. From P. Nolan, EsQ., Commissioner of the Rajshahi Division, to the Secretary

to the Government of Bengal, Revenue Department. (No. 574Met., dated Darjeeling, the 30th June 1897), progs. no. 417-418, Proceedings of the Hon'ble the Lieutenant Governor of Bengal during August 1897– Revenue Department. (Part II), WBSA.

127. From M. Finucane, EsQ., Secretary to the Government of Bengal, to the Commissioner of the Rajshahi Division. – (Agriculture – No. 461 T. R. / Fam., dated Darjeeling, the 31st May 1897), progs. no. 34, Proceedings of the Hon'ble the Lieutenant Governor of Bengal during August 1897– Revenue Department. (Part I), WBSA.

128. *Ibid.*

129. Malavika Chakrabarti, *op. cit.*, p. 433.

130. Since 'the estimated average cost of relieving each individual appear[ed] to be high, being in the case of relief workers equal to the maximum wage laid down in the Famine Code [therefore] in future the estimates should be framed on the basis of the numbers of individuals, men, women, and children, to be relieved, as [was] done in other Divisions.' From M. Finucane, EsQ., Secretary to the Government of Bengal, to the Commissioner of the Rajshahi Division. – (Agriculture – No. 461 T. R. / Fam., dated Darjeeling, the 31st May 1897), progs. no. 34, WBSA.

131. (No. 1452 (Fam.), dated Calcutta, the 24th July 1897, progs. no. 40, Proceedings of the Hon'ble the Lieutenant Governor of Bengal during August 1897– Revenue Department. (Part I), WBSA.

132. *Ibid.*

133. From C. A. Radice, EsQ., Officiating Collector of Pabna, to the Commissioner of the Rajshahi Division. (No. 730G., dated Pabna, the 18th July 1897), WBSA.

134. Malavika Chakrabarty, *op. cit.*, p. 381.

135. *Ibid.*

136. From M. Finucane, EsQ., Secretary to the Government of Bengal, to the Secretary to the Board of Revenue, Land Revenue Department. – (Agriculture – No. 5610 Agri., dated Calcutta, the 31st December 1896), progs. no. 42-43, Proceedings of the Hon'ble the Lieutenant Governor of Bengal during August 1897– Revenue Department. (Part I), WBSA.

137. In Bihar for digging tanks acre should be taken especially

from the areas which were selected and approved by the officers of Government with due regard to level, so that it might be possible to connect those tanks with rivers by pynes or channels, and thus to open them flushed with water when required, and so made permanently useful for purposes of irrigation and consequent prevention or mitigation of future scarcities from drought. *Ibid.*

138. *Ibid.*

139. In order to solve this problem, the Lieutenant Governor had followed the precedent of 1873-74, when Government agreed to defray up to one-third of the cost of village relief works (paragraph 70, page 131, Part III of the Report of the Indian Famine Commission). *Ibid.*

140. *Ibid.*

141. Notification No. 69, Modified Rules under the Land Improvement Loans Act, XIX of 1883, for tracts affected by scarcity or famine, progs no. 46, File No. 3A/9-5, Proceedings of the Hon'ble the Lieutenant Governor of Bengal during August 1897 – Revenue Department. (Part I), WBSA.

142. From P. Nolan, the Commissioner of the Rajshahi Division, to the Secretary to the Government of Bengal, Revenue Department, in Selection of papers relating to the famine of 1896-97 in Bengal. Revenue Department, Bengal, vol. IV (Jan. – Feb. 1897), IOR/V/27/830/40.

143. *Report of the Indian Famine Commission, 1898*, p. 47.

144. *Ibid.*, p. 67.

145. *Report of the India Famine Commission 1901*, Office of the Superintendent of Government Printing, 1901, p. 44.

146. L. S. S. O'Malley, *Bengal District Gazetteer: Rajshahi*, p. 67.

147. L. S. S. O'Malley, *Bengal District Gazetteers: Pabna*, pp. 39-40.

148. From N. K. Bose, the Collector of Rajshahi District, to the Commissioner of the Rajshahi Division, No. 586G., dated Rampur Boalia, the 17th May 1897, in Selection of papers relating to the famine of 1896-97 in Bengal. Revenue Department, Bengal, vol. VIII (May - June 1897), IOR/V/27/830/44.

149. Annexure E., Indian Famine Charitable Relief Fund. Bengal Fund. Bengal Branch, Report of the operations of the Bengal Branch of the Indian Famine Charitable Relief Fund, 1900.Calcutta, 1901. IOR/V/27/830/53: 1901.

150. *Ibid.*
151. *Report on the Administration of the Indian Famine Charitable Relief Fund in Bengal, 1898,* p. 13.
152. Tirthankar Roy, *op. cit.,* p. 61.
153. F. W. Strong, *op. cit.,* p. 67.
154. *Ibid.*
155. J. A. Vas, *op. cit.,* p. 72.
156. *Ibid.*
157. L. S. S. O'Malley, Bengal District Gazeetteer: Rajshahi, p. 92.
158. F. W. Strong, *op. cit.,* p. 67.
159. In the khiar tracts where the raiyats had practically only one crop (winter rice) to depend on, the sales were not so extensive, and even where stocks had been sold the money was not wasted. However, the circumstances were different in the *pali* area where, the raiyats with their extreme seriousness invested all their money and as a result the subsequent coming failure of successive crops left them without food-grain or money. *Ibid.*
160. *Ibid.,* p. 68.
161. *Ibid.*
162. J. A. Vas, *op. cit.,* p. 72.
163. *Ibid.,* pp. 72-73.
164. *Ibid.,* p. 73.
165. Since 1871 the increasing necessity of the improvement of the communication system was surfaced on the official circle in order to efficiently meet the agricultural distress. The improvement in the roads and railway communication, it was anticipated, would 'facilitate both import of food supplies and migration.' People were, however, criticized on account of not having the 'habits of thrift and Postal Savings Banka and Co-operative Credit Societies. *Ibid.*
166. L. S. S. O'Malley, *Bengal District Gazetteer: Rajshahi,* p. 92.

Conclusion

The Bengal famine of 1770 took a heavy toll of life and nearly a third of the population was perished in this famine. During the period of 1870-1910, as Mike Davis has argued, more than thirty million famine related deaths were occurred in British India, and this phenomenon has been considered by him as the "Late Victorian Holocaust".[1] Sugata Bose has remarked that since the establishment of colonial rule in Bengal and the great famine of 1770 to the post-colonial conditions of widespread endemic malnutrition and hunger poses all the conceptual problems of an agrarian society depending on a subsistence base which in course of time increasingly got connected to wider economic systems including a capitalist world market.[2] Hence, natural or ecological dislocations and their subsequent impact on the economy or production system during the colonial period were not confined only to the concerned regions, this had demonstrated an eclectic characteristic formed by their ultimate link with the broader world economic structure which was dominated by the British colonialism. It is evident from the analysis of the above famines that the colonized people had never been recognized beyond their minimum subsistence level and even though, during the time of scarcities the administration's concern was only to restore that minimum level, but public health and over-all well-being of the people was never a concern for them. Although the causation of famine had been chiefly and regularly attributed to the shortage of rainfall, the problem of irrigation or its practical absence was neither a part of relief operations nor public-works for the administration. The contradictory official reports sometime hindered the formulation of relief policy. On the other hand, despite of prevalence of widespread distress, the official pronouncement regarding the commencement of 'famine' came too late to introduce any timely organization of relief measures. Hence, the relief measures were bound to be a temporary solution for the victims instead of having any long-term development plan that could protect the famine affected areas from such future disasters.

Rainfall played a very crucial role in the occurrence of the 1873-74 famine. From the above analysis of district-wise study of rainfall during the later-half of 1873 and first part of 1874, it can be noticed that rainfall had been a major environmental reason behind the occurrence of the famine. However, there is no doubt that the colonial policy of import and export of food-grain to mitigate the disaster had a mixed impact upon the distressed people of this region. Though George Campbell had suggested for the 'prohibition of export', he was not supported by his own government and export continued even during the famine years. However, Campbell's insistence on prohibition of export, according to Bender, had reflected 'an element of British control over the impact of crop failure in India.'[3] It is very important to note here that though the government did not issue any ban on export from the affected tracts, only the amount of import had been shown by the government as part of their relief measures. Thus, the system of simultaneous inflow and outflow of grain from the affected areas to the outside areas or vice-versa was not successful enough to meet the situation. Bender further argues that 'the events of 1873-74 reflect the corrupt practices and/or alarmist tendencies of government officials.'[4]

The colonial government, from the very outset, had expressed its incapability to deal with the severity of famine and sought assistance from the local landlords and zamindars. The amount of grain and cash which were distributed by the Government as advance for the relief to the distressed had been obtained through the zamindars who were entrusted to realize the advance on behalf of the government. On the other hand, the government had to depend on the local zamindars and rich people who could help the administration by importing grain at their own cost and providing public works such as, repair of roads, digging tanks and works in the railway tracts etc. for the victims. The zamindars, as highlighted in the official reports, had neither forced the peasants to pay their rent nor put any pressure to realize the advances made by them during the famines years; whereas the government was pro-active in realizing the advances from the zamindars who paid to their tenants on behalf of the government. Thus, a considerable portion of relief works in the 1873-74 famine had been conducted by the local zamindars and landlords who were directed to relieve the burden of relief from the shoulder of the government. The zamindars, in many cases, had provided great assistance to the Government officers and to the people. In 1873-74, expansion of canal and railway lines were two major means of employment for the labourers who had been provided with minimum wages in order to survive in the famine-years. Though several canal and railway extension projects, like Gunduk canal, Sone Canal and North Bengal State Railway had been undertaken, the North Bengal State Railway had received the lowest numbers of labourers than the other areas. Despite of repeated official attempts, there was hardly any improvement in the numbers of labouers in the railway-works. This reflected that till 1873-74, railways were not used by the government to distribute relief in the districts of North Bengal. River traffic and rural transport had remained the main medium of grain transportation.

Another important feature of the relief operations was the participation of women and children in the government and private relief works during the advancement of the famine. This participation of women and children had displayed a very critical condition of the households which were suffering from acute shortage of food grain. It is argued that the 1873-74 famine had not been attended with any large-scale mortality. Mike Davis, who criticizes the colonial state for its imbalanced famine policies, argues that the 1873-74 famine 'was the only truly successful British relief effort in the nineteenth century and might have been celebrated as a template for dealing with future emergencies.'[5] Relief works of the 1896-97 famine had also included a large number of women and children, which showed the growing intensity of the famine in North Bengal.[6] Famines were attended by serious outbreak and diseases. The famine of 1770 had become more severe and deadly after the outbreak of small-pox which alone killed thousands of lives. The subsequent famines had also witnessed serious health issues. The famine of 1896-97 in Bengal was accompanied with numerous cases of cholera in different parts of Bengal. Due to the scarcity of water during the shortage of rainfall people used to consume polluted water from their old sources. Several tanks were opened as part of test-relief works during the period of drought without taking into notice that shortage of rainfall would not fill the tanks with water. The problem of drinking water thus continued for a long time which caused cholera and other diseases. The deteriorating condition of food-habit during the famine years had aggravated this tendency. Thus, public health become a serious issue for the colonial administration to deal with. However, in reality, the colonial government did not pay adequate attention to this problem and as a result the outbreak of diseases which was started with the commencement of famine had taken the shape of epidemics in course of time. In regards to the demographic implications of the famines, Roy argues that the famines which had occurred during the late-nineteenth century had 'killed their victims directly by making food unaffordable and indirectly by exposing the vulnerable population to epidemic outbreaks.'[7]

Though in all cases famines had been examined through the perspectives of entitlement, drought, ecology, market, subsistence and colonialism, there are certain continuities and changes between the approaches on nineteenth and twentieth century famines. The devaluation of currency that began in 1873 and continued over the next twenty years increased not only the burden of Home Charges but also heightened the demand for compensation from the British officers in India. The principal sources of revenue, at the time, were land revenue, excise, salt tax, stamps and opium. The burden of all these taxes fell on the rural classes in general and the poorer classes in particular.[8] At the beginning of the twentieth century, the British government had considered the necessity to prevent recurrence of famines 'by moderating the Land Tax, extending irrigation works, and relieving as far as possible the annual burdensome drain on the financial resources of India'.[9] The 'remedies' which were adopted by the British administration were too late to alleviate the condition of the poorer classes because by that time widespread famines and hunger had swept across the country. Thus, human survival and subsistence became a subject of State's relief and private charity. Agriculture had suffered the worst fate. The famines had transformed the arable land into deserted lands which provided a serious blow to the overall agricultural production system. Historians have traced the relationships between the process of commercialization of agriculture, which was driven by international market-economy, and the Indian famines, which were partially caused by changing pattern of crop production that was further instigated further by overseas demands. According to Bhatia, the impact of this commercialization was felt in the recurrence of famines in India. Bhatia argues that the famines that 'took a heavy toll of life among the poor were caused by a variety of factors of which the principal ones were the growing proletarianization of the rural society and impoverishment of the rural masses.'[10] Landless agricultural labourers and rural artisans, Bhatia further argues, were the chief 'victims of the famine ravages.'[11]

Apart from the seasonal migrations, natural calamities had generated sometime large-scale migration or displacement of population from the affected areas to the non-affected areas that had altered not only the existed demographic scenario of the affected region but to a great extent changed the population profile of the neighbouring or distant regions. This process resulted in the creation of new lands of habitation one the one hand, and the desertion of old settlements on the other. The desertion of agricultural lands in the post-famine period had greatly influenced the agricultural production and livelihood pattern as a whole. Displacement of the sufferers had affected their rights on property and belongings which had been left on the mercy and mutual arbitration between the nature and human on the one hand and the market, State and society on the other hand. It can be observed from the above discussion that the study has shown a changing relationship between the environment, political economy and socio-economic pattern of a particular region namely northern Bengal, as a case study, where recurrence of droughts, famines and scarcities during the late-nineteenth century had introduced and developed a complex scenario of changing livelihood which was further influenced by the changing dialogue between the state, market, production and social agencies. The multiple frontiers of suffering of people caused by the famines and successive human effort to control the recovery and relief is not only a part of environmental or socio-economic research, rather it formed the basis of the historical transformation of the region as a whole, that was re-constructed and transformed by the natural disasters in many ways.

The second half of the nineteenth century in North Bengal had witnessed the emergence of a new type of relief policies along with other parts of Bengal. The famine relief operations during 1873-74 and 1896-97 had reflected new pattern of administrative and private involvement which was different from the previous famine-relief operations. Roy argues that the 'contents of famine policy changed not due to a change in mindset. Rather it evolved in the course of a progressively better understanding of the way failure of rains developed into full-blown famines.'[12] The famine relief policies which were adopted by the colonial state had redefined the relationships between the ecology, state and market, which were all critical to the minimum maintenance of subsistence level for the poorer classes of the society. Roy, most interestingly, comments that 'lawlessness, breakdown of cooperation, and anarchic markets meant that one life saved would be another life lost.'[13]

So far the regional variations of famine was concerned, North Bengal had reflected certain distinctive characteristics in terms of rainfall, crop-production, market and relief. Despite of being a fertile region for cultivation this region had to suffer from a series of famines and scarcities. There is no doubt that rainfall had been the most important element for cultivation during the second half of the nineteenth century, but the hostile market, the ineffectiveness of the state to control the private trade and above all the colonial taxation policy had brought the poor people to the threshold of subsistence crisis and starvation. There were several instances of small-scale scarcities in different parts of North Bengal during the second half of the nineteenth century and first decade of the twentieth century. These scarcities till date do not receive any adequate historical consideration despite of the fact that these can be essential to examine the issues of drought, market and subsistence-crisis in a very small area. The ecological dimensions of the famines, especially in North Bengal, remain a crucial issue due to the existence of a large number of aboriginal populations which included several tribes and castes.

The book has tried to reassert the dynamics of sufferings and vulnerability of the people of colonial North Bengal where issues of rainfall, drought, crop-failure and subsistence crisis had appeared in a distinctive form than the other regions of undivided Bengal. The agrarian society of North Bengal had witnessed the development of a complex relationship between the state, market and people during the time of scarcities which had brought new challenges to the survival and continuation of pre-existing norms of social cooperation and economic dependence. The recovery of the famine-victims had been affected by the imbalances between import and export of food-grains which was further caused by a sharp competition between the rate of success of governmental relief and the artificial increase of prices of food grains. Thus, the condition of market during and after the calamities had been very crucial for the recovery of the people of North Bengal. Though the present study provides much emphasis on the relationship between rainfall, crop failure and price-rise; the nature of response and involvement of the state in the relief-works had explored a new dimension of famine-relief which remains very critical for the region like, North Bengal where agrarian class structure and land-holding patterns were different from the rest of Bengal. The governmental apathy (/rigidity) towards the banning of remission of revenue during the famine years had inflicted additional burden upon the poor peasants who were left at the mercy of the state and private charity. The policy of mere controlling the import-export ratio had revealed that the government had paid little attention to the develop the communication system and agrarian infrastructure in North Bengal. The slow and negligible growth of modern communication system, like roadways and railways, had hindered the success of famine-relief in North Bengal, and that is why famine conditions prevailed for a longer time. Thus, the period between 1866 and 1909 has a larger significance in the history of colonial North Bengal where social and economic life of the poor people had been greatly influenced by ecological dislocations and the political economy of the colonial state.

REFERENCES

1. Mike Davis, *Late Victorian Holocausts: El Nino Famines and the Making of the Third World,* Verso, London, 2001.
2. Sugata Bose, *op. cit.*, p. 4.
3. Jill Bender, 'The Imperial Politics of Famine: The 1873–74 Bengal Famine and Irish Parliamentary Nationalism', Éire-Ireland, Volume 42:1&2, Spring/Summer 2007, p. 144.
4. *Ibid.*
5. Mike Davis, *op. cit.*, p.

6. For a detail analysis on gender aspects of famine of 1896-97, see Tirthankar Ghosh, 'Ecology, Gender and Social Crises: North Bengal in 1896-97 Famine,' in *Contemporary Voice of Dalits*. (forthcoming)
7. Tirthankar Roy, *Natural Disasters and Indian History*, New Delhi: Oxford University Press, 2014, p. 56.
8. B. M. Bhatia, *Famines in India: A Study in Some Aspects of the Economic History of India, 1860-1945*, Asia Publishing House, Bombay, 1968, p. 22.
9. Romesh Dutt, *Indian Famines: Their Causes and Prevention*, London: P. S. King & Son, 1901, p. 2.
10. B. M. Bhatia, 'Famine and Agricultural Labour in India: A Historical Perspective', *Indian Journal of Industrial Relations*, Apr., 1975, Vol. 10, No. 4 (Apr., 1975), pp. 575-576.
11. *Ibid*.
12. Tirthankar Roy, *Natural Disasters and Indian History*, p. 70.
13. *Ibid*.

Bibliography

1. Primary Sources

I. Unpublished Government Records

(A) Asian and African Studies, British Library, London

India Office Records and Private Papers

Remarks of Government on the report of the Commission appointed to enquire into the circumstances connected with the famine in Orissa and other parts of Bengal in 1866, with other papers relating to the famine, IOR/L/PJ/3/1100 No.99: Mar 1867-Jul 1867. Letters. Bengal famine, Mss Eur F86/121: Unspecified Papers.

Bengal famine, Mss Eur F86/125: 1873-1874.

Bengal famine papers, Mss Eur F86/126: 1873-1874.

Papers. Bengal famine, Mss Eur F86/127: 1874.

Narrative. Bengal famine, Mss Eur F86/131: 1873-1874.

Journal. Bengal famine, Mss Eur F86/132: 1874.

Bengal famine correspondence, Mss Eur F86/133: 1873-1874.

Correspondence between the Government of India and the Secretary of State in Council relative to the Famine in Bengal, Part I, Her Majesty's Stationary Office, London, 1874.

Offprints of articles by Sir George Campbell on famine administration, anthropology and land tenure. Also report of House of Lords debate on the Bengal famine, from The Mail, Apr 27, 1874. Mss Eur E349/17: 1874-1886.

Minute by the Hon'ble Sir Richard Temple, K. C. S. I., Lieutenant Governor of Bengal, dated the 31st October 1874, MSS EUR F486/21.

Temple, Sir Richard, [Minute on the famine in Bengal and Behar in 1873-74, dated 31 October 1874], IOR/V/27/830/35: 1874.

Correspondence relating to the famine in Bengal and Behar from October 1873 to 31 May 1874. Calcutta 1874, IOR/V/27/830/33: 1874.

Famine Minutes. Bengal, Mss Eur F86/129: 1874.

Selection of papers relating to the famine of 1896-97 in Bengal. Revenue Department, Bengal, vol. I (Oct. – Nov 1896), IOR/V/27/830/37.

Selection of Papers relating to the Famine 1896-97 in Bengal, Revenue Department, Bengal, vol. II (Nov – Dec 1896), IOR/V/27/830/38.

Selection of papers relating to the famine of 1896-97 in Bengal. Revenue Department, Bengal, vol. III (Dec. 1896 – Jan. 1897), IOR/V/27/830/39.

Selection of papers relating to the famine of 1896-97 in Bengal. Revenue Department, Bengal, vol. IV (Jan. – Feb. 1897), IOR/V/27/830/40.

Selection of papers relating to the famine of 1896-97 in Bengal. Revenue Department, Bengal, vol. VI (March – April 1897), IOR/V/27/830/42.

Selection of papers relating to the famine of 1896-97 in Bengal. Revenue Department, Bengal, vol. VII (April - May 1897), IOR/V/27/830/43.

Selection of papers relating to the famine of 1896-97 in Bengal. Revenue Department, Bengal, vol. VIII (May - June 1897), IOR/V/27/830/44.

Selection of papers relating to the famine of 1896-97 in Bengal. Revenue Department, Bengal, vol. IX (June – July 1897), IOR/V/27/830/45.

Selection of papers relating to the famine of 1896-97 in Bengal. Revenue Department, Bengal, vol. X (July - August 1897), IOR/V/27/830/46.

Selection of papers relating to the famine of 1896-97 in Bengal. Revenue Department, Bengal, vol. XII (Sept. 1897 – March 1898), IOR/V/27/830/48.

Indian Famine Charitable Relief Fund. Bengal Fund. Bengal Branch, Report of the operations of the Bengal Branch of the Indian Famine Charitable Relief Fund, 1900. Calcutta, 1901. IOR/V/27/830/53.

Selection of papers relating to the famine of 1896-97 in Bengal, Vol. 1, Vol. 2, and Vol. 3, Shelfmark: W 835. IOL.

(B) West Bengal State Archives, Kolkata

Files of the Department of Agriculture, Commerce and Land, Bengal.

Annual Reports on Agriculture, Rainfall, Land Settlements, Production and Distribution, Weather, Crops and Land Revenues of Bengal (1860-1943)

Proceedings of the Lieutenant-Governor of Bengal. Scarcity and Relief department, Calcutta, January 1875, West Bengal State Archives

Proceedings of the Lieutenant Governor of Bengal. General Department (Land Revenue Branch, Industry and Science Branch – Meteorological Records), and Medical Department.

Files of Government of Bengal. Revenue Department, Revenue Department –Land Revenue Branch, Famine Branch, Miscellaneous Branch.

Proceedings of the Hon'ble the Lieutenant Governor of Bengal during August 1897 – Revenue Department, Part I, Part II, and Part III.

Proceedings of the Government of Bengal. Revenue Department (Agriculture Branch. Famine Relief, Famine Statement, Weather and Crop Report.1909-16.

II. Published Primary Sources, Government Publications and Reports (Selected)

(A) Bengal District Gazetteers:

Dash, Arthur Jules., *Bengal District Gazetteer: Darjeeling*, Bengal Government Press, Alipore, 1947.

Grunning, John F., *Eastern Bengal and Assam District Gazetteers: Jalpaiguri*, Pioneer Press, Allahabad, 1911.

Gupta, J. N., *District Gazetteers of Eastern Bengal and Assam: Bogra*, Pioneer Press, Allahabad, 1910.

Lambourn, G. E., *Bengal Districts Gazetteers*: *Malda*, The Bengal Secretariat Book Depot, Calcutta, 1918.

Mazumdar, Durgadas., *West Bengal District Gazetteer: Koch Behar*, Calcutta, 1977.

O'Malley, L. S. S., *Bengal District Gazetteers: Darjeeling*, Bengal Secretariat Book Depot, Calcutta, 1907.

Bengal District Gazetteers: Murshidabad, Bengal Secretariat Book Depot, Calcutta, 1914.

Bengal District Gazetteers: Rajshahi, Bengal Secretariat Book Depot, Calcutta, 1916.

Bengal District Gazetteers: Pabna, The Bengal Secretariat Book Depot, Calcutta, 1923.

Strong, F. W., *Eastern Bengal District Gazetteers: Dinajpur*, Pioneer Press, Allahabad, 1912.

Vas, J. A., *Eastern Bengal and Assam District Gazetteer: Rangpur*, Pioneer Press, Allahabad, 1911.

(C) Census, Reports and other Official Publications.

A Fortnight in the Famine Country of Bengal, March 1874, Serampore Press, Serampore, 1874.

Annual Report of the Department of Land Records and Agriculture for the year ending 30th September 1891, Calcutta, 1892.

*Annual Administration Report of the State of Cooch Behar for the year*1878-79, 1880-81, 1884-85, 1887-88, 1893-94.

Bagchi, Amiya Kumar and BandopadhyayArun (eds.), *Documents on Economic History of British Rule in India, 1858-1947: Eastern India in the Late Nineteenth Century, Part I: 1860s-1870s* (New Delhi, 2009) and *Part II: 1880s-1890s*, Manohar, New Delhi, 2011.

Buchanan-Hamilton, Francis, *A Geographical, Statistical and Historical Description (1908) of the District, A Zillah of Dinajpur in the Province, or Soubah of Bengal*, Calcutta, 1883.

Buckland, C. E., *Bengal under the Lieutenant Governors: A Narrative of the Principal Events and Public Measures during Their Periods of Office from 1854 to 1898, Vol. I & Vol. II* , S. K. Lahiri & Co., Calcutta, 1901.

Campbell, A., 'On the Tribes around Darjeeling,' *Transactions of the Ethnological Society of London*, Vol. 7, No. (1869).

Chaudhury, Harendra Narayan, *The Cooch Behar State and its Land Revenue Settlements*, Cooch Behar State Press, Cooch Behar, 1903.

Dalton, E. T., *Descriptive Ethnology of Bengal*, Calcutta, 1872.

Dass, Gopal Chandra., *Report of the Statistics of Rangpur for the year, 1872-73*, Calcutta, 1874.

Famine Inquiry Commission Report on Bengal, 1878-80, 1898, 1900.

First Annual Report of the Sanitary Commissioner for Bengal for 1868, Calcutta, 1869.

Gait, E. A., *Census of India, 1901 Vol. VI Part I: The Report*, Bengal Secretariat Press, Calcutta, 1902.

Gregg, Surg. Maj. W. H., *Twenty-second Annual Report of the Sanitary Commissioner for Bengal, 1889*, Calcutta, 1890.

Holderness, T. W. (1897). *Narrative of the famine in India in 1896-97*, Simla: Government Central Printing Office.

Hunter, W. W., *The Annals of Rural Bengal*, New York: Leypold and Holt, 1868.

Famine Aspects of Bengal Districts, Trubner & CO., London, 1874.

A Statistical Account of Bengal, Vol. VII: Districts of Malda, Dinajpur and Rangpur;

Vol. VIII: Districts of Rajshahi and Bogra;

Vol. IX: Districts of Murshidadbad and Pabna; and

Vol. X: Districts of Darjiling, and Jalpaiguri and State of Kuch Behar (Trubner & Co., London, 1876)

MacDonnell, A. P., *Report on the Food Grain Supply and Statistical Review of the Relief Operations in the Distressed Districts of Behar and Bengal During the famine of 1873-74*, Calcutta, 1876.

O'Malley, L. S. S., *Census of India 1911, Vol. V: Bengal, Bihar and Orissa and Sikkim, Part I – Report*, Bengal Secretariat Book Depot, Calcutta, 1913.

Thompson, W. H., *Census of India, 1921 Vol. V Bengal, Part II – Tables*, Bengal Secretariat Book Depot, Calcutta, 1923.

(D) Memoirs, Diaries and Travelogues

George Campbell, 'The Famines which affected Bengal in the last Century,' in *Further Report on the Famine in Bengal and Orissa in 1866 with Appendices*, 1867.

Memoirs of My Indian Career, Vol. I & II, Macmillan, London, 1893.

Temple, Richard., *Men and Events of my Time in India*, London, 1882.

The Story of my Life in 2 *vols*., London, 1890 and 1896.

2. Secondary Sources

I. Books

Arnold, David, *Famine: Social crisis and historical change*, Oxford: Basil Blackwell Ltd, 1988.

'Hunger in the Garden of Plenty: The Bengal Famine of 1770, in Alessa Johns,' *Dreadful Visitations: Confronting Natural Catastrophe in the Age of Enlightenment*, London and New York: Routledge, 2013, pp. 81-112.

Bhatta, Braja Bandhu., *The Natural Calamities in Orissa in 19th century*, New Delhi: Commonwealth Publishers, 1997.

Blyn, George., *Agricultural Trends in India, 1891-1947: Output, Availability and Productivity*, Philadelphia: University of California Press, 1966.

Bose, Sugata. *Peasant Labour and Colonial Capital: Rural Bengal since 1770*. Cambridge: Cambridge University Press. (digital version), 2008.

Agrarian Bengal: Economy, Social Structure and Politics, 1919-1947, Cambridge: Cambridge University Press, (digital version), 2008.

Chakrabarty, Malavika. Famine of 1896-97 in Bengal: The availability or entitlement crisis, New Delhi: Orient Blackswan, 2004.

Chandra, A. N., *The Sannyasi Rebellion*, Calcutta: Ratna Prakashan, 1977.

Chattopadhyay, Haraprasad., *Internal Migration in India: A Case Study of Bengal*, K. P. Bagchi & Co., Calcutta, 1987, pp. 80-81.

Chaudhury, B., 'Eastern India', in Daharma Kumar (ed.), *The Cambridge Economic History of India, Vol. II: c. 1757-2003*, New Delhi: Orient Blackswan, 2008.

Chaudhury, Nani Gopal., *Cartier: Governor of Bengal, 1769-1772*, Calcutta: Firma K. L. Mukhopadhyay, 1960.

Damodaran, Vinita., Famine in a forest tract: Ecological change and the causes of the 1897 famine in Chotanagpur, Northern India,' in Arun Bandopadhyay (ed.), *Nature Knowledge and Development: Critical Essays on the Environmental History of India*, New Delhi: Primus Books, 2016, pp. 09-142.

'The East India Company, Famine and Ecological Conditions in Eighteenth-Century Bengal', in Vinita Damodaran et el (eds.), *The East India Company and the Natural World,* Palgrave Macmillan, 2015, pp. 80-101.

Das Gupta, Sanjukta. Accessing nature: Agrarian change, forest laws and their impact on an adivasi economy in colonial India,' in Arun Bandopadhyay (ed.), *Nature Knowledge and Development: Critical Essays on the Environmental History of India*, New Delhi: Primus Books, 2016, pp. 81-108.

Datta, Rajat., *Society, Economy and the Market: Commercialization in Rural Bengal, C.1760-1800,* New Delhi: Manohar, 2000.

'Subsistence Crisis and Economic History: A Study of Eighteenth Century Bengal,' in Ayesha Mukherjee (ed.), *A Cultural History of Famine Food Security and the Environment in India and Britain*, London and New York: Routledge, 2019, pp. 38-39.

Davis, Mike. *Late Victorian holocausts: El nino famines and the making of the Third World*, New York: Verso, 2002.

Dhir, Anil and Mohapatra, Ramesh Chandra (eds.), *The Great Orissa Famine 1866 (Na'anka Durbhikshya)*, Bhubneswar: Amadeus Press, 2017.

Dutt, Romesh., *Indian Famines: Their Causes and Prevention*, P. S. King & Son, London, 1901.

Fiske, John., *The Unseen World, and Other Essays*, Boston and Cambridge: Houghton, Mifflin and Company ,1876 (tenth edition).

Forrest, G. W., *The Famine in India*, Horace Cox, London, 1897.

Gadgil, Madhav and Guha, Ramchandra, *This Fissured Land: An Ecological History of India*, New Delhi: Oxford University Press, first published 1992, thirteenth impression, 2010.

Ghose, Hemendra Prasad., *The Famine of 1770*, Calcutta: The Book Company Limited, no date.

Ghosh, Jamini Mohan., *Sannyasi and Fakir Raiders in Bengal*, Calcutta: Bengal Secretariat Book Depot, 1930.

Hall-Mathews, David. *Peasants, famines and the state in colonial western India*, New York: Palgrave Macmillan, 2005.

Hughes, J. Donald. 'What Does Environmental History Teach?' In Angela Mendonca, Ana Cunha & Ranjan Chakrabarty (Eds), *Natural Resources, Sustainability and Humanity: A*

Comprehensive View, Springer: New York, 2012, pp. 1-15.

Loveday, A., *The History and Economics of Indian Famines*, London: G Bell and Sons Ltd., 1914.

Majumdar, S. C., *Rivers of the Bengal Delta*, University of Calcutta, Calcutta, 1942.

Mann, Michael., 'Forestry and Famine in the Chambal-Jamna Doab, 1879-1919,' in Mahesh Rangarajan and K. Sivaramakrishnan (eds.), *India's Environmental History, Vol. 2: Colonialism, Modernity, and the Nation*, Permanent Black, Ranikhet, 2014.

McMinn, C. W., *Famines: Truths, Half-Truths, Untruths*, Calcutta, 1902.

Ray, Ratnalekha., *Change in Bengal Agrarian Society, c.1760-1850*, New Delhi: Manohar, 1979.

Roy, Tirthankar. (2014), *Natural Disasters and Indian history*, New Delhi: Oxford University Press. (first published 2012).

The Economic History of India, 1857-1947, New Delhi: Oxford University Press. (second edition, third impression), 2009.

Scott, J. E., *In Famine Land: Observations and Experiences in India during the Great Drought Of 1899-1900*, New York and London: Harper Brothers and Publishers, 1904.

Sen, Amartya. *Poverty and famines: An essay on entitlement and deprivation*, New Delhi: Oxford University Press. (first published 1981), 2007.

Sen, Asoke and Others, *Perspective in Social Science Vol.2: Three Studies on the Agrarian Structure in Bengal, 1850-1947*, Calcutta, 1982.

Sinha, Narendra Krishna., *The Economic History of Bengal: From Plassey to the Permanent Settlement, Vol. II*, Calcutta: Firma K. L. Mukhopadhyay, 1960.

II. Journal Articles

Agarwal, Bina., 'Gender, Environment, and Poverty Interlinks: Regional Variations and Temporal Shifts in Rural India, 1971-1991,' in Mahesh Rangarajan and K. Sivaramakrishnan (eds.), *India's Environmental History, Vol. 2: Colonialism, Modernity, and the Nation*, Permanent Black, Ranikhet, 2014.

Ambirajan, S., 'Malthusian Population Theory and Indian Famine Policy in the Nineteenth Century', *Population Studies*, Vol. 30, No. 1 (Mar., 1976), pp. 5-14.

Bender, Jill., 'The Imperial Politics of Famine: The 1873–74 Bengal Famine and Irish Parliamentary Nationalism,' *Éire-Ireland*, Volume 42:1&2, Spring/Summer 2007, pp. 132-156.

Bhatia, B. M., 'Famine and Agricultural Labour in India: A Historical Perspective' *Indian Journal of Industrial Relations*, Apr., 1975, Vol. 10, No. 4 (Apr., 1975), pp. 575-594.

Bhattacharya, Ananda, 'The Wandering Fakirs of Bengal: Heroes or Villains,' *South Asia Research*, Vol. 36(1), 2016, pp. 1-23.

Bhattacharya, Nandini., *Leisure, Economy and Colonial Urbanism: Darjeeling, 1835–1930, Urban History*, August 1, 2013, 40(3), pp. 442-461.

Brennan, Lance., Heathcote, Les., and Lucas, Anton., 'The causation of famine: A comparative analyses of Lombok and Bengal, 1891–1974,' *South Asia*, 7 (1), 1984, pp. 1–26.

Brewis, Georgina. 'Fill Full the Mouth of Famine': Voluntary action in famine relief in India 1896— 1901', *Modern Asian Studies*, 44 (4), July 2010, pp. 887-918.

Campbell, A., 'On the Tribes around Darjeeling,' *Transactions of the Ethnological Society of London*, Vol. 7, No. (1869), pp. 145-46.

Carlyle, R. W., 'Famine administration in a Bengal district in 1896-7,' *The Economic Journal*, 10 (39), September, 1900, pp. 421-430.

Damodaran, Vinita., 'Gender, forests and famine in 19th-century Chotanagpur, India,' *Indian Journal of Gender Studies*, 9 (2), 2002, pp. 133-163.

'Famine in Bengal: A Comparison of the 1770 Famine in Bengal and the1897 Famine in Chhotanagpur,' *The Medieval History Journal*, 10, 1&2, 2007, pp. 143-181.

Dasgupta, Atis., 'The Fakir and Sannyasi Rebellion,' *Social Scientist*, Jan., 1982, Vol. 10, No. 1 (Jan., 1982), p. 44-55.

Dyson, Tim and Ó Gráda, Cormac., 'Famine Demography: An Introduction,' *Working Paper Series, Centre for Economic Research, WP01/25*, October 2001, Department of Economics, University College Dublin.

Ghose, Ajit Kumar., 'Food Supply and Starvation: A Study of Famines with Reference to the Indian Sub-Continent', *Oxford Economic Papers*, New Series, Vol. 34, No. 2 (Jul., 1982).

Ghosh, Tirthankar, 'Ecology, Gender and Social Crises: North Bengal in 1896-97 Famine,' in *Contemporary Voice of Dalits*. (forthcoming).

Ghosh, Tirthankar, 'Climate and Colonialism: Rainfall Drought and Famine in North Bengal, 1873-74', in *Crossroads: The Journal of Transdisciplinary Studies*, Vol. I, No. I, May 2015, pp. 47-63.

Ghosh, Tirthankar, 'Nature, Famine and Economy: Ecological Dislocations and Subsistence Crises in Select Districts of Northern Bengal (1866-1874)', in *The Quarterly Review of Historical Studies*, April-Sept. 2014, pp. 4-19.

Kenny, Judith T., *Climate, Race, and Imperial Authority: The Symbolic Landscape of the British Hill Station in India, Annals of the Association of American Geographers*, Vol. 85, No. 4, Dec., 1995, pp. 694-714.

Maharatna, Arup, 'Infant and Child Mortality during Famines in Late 19th and Early 20th Century India,' *Economic and Political Weekly*, Vol. 31, No. 27 (Jul. 6, 1996), pp. 1774-1783.

Mahato, Nirmal Kumar., 'Environmental Change and Chronic Famine in Manbhum, Bengal District, 1860-1910,' *Global Environment*, 6, 2011, pp. 68-94.

McAlpin, Michelle Burge., 'Dearth, famine and risk: The changing impact of crop failures in western India, 1870 – 1920,' *Journal of Economic History*, 39 (1), March 1979, pp. 143-157.

Mukherjee, Arun, 'Scarcity and Crime: A Study of 19th Century Bengal,' *Economic and Political Weekly*, Vol. 28, No. 6 (Feb. 6, 1993), pp. 237-243.

Ray, Ratna and Ray, Rajat, 'Zamindars and Jotedars: A Study of Rural Politics in Bengal,' *Modern Asian Studies*, Vol. 9, No. 1 (1975), 81-102.

III. Unpublished PhD. Dissertation

Ghosh, Tirthankar, Natural Calamities, Economy and Ecology: A Study on Northern Bengal during the Second half of the Nineteenth Century and First half of the Twentieth Century, Unpublished Ph. Dissertation, University North Bengal, 2018.

Khasnobish, Sudip., *Socio-economic and Political Transition of Darjeeling Terai (1864-1994)*, Unpublished Ph. D dissertation, University of North Bengal, 2016.

IV. Digital sources/Repository

Archive.org

Digital Library of India

Jstor.org

National Library (Kolkata), Digital Collection

Shodganga.inflibnet.ac.in

South Asia Archive

West Bengal Public Library Network

Index